EAST-WEST PARALLELS

EAST-WEST PARALLELS

SOCIOLOGICAL APPROACHES
TO
MODERN ASIA

by

W. F. Wertheim

Professor of Modern History and Sociology of Southeast Asia

University of Amsterdam

QUADRANGLE BOOKS – CHICAGO

First American edition published 1965

Published in The Netherlands by N.V. Uitgeverij W. van Hoeve, The Hague

Library of Congress Catalog Card Number: 63-11847

Printed in The Netherlands

FOREWORD

To find time to write a book is difficult enough for a university professor, who has the privilege of being responsible for guiding the studies of quite a number of students. It is even more difficult for one who has the task of running a department and is fully engaged in the administrative and organizational chores of faculty, committee, and staff meetings which are ever expanding according to the Parkinson rate. It is well-nigh impossible in a country like Holland, where the institution of 'sabbatical years' is unknown in the academic tradition.

When I realized this, I decided to publish what is nowadays called in the United States 'a no book'. I found that a number of papers and articles dealing with the social structure and social dynamics of modern Asia, which had been read or published in the past few years in English, could be brought together to form a more or less coherent whole.

I had to delete a few paragraphs which amounted to a repetition of what had been said elsewhere in this volume. On the other hand, I had to add a few new articles, two of which had to be written especially for this purpose, while another one could be largely adapted from a Dutch text which was already extant. Together, these articles constitute an attempt to provide a theoretical frame for sociologists who are interested in the contemporary study of Asian countries. Though most of the articles are restricted in scope to the area of Southeast Asia, and a few of them deal exclusively with Indonesia, the Asian country with which I am personally best acquainted, nevertheless the approach to these countries is generally such that it can be used in a wider context, for countries with a comparable social structure or in a comparable phase of historical development.

The articles deal with such divergent problems as the general social and economic structure of these societies, minority problems, the urbanization process, migration and overpopulation, characteristics of the state apparatus and political leadership, religious reform movements and the dynamics of historical change.

The basic issue in most of the contributions is the question to what extent a certain parallelism between Western and Asian societies can be demonstrated. First of all, this is a problem of methodology. To what extent does sociology, born as a discipline in the West and largely adapted to Western social structures and institutions, provide a conceptual frame for the study of the emerging nations in Asia?

That this task has not yet been performed in a satisfactory way can be deduced from Lloyd Braithwaite's pronouncement, that 'the anthropological concern with the problems of Western society has not been paralleled by a like concern of the sociologists with the problems of colonial societies'.[1]

But a second problem is still more relevant: to what extent do historical developments in modern Asia run parallel to what happened in Western Europe a few centuries ago? Whereas 'evolutionism' was, some time ago, declared to be as dead as a doornail, the concept appears to be in full swing again. Economic theories, starting from the assumption of a repetition of the 'take-off' process all over the world, assume without questioning and without any philosophic analysis that history repeats itself. Most of the political leaders in the West may be influenced in their actions by the same naive assumption.

The problem of East-West parallels runs like a red thread through most of the chapters of the present volume. One of the basic theories developed in the following pages is that such a parallelism really exists, but that its realization in history is much less simple than is generally assumed. A most enlightening concept is that of the 'dialectics of progress', as elaborated by my late

[1] Lloyd Braithwaite, 'Social Stratification and Cultural Pluralism', in Vera Rubin (ed.), 'Social and Cultural Pluralism in the Caribbean', *Annals of the New York Academy of Sciences*, Vol. 83 (1960), p. 816.

colleague and friend Jan Romein, to which I refer in the first paper included in this volume. His view makes the term 'parallel' much less mechanical than the customary usage of evolutionary concepts would appear to involve. Just as the East-West parallels on our globe do not preclude that some natural and social phenomena, such as the cultivation of wheat which in East Asia hardly extends beyond the 40th parallel, can be found in Western Europe even as far North as the 60th owing to climatical conditions created by the Gulf Stream, in the same way historical sequences in Asia may essentially differ from those in the Western world over an equal span of time. Distance in time in history does not necessarily coincide with distance in social phase, just as distance in latitude in geography does not necessarily imply distance in climatical conditions and social environment.

The general objective of this book is to provide a more elaborated and refined theoretical frame for applying East-West parallels in human history.

Acknowledgements are due to Mrs. Nell Clegg-Bruinwold Riedel for her kind help in translating two of the papers included in this volume; to Mme A. M. de Bruin-Cousins for her valuable assistance in editing a large part of the present text and correcting its English style; to Mme H. van Weel-Frankenhuis and Mme S. Sie-Ockeloen for typing and again retyping parts of the manuscript; to Mr. W. G. Wolters who assisted the author in checking the bibliographical references; to Mr. O. D. van den Muijzenberg for his help at proof reading; again to Mme H. van Weel-Frankenhuis for her assistance in making an index; to many scholars who furnished useful comments on one or more papers included in the volume; to the publisher and his staff with whom it was, as usually, a pleasure to collaborate; and finally to Cornell University Press for their kind permission to incorporate the article on 'The Sociological Approach to Indonesian History' within this volume.

Amsterdam, May 1964   W. F. WERTHEIM

Contents

The present article has been first published in Dutch, under the title 'Sociologische aspecten der achtergebleven gebieden' (Sociological aspects of underdeveloped areas), in *Mens en Maatschappij*, Vol. 35 (1960), pp. 346–358. The English translation has been prepared by Mrs. Nell Clegg-Bruinwold Riedel after a somewhat abridged text; the last few pages, touching on the patterns of human evolution, have been added by the author with the present volume in view.

ONE

A SOCIOLOGICAL APPROACH
TO THE PROBLEMS OF UNDERDEVELOPMENT

The purpose of this essay is to try to give a sociological description of those countries, areas and communities which are
usually regarded as 'underdeveloped' technically and economically.

This is no simple task. For indeed, far from showing uniform
traits, it is on the contrary the great diversity of the 'underdeveloped' world which impresses us. This is understandable considering the fact that only a few centuries ago the whole inhabited
world was underdeveloped judging by present European or
North American standards. Not until the Industrial Revolution
did what Romein calls the *Western European Deviation* from the
Common Human Pattern[1] begin to stand out clearly.

On closer scrutiny, however, the *Common Human Pattern* turns out
to be a 'mosaic of cultural patterns'[2] – in the 'underdeveloped
world' practically uninhabited desert regions can be found side by
side with unimaginably densely populated river valleys, where
wet rice cultivation is the prevailing means of existence; nomadic
tribes practising cattle breeding or hoe-culture side by side with
peasant populations which for tens of centuries have been living
within an organized state structure; isolated little mountain

---

[1] Jan Romein in co-operation with Annie Romein-Verschoor, *Aera van Euro-
pa: De Europese geschiedenis als afwijking van het Algemeen Menselijk Patroon* (Era
of Europe: European history as a deviation from the Common Human Pattern, Leiden, 1954). See for an English version of the basic idea also Romein's
paper mentioned on p. 6, note 1.

[2] Expression used by A. J. F. Köbben, in a critical appraisal of Romein's
Common Human Pattern concept from the point of view of a cultural anthropologist, 'Het A.M.P. en de volkenkundige' (The C.H.P. and the cultural anthropologist), *Mens en Maatschappij*, Vol. 32 (1957), pp. 193 ff.

peoples living close to nature side by side with groups of small traders and artisans huddled together in closely built-up, stinking urban quarters; peoples which for centuries have been living under an omnipotent colonial authority side by side with only recently discovered tribes without the slightest notion of the existence of a world outside their own. A sociological approach to this 'underdeveloped world' would be more in place in an encyclopaedia of eighteen volumes than in an article of eighteen pages.

What then does lie within our scope? At most an attempt to seek, not the diversity, but the common characteristics of this underdeveloped world. In practice this must amount to emphasizing such sociological aspects as are closely connected with the distinctive feature of this particular part of the world – namely the low level of its technical and economic development.

The first and most obvious economic characteristic of such countries, areas and communities is low productivity per head of the population. This is in turn a consequence of the low degree of mechanization of labour coupled with lagging technical development. Next is an economic structure which, according to our present standards, is one-sided with a strong emphasis on primary production, in the first place agriculture. The economic superstructure, and connected with it the sectors of 'secondary' and 'tertiary' production – however one may circumscribe these – has reached only a limited development. The low mechanization and the predominant role of agriculture again generally result in a great dependence on natural forces and climatic conditions and in the great vulnerability of the most elementary means of existence. The dependence of agriculture on the cycle of nature furthermore causes a large number of man-hours per year to remain unproductive – and this sometimes applies even more forcibly to woman-hours.

This links up with the phenomenon we call, according to our present standards of efficiency, 'hidden unemployment' – wisely ignoring how much of our present expenditure of time will be deemed inefficient according to the norms of the future.

This brief summary of some essential economic traits also indi-

cates in which direction we must seek the sociological characteristics of our underdeveloped societies. First of all the low per
capita productivity of labour and the dependence on natural
forces engenders an intense feeling of insecurity. For the large
majority of the members of the community the margin between
production and the minimal necessities of life remains alarmingly
narrow. This sense of insecurity leads in turn to an attitude to life
which attaches great value to behaviour in accord with ancient
traditions. Disasters and bad harvests are regarded as normal; the
only possible way to meet them is by maximum solidarity and
mutual support. Such a society affords little room for adventurous
individualism. In such an environment religious or quasi-religious ideas tend towards acceptance of suffering and of the ever-
recurring disasters as an inevitable fate. Ignorance of technical
means to avert natural disasters furthers the use of expedients
which we, from the viewpoint of our present knowledge, designate
as magic. In the religious sphere, too, the emphasis lies on a collective following of traditions rather than on personal experience.

The changing cycle of nature leads to a labour ethos which is
essentially different from our Western-industrial ideal of constant
and continuous labour. Neither labour nor time are measured in
standardized units. Labour is performed discontinuously – in
some seasons with great intensity, while in others the expenditure
of labour is characterized, according to the standards of the urban
observer from an industrialized world, by an extremely uneconomic management of time.

The loyalties of the rural inhabitant of the underdeveloped world
are in general confined to a circle with which he is familiar, in
conformity with his limited mental horizon. His relations to his
fellow humans are not abstract, but concrete and personal. Even
in the urban centres the modern, impersonal business relationship is unknown. Trade is carried on in the traditional way, in an
atmosphere of genial haggling which leaves the man to man relationship intact. But wherever people face one another not as
equals, traditional authority based on birth can be exercised and
accepted in a way which approaches the absolute.

If one compares the above-mentioned characteristics of the un-derdeveloped world with the traits Romein calls typical of the *Common Human Pattern*, one is struck by their great similarity to his description.[1] Romein mentions in particular the attitude of 'the C.H.P.-man towards nature', which does not objectify but is sub-jective, *i.e.* experiencing and enduring. He points furthermore to the habit of thinking in images, *i.e.* concretely instead of abstract-ly, and to the character of community life which is organic in-stead of organizational. He also mentions the absence of a con-scious struggle against natural disasters and, in connection with this, the predominance of a religious-magical world of ideas. He stresses the absence in the underdeveloped world of time as an economic commodity. Finally he points out the absolute charac-ter of authority.

So it appears that Romein, with his concept of the *Common Human Pattern*, has succeeded in most strikingly characterizing whatever the pre-industrial world, in spite of all its diversity, has in common.

But if the above outline should be considered too vague, since it describes underdeveloped society only in qualitative terms, we could try to approach it in quantitative ones. We can do this in the main by falling back on Alfred Sauvy's attempt to enumer-ate the demographic aspects of the underdeveloped world.

In his *Théorie générale de la population* this French demographer mentions ten tests for recognizing the underdeveloped coun-tries.[2] These are:

1. High level of mortality, especially of infant mortality; low average expectation of life, between thirty and forty.
2. High birth rate, not far from the physiological fertility limit; at least the absence of birth control.

[1] Jan Romein, 'The Common Human Pattern: Origin and Scope of Histori-cal Theories', Journal of World History, Vol. 4, no. 2 (1958), pp. 449 ff.; also published in Delta, Vol. 2 (1959), pp. 5 ff.

[2] Alfred Sauvy, *Théorie générale de la population*, Part One: *Economie et population* (Paris, 1952), pp. 241–242.

3. Insufficient nutrition, on the average below 2500 calories per day, and a diet especially weak in proteins.
4. High percentage of illiterates, often close on eighty per cent.
5. High percentage of peasants or fishermen.
6. Lack of opportunity for employment as a result of the absence of means of production.
7. Inferior position of women; no outdoor labour for women.
8. Child labour from the age of ten or less.
9. Absence or weakness of middle classes.
10. Authoritarian regime in various forms; absence of democratic institutions.

There is something to be said against several of these descriptions, notably against the general character which is ascribed to these demographic traits. Thus for example, though a high birth rate is characteristic of the large majority of types of 'underdeveloped' countries – as is shown by a comprehensive and comparative study by Frank Lorimer *c.a.*, *Culture and Human Fertility* – there are some striking exceptions particularly in Africa.[1] Insufficient nutrition is acceptable as a general characteristic, but point seven – the absence of outdoor labour for women – is very controversial. In the 'underdeveloped' countries many peoples can be found among whom the women fulfil a vital function in agriculture, in gathering forest products or in fishing. The subordinate position of women is therefore rather an urban phenomenon and widespread in oriental commercial districts. For rural societies this subordination of women certainly cannot be taken as an omniprevalent characteristic.

But the strongest objections arise when Sauvy asserts that these ten tests apply nearly as well to the underdeveloped countries of 1952 as to the Western countries at the time before economic development started. For when we subject the quantitative aspects of the underdeveloped countries to a closer investigation we

[1] Frank Lorimer *c.a.*, *Culture and Human Fertility: A Study of the Relation of Cultural Conditions to Fertility in Non-Industrial and Transitional Societies* (Unesco, Paris, 1954); for divergent birth rates in African areas see p. 118.

realize with a shock that the identification of the pre-industrial
'West' with the present 'East' does not hold good in every particular, and that the present specific problems of the underdeveloped
countries are partly due to the very existence, in the middle of the
twentieth century, of an 'underdeveloped' part of the world side
by side with a 'developed' one.

For the *Common Human Pattern* as sketched by Romein is connected with a certain stability of social relations which, in spite of all
the uncertainties of material existence, continues to dominate the
activities of life. The ten demographic characteristics of Sauvy
reflect a certain long-term equilibrium. The high birth and mortality rates on the one hand ensure a safe old age for the parents
despite the high child mortality, and on the other hand prevent a
too sudden disturbance of the equilibrium between population
and means of subsistence. And insofar as the modest though constant population increase drew too heavily on the productive capacity of pre-industrial man, there were 'the three Fates' – famine,
epidemic, and war – which brusquely restored some of the demographic equilibrium.[1] According to Sauvy's calculations, the
world population from the beginning of our era until 1650 or
thereabouts did not on an average increase faster than at a rate of
one per thousand a year.[2] And even from about 1650 to the
middle of the nineteenth century the average annual increase was
still no higher than four or five per thousand.[3] But one of the most
important differences between the mediaeval West and the present-day East is that Sauvy's first demographic 'test' – high mortality – is no longer valid otherwise than in a relative sense. For
although mortality, and notably child mortality, is in general still
considerably higher in the 'underdeveloped' than in the 'developed' part of the world – all the more so if one takes into account
the composition of the population according to age groups, since
the percentage of young people is as a rule much higher than in

[1] Alfred Sauvy, *Fertility and Survival: Population Problems from Malthus to Mao
Tse-tung* (New York, 1963), p. 38.
[2] Sauvy, *Fertility and Survival* (*op. cit.*), pp. 27–28.
[3] *Ibidem*, p. 26.

Western countries – the rapid decline that has gone on in mortality while all other structural traits of the underdeveloped country are retained lends the present problems in those areas their specific character. This is because the rapid decline in mortality, due not to internal factors but to intervention from outside, has brought about the present 'population explosion'.

Therefore the preceding description of the social structure of the underdeveloped countries is too static. In order to be complete it would simultaneously have to do full justice to the fact that for the first time in world history a situation which until recently formed the *Common Human Pattern* is now experienced as *under*development, as a pathological deviation. And it is not only the leading groups in the developed world, with their sense of responsibility for world events, who want to eliminate or reduce the gap between the two types of society. In the underdeveloped world itself, too, awareness of 'underdevelopment' and dissatisfaction with this state of affairs is beginning to penetrate more and more deeply and more and more widely. This is the biggest essential difference with the pre-industrial West.

The existence of a developed part of the world presents a challenge to the part which is not yet developed. It sets in motion processes which irreparably destroy the relative equilibrium within the societies hitherto corresponding with the typology of the *Common Human Pattern*. For the same reason it is impossible to approach the underdeveloped societies sociologically in terms of static structures and conditions. It is the task of the sociologist to awaken understanding of the dynamic processes taking place in those societies. In order to approach these he will yet again have to use qualitative terms.

True, there are some quantitative indications of the presence of new dynamic factors. For example, if we once again look at Sauvy's ten tests we see that the decline in mortality is not the only quantitative pointer to the existence of such dynamic tendencies. Thus the percentage of illiterates in the underdeveloped world has been rapidly decreasing since the end of the Second World War. Also those young governments which have not succeeded in

changing the economic structure noticeably nor in raising nutrition above the 'underdeveloped' level, often score big successes in
the spheres of hygiene and education and thereby, voluntarily or
involuntarily, arouse the revolutionary forces which want to abol-
ish the underdevelopment at an accelerated tempo.

But when one describes the 'underdeveloped' areas euphemis-
tically as countries in a process of 'accelerated development' one
simply overlooks the most essential element of what is actually
going on in those areas.

For – and now I shall try to describe these processes in qualitative terms – in the first instance the economic influence which the
developed world exerts on the underdeveloped world has often
been inhibiting rather than stimulating. The present underdeveloped world presents a picture not only of backwardness, but also
of artificial petrifaction in that underdeveloped state. In this
artificial situation there are tensions – social, psychological, ideological and also purely economic and technical – which make the
present conditions in that world differ so widely from the Western
pre-industrial world that they are poles apart. For as J. H. Boeke
hast justly argued all his life, the present 'East' is not characterized by a pre-capitalist economy, but by the existence of a pre-
capitalist system side by side with a high-capitalist one mutually
influencing one another.[1] The capitalist system, an extension of
the Western industrialized world, has for many years influenced
the rural East and put its stamp on it.

In this interaction capitalism, coming from outside, was in the
main the active factor, the indigenous rural society in the main
the passive. The West appeared in the East in various guises – as
the colonial ruler who brought into existence a stratification
according to race; as the colonial administration which introduced medical and hygienic provisions – such as mass inoculation
against smallpox; as the plantation owner in search of cheap land
and cheap labour; as the engrosser and money-lender who

---

[1] J. H. Boeke, *Economics and Economic Policy of Dual Societies as Exemplified by
Indonesia* (Haarlem, 1953). For a discussion of Boeke's views see *Indonesian
Economics: The Concept of Dualism in Theory and Policy* (The Hague, 1961).

brought the money economy deep into the interior; as the missionary who founded schools or hospitals.

A perceptive analysis of the social processes set in motion by these contacts has been undertaken by the American social anthropologist Clifford Geertz for pre-war Indonesia. In a recent book which elaborates ideas previously forwarded in a series of mimeographed studies he has described such processes in Central and East Java.

One of his main conclusions is that the processess set in train by the sugar plantations must be characterized, for the great mass of the Javanese peasants, not as a 'development' – *evolution* – but as the opposite – *involution*.¹ The rapid growth of the population caused by improved hygienic conditions resulted in increasing pressure on agricultural land. The plantation economy led to an artificial preservation of the traditional forms of communal land tenure, and to a capitalist stimulus introduced in this way the population could react only by a rigidifying of traditional structures and institutions. Thus a social pattern emerged which Geertz has defined as a 'shared poverty system',² in which at least some sort of security is sought by spreading out the available goods over as many people as possible.

Raised to an extreme, the density of the population makes it more and more difficult to find elbow room for economic and social renewal in the countryside. Technical renewal usually boils down to the release of labour, and in a chronic condition of hid-

¹ Clifford Geertz has launched this concept of *involution* in *The Development of the Javanese Economy: A Socio-Cultural Approach* (mimeographed paper, M.I.T., Cambridge, Mass., 1956), pp. 29 ff., 112–113 (note 24). The effect of the sugar plantation economy upon traditional agriculture in Java has been analysed by Geertz, *The Social Context of Economic Change: An Indonesian Case Study* (mimeographed paper, M.I.T., Cambridge, Mass., 1956), pp. 29 ff. The basic ideas have recently been elaborated in much greater detail in Geertz, *Agricultural Involution: The Processes of Ecological Change in Indonesia* (Berkeley/Los Angeles, 1963).

² Geertz, 'Religious Belief and Economic Behavior in a Central Javanese Town: Some Preliminary Considerations', *Economic Development and Cultural Change*, Vol. 4 (1956), p. 141.

den unemployment there is not the slightest incentive to this. On the contrary, the 'shared poverty' system serves, at any rate to provide a minimum of social security for the many economically weak members of the village.

Originating in rural society, the 'shared poverty' pattern also spreads to Eastern urban society. Of this Geertz has also given striking illustrations in an analysis of life in the town of 'Modjokuto'.[1] The lack of opportunity for employment in the town, the growing stream of impoverished rural inhabitants moving there, and the generally low standard of living lead to the available opportunities for work being spread over large numbers of applicants each of whom has too little to do and is living on the very margin of minimal subsistence. The innumerable street-vendors, pedicab drivers, 'peons' and little clerks in the offices all testify to the same system, in which social justice takes precedence over efficiency and a minimum output per head is put up with so that the available means of subsistence can be spread out over a maximum number of people. In urban industry, too, the efficiency and viability of an enterprise suffer from the social pressure of the environment, which demands that the factory owner takes on and maintains so many male or female workers that each has too little to live and too much to die, while there is no incentive to and possibility of further investment left.

Hence the paradox that the same capitalism which in the West formed a stimulus for technical development, in the East has in many cases had the opposite effect, because the colonial or semi-colonial form in which capitalism appeared there often had a petrifying effect on the social institutions and consequently paralysed economic-technical adaptability.

Since the decline in mortality occurred before the industrialization, Eastern society was forced into an attitude of passive resistance which for many years excluded active adaptation. And this while the dynamic development in the demographic sphere – a population growth of hitherto unprecedented rapidity, in Java

[1] *Modjokuto* – a fictitious name for a small town in the Western part of East Java.

as early as the first half of the nineteenth century, in other non-Western areas some time later – presents a challenge to which the correct answer would have to be at least as dynamic as the original stimulus. For it is clear that, if the cause of 'underdevelopment' lies in low *per capita* productivity, development can never be achieved in any other way than by increasing this labour productivity. A purely passive resistance, either in the form of 'shared poverty' or in that of birth control (in Sauvy's terminology: 'the demographic solution') or emigration, can provide no more than temporary relief and by no means removes the cause of the 'disease' – on the contrary, it tends only to divert the energy necessary to give the correct answer: the 'economic solution' to use Sauvy's terminology again.[1]

Now it becomes clearer why there are still so many countries for which Sauvy's ten tests are largely valid. In many non-Western countries the protracted colonial or semi-colonial expansion has not furthered, but retarded economic development. Consequently for many of those countries the traits mentioned by Sauvy still apply: one-sided economic structure, high percentage of agriculturalists, low standard of living and of nutrition, low degree of mechanization. If, however, we want fully to understand the social processes in these areas we must also take into account the positive dynamic forces which are also operative there. For simultaneously with the petrifaction of many social institutions a process is found which has a solvent effect on those institutions. The penetration of monetary exchange has disrupted many traditional bonds, has mobilized landed property and thus uprooted the traditional protection surrounding the individual. A process of atomizing and proletarianizing of the peasant population is going on as a result of which the traditional structures, preserved in a petrified form, are often no more than an empty shell. Both a rural and an urban proletariat have begun to move. Dissatisfied with the present, they no longer regard poverty and destitution as inevitable, partly as a result of visual confrontation either in reality

[1] Sauvy, *Fertility and Survival* (*op. cit.*), pp. 105 ff., 185 ff.

or via the film with the way of life of the neighbouring whites – colonial administrators or businessmen. And the small clerks crowding urban offices have also become a turbulent element in society. These groups, moreover, freely make use of modern forms of organization (trade unions, peasant organizations, district associations) which replace the community bonds rooted in tradition.

For this reason, too, present Asian society cannot be put on a par with the pre-industrial West. Although in Western history expressions of social dissatisfaction also occurred again and again, they usually sought an outlet in religious, messianic movements which turned away from reality.

In the present underdeveloped areas the dissatisfaction expresses itself in new forms often derived from the modern West. The loyalties of the present rural population in the East are no longer predominantly particularistic. Even though their new ideals, whether these present themselves in a nationalistic, a religious, or a socialist or anti-imperialist garb, can not yet be called 'universalistic' in a true sense, their universe is still an expanding one. Even if the society itself does not yet harbour a social dynamic sufficiently powerful to bring about economic and technical innovations, there is an inner, psychological motive force which contrasts sharply with the traditional, fatalistic-religious attitude to life.

A philosophically resigned East exists nowadays almost exclusively in the imagination of sentimental Westerners.

A review of the actual sociological aspects of the underdeveloped part of the world cannot be confined to the broad mass of agriculturalists and townspeople. It must embrace the elite groups which in the present situation contend with each other and with the foreign rulers for supremacy.[1] Naturally, modern industrial culture influences these groups even more than it does the mass of simple peasants and workers.

[1] For a more detailed treatment of the elite in Asian countries see the fourth paper of this volume. The corruption issue is dealt with in the fifth paper.

In the attitude and way of life of these groups there are still many remnants of the traditional pre-industrial society. Their behaviour shows many relics of an aristocratic-traditional life pattern, while their loyalties towards relatives or persons belonging to the same ethnic group also frequently display particularistic traits. On the other hand these groups are often more strongly affected by universalist or quasi-universalist ideals which can serve to bridge traditional local particularisms. It is especially this clash of two conflicting worlds meeting within one and the same person which causes a certain lability in social norms and attitudes to life. The phenomenon of corruption, so widespread in the present underdeveloped world, should also be seen in the first place as the expression of a chronic conflict between universalist norms and particularist loyalties. Purely economic factors such as low remuneration, or exorbitant power for individual civil servants in deciding matters involving large interests, play only a secondary role in this respect. Nor is the pre-industrial pattern of nepotism and 'squeeze', the decisive point, but the marginal position between traditional-particularist and modern-universalist norms. Even more than the great mass of the people, the new leading group moves on the borderline between two worlds. In many underdeveloped areas this leading group fulfils a dynamic and revolutionary function – but it is able to do so only because and insofar as the social dynamic has to a certain extent also affected the masses.

At this point the question arises, to what extent the social dynamics in Asian countries can be expected, in the near future, to take a similar course as previously in the West.

According to Romein's view of Western modern history as a deviation from the *Common Human Pattern*, the new way of life which originated in the West gradually spreads to other parts of the world. As a result, the original deviation is gradually developing into a new *Common Human Pattern*. The prospect, in that case, would appear to be such that, despite many retarding or impeding factors, the dynamics of development in Asia could be expected, in the long run, to create a counterpart of Western society.

But in addition, Romein has formulated in one of his pre-war essays which, unfortunately, has never been published in an English translation,[1] a hypothesis on the way human evolution tends to proceed.

Contrary to the nineteenth-century belief in a unilinear evolutionary pattern according to which any human society develops through a series of distinct, identical phases, Romein tries to establish a different pattern of evolution, which he calls a 'dialectical' one.

He demonstrates, with a wealth of examples drawn from human history, that far from developing in a gradual way, human history progresses with leaps and bounds, comparable to the mutations known from the world of living nature. A next step in human evolution is not at all likely to occur within the society which has achieved a high degree of perfection in a given direction. On the contrary, the progress once achieved in the past is liable to act as a brake upon further progress. Both an atmosphere of complacency and vested interests tend to oppose further steps which might involve a complete overhaul of established institutions or equipments.

Therefore, further progress on the road of human evolution is, time and again, much more likely to occur in a more backward society, where resistances against social change are weaker. Romein shows that leadership in human evolution perpetually shifts from one society to another, after over-specialization has led yesterday's leader into a blind alley. He draws his examples both from the realm of technique (including armaments and warfare)

[1] Jan Romein, 'De dialektiek van de vooruitgang: Bijdrage tot het ontwikkelingsbegrip in de geschiedenis' (The dialectics of progress: a contribution to our understanding of evolution within history), *Forum*, Vol. 4, Part Two (1935), pp. 752–777 and 828–855; reprinted in Romein, *Het onvoltooid verleden: Cultuur-historische studies* (The Imperfect Past: Studies in cultural history, Second Ed., Amsterdam, 1948), pp. 13–69. A German version has been published with the title 'Dialektik des Fortschritts', in *Mass und Wert*, Vol. 2 (1939), pp. 305 ff.

and the birth of social institutions. A few of his most striking illustrations of his thesis are the following: retardation in the introduction of electric lighting in London, which was the first city to
develop illumination with gas and to carry it forth to a remarkable
perfection; the lagging behind of the productivity of collieries in
Britain, France and Belgium, the countries which were the first to
develop large scale coal mining; the advantage of late-comer
Japan over Britain as far as modernization and rationalization of
textile industries is concerned; and finally the occurrence of the
proletarian revolution in backward Russia contrary to the prophecies of those Marxists who had expected this revolution to
take place in Germany, at that time industrially the most developed country. The general design of his argument is to show that
backwardness may, under certain circumstances, act as an advantage and a spur to further effort, whereas rapid advance in the
past may act as a brake. This is what he calls 'the dialectics of
progress', or the 'law of the retarding lead'.

  Romein's thesis, which could be substantiated with many more
instances from the history of mankind, seems to me highly relevant
to the problem as to how far repetition of a Western pattern of
evolution is to be expected in Asian countries. If Romein's view
of the way human evolution proceeds is essentially correct, this
means that it would be futile to look for a pure copying, in Asia,
of patterns familiar from the West. Even though the general
trend in Asia may, in general terms and to a certain extent, run
parallel with recent Western developments, the statement that
the 'Western deviation' is going to develop into a *Common Human
Pattern* may be accepted only in its most general sense. The rate at
which social change occurs, and the exact shape which it takes,
will vary from one single society to another. It is, more in particular, the time factor which is subject to significant variations.[1]
If it is true, as elaborated by Romein, that under certain circum-

---

[1] Romein, 'National and Social Revolution in Asia and the Time Factor',
in: Soedjatmoko *c.s.* (ed.), *An Introduction to Indonesian Historiography* (Ithaca,
1964), Chapter 20.

stances an initial handicap may function as an advantage, short-cuts and the skipping over of phases are possible in human history. This means that mankind is able to repeat a certain process within a much shorter period than in a parallel case, thus avoiding the many detours which had to be made in the original model.

This insight has an enormous importance for our theoretical approach to modern Asia. For it enables us to keep clear from any forced search for institutional parallels, even though the general direction of developing trends may be largely comparable. If human evolution is not, as a matter of course, a gradual one, then actual processes need not necessarily be developments in the direction which we have witnessed in the West. They may even present 'involutionary' trends as defined by Clifford Geertz. For example, if we evaluate the present trends of development in the majority of Asian cities and small towns, we may be forced to conclude that, for the time being, these do not move in the direction which urbanization has taken in the West, but exactly in the opposite one.[1]

On the other hand, factors of stagnation may be compensated for by other dynamic factors that can occasionally lead to a development which should no longer be called 'evolutionary' but 'revolutionary'. In such a case the period within which a social process is completed would be appreciably abridged in comparison with the original model, though numerous remnants of the pre-revolutionary structure may stay on for a long time, representing a cultural lag in comparison with the main body of society. Such a revolutionary process may even take the social structure beyond the point achieved by the society which had taken the lead in the first instance, in particular if, according to the 'dialectics of progress', 'involutionary' factors are retarding a continuous growth in the advanced society.

In practice this might imply that modernization and industrialization in Asia need not necessarily follow the course taken in the West, via private capitalistic enterprise. Certain phases from

[1] I may refer to the eighth paper of this volume, dealing with urban characteristics in Indonesia.

Western development can be skipped over, taking a definite Asian society beyond the level of technical and institutional perfection achieved in the countries which, in the past, led the way towards modern industrial development. But even so, the new type of society produced in Asia may show, for a long time to come, a combination of elements which are hyper-modern with other ones which represent, in our Western history, a much less advanced phase of social development.

This view of social transformation appears more enlightening than a theory such as Rostow's, which takes a universal pattern of economic development for granted, though even he acknowledges that there is no need for a growing society to recapitulate the course of events in the older industrial societies.[1] The stereotype of a perpetual transition via a take-off period of a relatively short, equal duration (two or three decades) into a phase of 'self-sustained growth' does not take account of the differential inherent in the time-factor; it neglects the possibility of short-cuts from a backward state into a more advanced one; and it overlooks the 'involutionary' elements within Western society by viewing the 'self-sustained growth' as proceeding more or less automatically, if necessary without appreciable interference by the government. Rostow recognizes, that Britain's lead was gone, as soon as the United States and continental Western Europe had 'completed their take-off'. But in his view this is not a dialectical process, but simply an equalization of chances for 'a latecomer with a big unapplied backlog of technology available'. In Russia nothing extra-ordinary has happened, according to Rostow: the take-off had occurred before the Revolution; at present 'Russia closes the technological gap on the West; China, India, Brazil and others

---

[1] See for example W. W. Rostow, 'The Take-Off into Self-Sustained Growth', *The Economic Journal*, Vol. 66 (1956), pp. 25 ff.; Rostow, *The Stages of Economic Growth: A Non-Communist Manifesto* (Cambridge, 1960); 'Rostow on Growth', *The Economist*, August 15 and 22, 1959.

For a critical appraisal of Rostow's and Gerschenkron's schemes I may refer to Witold Kula, *Les débuts du capitalisme en Pologne dans la perspective de l'histoire comparée* (Rome, 1960).

promise to repeat the trick again on the older mature powers, including Russia, in the next half century or so'.[1]

It may be difficult for a Western scholar to imagine that the type of social development with which he is familiar is not the most advanced one conceivable; and that the advantage achieved by the West, which is, by the way, rather a recent phenomenon in world history, is not likely to be permanent. Rostow's theory aims clearly at explaining away the specific upsurge of the Soviet-Union under communist rule by defining its development as fitting within the usual pattern and the usual time-table.

But then, a scholarly attitude is always characterized by a relativistic attitude which does not put one's own society, nation or race in the centre of the world. A deeper concern with the social dynamics of the Eastern world might rescue us, Westerners, from complacency – the most retarding factor in human evolution.

[1] 'Rostow on Growth', *loc. cit.*, p. 413.

'Society as a composite of conflicting value systems' is a paper read at the Fourth World Congress of Sociology (Milan–Stresa, 1959) as a contribution to the Seminar on the Approaches of Social Anthropology. Earlier the basic idea of this paper had been formulated by the present author in Dutch, in 'Het contrapunt in de samenleving' (The counterpoint in society), a contribution to *Weerklank op het werk van Jan Romein: Liber Amicorum* (Resonance upon Jan Romein's works: Liber amicorum), a collection of essays, presented to Professor Jan Romein by colleagues, disciples, and friends on the occasion of his sixtieth birthday (Amsterdam, 1953), pp. 210–217.

An abstract of the paper has been published in the *Transactions of the Fourth World Congress of Sociology*, Vol. 3 (Louvain, 1961), pp. 365–368. A French translation of the complete text has been published under the title 'La société et les conflits entre systèmes de valeurs', *Cahiers Internationaux de Sociologie*, Vol. 28 (1960), pp. 33–46.

The present text has been slightly revised; a paragraph on the 'plural society' concept has been added.

TWO

SOCIETY AS A COMPOSITE
OF CONFLICTING VALUE SYSTEMS

The view of non-literate society generally held by the classic social anthropologists was one of a well-integrated structure. Though the existence of conflicts was, of course, never denied, society was looked upon as an essentially organic whole, in which each element has its special function, in harmony with a value system commonly accepted as a basis of social hierarchy. Accordingly, the functioning of a society is described in synchronic terms, whereas diachronic elements are taken account of only in as far as they produce a change in the overall structure of society. Instead of the concept of the happy savage, the concept of the well-integrated primitive society was held out as a paradise lost to modern man.

Gradually, social anthropologists are becoming aware of the existence of elements within each society that are contrary to the notion of complete harmony. Radcliffe-Brown developed his theory of 'opposition' as a widespread structural principle in non-literate societies.[1] But the antagonism between social groups which may find expression in such institutions as 'joking relationships' is not allowed to develop into a real conflict. Opposition 'is not at all the same thing as strife or enmity, but is a combination of agreement and disagreement, of solidarity and difference'. Essentially, in Radcliffe-Brown's view opposition functions 'as a mode of social integration'.

A further step has been made by Professor Gluckman and his associates, who have called attention to social conflict as a persistent feature of non-literate societies. Social anthropologists are

---

[1] A. R. Radcliffe-Brown, *Method in Social Anthropology* (Chicago, 1958), p. 118.

at present much less convinced than the leading scholars of the
past generation that non-literate societies should be looked upon
as models of a harmonious well-integrated structure. Their view
of these tribal societies has been strongly influenced by the inroads into primitive life made by cultural contacts and colonial
rule. They refuse to view those tribal communities, as they exist
and function to-day, as separate and relatively self-contained entities and to make abstraction from the overall colonial structure
which permeates their original value system as well.[1] The way
those tribal societies react at such modern contacts and forces
gives expression to a constant interplay of synchronic and diachronic factors, which calls for a more complicated analytical model
than that applied by Malinowski's functionalist school.[2] In the
process of analysing social conflict in present-day African society,
the modern social anthropologists are discovering that this phenomenon played an important role in the tribal communities
even before they came into contact with Western powers and that
those societies had developed special devices for solving such conflicts, a kind of 'redressive mechanism deployed to handle conflict'.[3] In the present constellation those devices are still being
applied in modified form. One of the adherents of the new school
of thought among British social anthropologists, V. W. Turner,
no longer looks upon a social system as 'a static model, a harmonious pattern'. 'A social system is a field of forces in which, to
quote Fortes, centrifugal tendencies and centripetal tendencies
pull against one another and whose power to persist is generated
by its own socially transmuted conflicts'.[4] Even so, the community
as a whole tends, according to that school of thought, towards a
reintegration of the prevalent communal values, which are held

[1] Max Gluckman, *An Analysis of the Sociological Theories of Bronislaw Malinowski* (London, 1949), pp. 9 ff.; Georges Balandier, *Sociologie actuelle de
l'Afrique noire: Dynamique et changements sociaux en Afrique centrale* (Paris, 1955).

[2] Gluckman, *op. cit.*, pp. 22 ff.

[3] See for example V.W. Turner, *Schism and Continuity in an African Society: A
Study of Ndembu Village Life* (Manchester/New York, 1957).

[4] Turner, *op. cit.*, Preface, p. XXII.

to persist throughout the process of dynamic, social change. Ultimately, in Professor Gluckman's view, conflict remains 'a mode
of integrating groups', and hostility between groups 'is a form of
social balance'.[1]

A further departure from the classical approach is embodied in
Dr. Leach's illuminating study of Kachin social structure in the
highlands of Burma.[2] Leach argues 'that equilibrium theory in
social anthropology was once justified but that it now needs drastic modification... Few if any of the societies which a modern
field worker can study show any marked tendency toward stability'.[3] 'If ritual is sometimes a mechanism of integration, one could
as well argue that it is often a mechanism of disintegration.'[4] The
main theme of the study is to demonstrate the oscillation of Kachin communities between two conflicting social systems, two
polar types of political organization. Leach opposes the aristocratic structure of the Buddhist *Shans* dominating the lowlands
to the democratic *Gumlao* principles characteristic of the highland
Kachin communities. His main thesis is that only if account is tak-
en of the precarious equilibrium between the two contradictory
value systems, which expresses itself in an intrinsically unstable
intermediate type of social structure, can a more or less satisfactory sociological description of the functioning of such a complex
society be attempted. But even so Leach holds the view that 'the
anthropologist must always treat the material of observation *as if*
it were part of an overall equilibrium, otherwise description becomes almost impossible.'[5] The author conceives the process of
social change as a consequence of the interpenetration of the
component unstable ideal systems. In Leach's view, it is no longer
conflict as an element of social structure that matters but an op-

---

[1] Gluckman, *op. cit.*, p. 10; see also from the same author: *Custom and Conflict
in Africa* (Oxford, 1955), pp. 47–48.
[2] E. R. Leach, *Political Systems of Highland Burma: A Study of Kachin Social
Structure* (London, 1954).
[3] Leach, *op. cit.*, p. 285.
[4] *Ibidem*, p. 278.
[5] *Ibidem*, p. 285.

position between conflicting value systems discernible within one and the same society.

It appears to me that we could carry Leach's argument much further, in a most fruitful manner. I do not see why a qualitative distinction should be made between the African societies as described by Evans-Pritchard and Fortes, where 'hostility and friendship, social solidarity and social opposition necessarily balance out to form a system which, regarded as a whole in long term, is a system in structural equilibrium',[1] and the Kachin Southeast Asian communities, which at no point in his studies gave Leach 'the impression of being part of a system that tended towards equilibrium'. It looks much more probable that the difference is rather one of approach and of a pre-conceived model of a social structure, and that Leach's pattern of analysis could, in essence, be applied to any society.

I would suggest, then, that no human society is a completely integrated entity. In any community there are hidden or overt forms of protest against the prevalent hierarchical structure. In general a more or less dominant set of common values can be discerned – else the society would not have sufficient cohesive power to subsist. But beneath the dominant theme there always exist different sets of values, which are, to a certain degree, adhered to among certain social groups and which function as a kind of counterpoint to the leading melody.

In general those counterpoints only manifest themselves in some veiled form – for example, in tales, jokes and myths, which give expression to the deviant sets of values. From the fact that the contrary set of values expresses itself in an institutionalized form, it can be deduced that it is not merely an individual expression of protest against an over-rigid cultural pattern, but a group protest which has a certain sociological meaning. On the other hand, in diverting the contrary elements into an institutionalized form, the society at the same time canalizes those forces and prevents them from becoming disruptive factors for the overall social

[1] *Ibidem*, pp. 86–87.

structure. In so far the institutionalizing process may be called an integrative function of society. But the basic protest elements remain dormant and may resume, under circumstances favourable to them, their tendency to produce a basic change within the dominant structure. Therefore, any description of a given society has to take account of the deviant value systems as basic elements in the total fabric of social life.

I would like to illustrate my argument with a few peculiarities from Balinese society. Margaret Mead,[1] after having described the rigidity of the caste system and the severe restrictions surrounding personal relationships in terms of seniority, demonstrates a number of anomalies and points of contradiction in the use of fixed levels. Especially 'the hierarchical position of brothers, in which the younger is supposed to use self-deprecating pronouns in addressing the elder, is one of the least stable and most uncomfortable points in Balinese inter-personal relations'.

This uneasiness finds expression in theatrical performances. These relationships are constantly being skitted at such occasions. 'The stock theatrical servants are an elder brother, elegant, pompous, and dull, and a younger brother, gauche, mischievous and hyperactive', who relish in thoroughly confusing their relationship to each other, and afterwards 'proceed to overdo and caricature their relationship to their prince, who remains charming and aloof and continues to sing unintelligible archaic words while the two brothers posture around him'. According to Margaret Mead, 'this freedom of theatrical caricature, from which neither the possessed seer nor the Brahman high priest escapes, though running the whole gamut of Balinese life, concentrates on the points of strain in the system, and so provides continual release in laughter for an audience which has learned to count upon the recurrence of just these themes'.

Margaret Mead discerned in this laughter the same overtones which, in other cultures, distinguish 'the sudden roar of pornographic laughter' from laughter at themes other than sex. This means,

[1] Gregory Bateson and Margaret Mead, *Balinese Character: A Photographic Analysis* (New York, 1942), pp. 11 ff.

that the restrictions surrounding personal relationships in terms of seniority and caste are felt as oppressive, in the same way as restrictions surrounding sex in other civilizations.

In a similar way the respect system between siblings is purposely reversed in stereotyped jokes, when for example a mother teases her child by placing a younger baby over his head. As the position of the elder brother as the person of rank and the sacredness of the head have been impressed upon the child from his infancy, he will shriek with rage in such occasions.

Other institutions to escape the rigidity of formal relationships in Balinese society are provided by the cremation ceremonies, where the Balinese, in contrast to their habitual pose of guarded self-control, show intense emotion – 'a riotous, hysterical gaiety', to quote Margaret Mead again. Another instance is provided by 'eloping' as a means for a young couple to escape an oppressive marriage project imposed by the elders. For younger children who want to protest against the rigidity of discipline in their home there is an institutionalized protest form in running away to the house of some relative.[1]

In the preceding examples the protest against the official hierarchy and against the formal social values manifests itself in veiled, institutional forms. By allowing these kinds of protest behaviour in prescribed and culturally accepted forms the strains of the social system are, to a certain degree, mollified and consequently the overall structure is, if anything, strengthened. In such cases one could argue that the institutionalized protest patterns have an integrative function.

But there are expressions of protest against the formal caste structure which indicate the existence of a more consistent set of values opposed to the official one. The division of the population of Bali according to a caste system adopted from India via Java has never been accepted among the majority of the Balinese themselves. Though the prince and his followers will call the common people *Sudra* as distinct from the *Triwangsa*, the people themselves

[1] Jane Belo, 'The Balinese Temper', *Character and Personality*, Vol. 4 (1935), pp. 120 ff.

use a different hierarchical system and a different terminology.[1]

In general the mountain villages, the so-called *Bali-aga* communities, where a relatively large portion of the original Balinese culture has been preserved, represent a type of social organization which is, to a certain extent, opposed to the aristocratic caste structure imported from without. The relationship between Hindu-Balinese society and *Bali-aga* society is, thus, comparable with the *Shan-Gumlao* opposition analysed by Leach in his study of Kachin communities. The *Bali-aga* have their own hierarchical system and Hindu priests are excluded from their temples.

Among Balinese village people there are many tales circulating which give overt expression to their hostility to the Brahmin priests (*Pedanda*). A tale of the *Uylenspiegel* type, in which the priests are ridiculed, is very popular. Nor are the aristocrats exempt from censure in popular literature.

In 1949, in the village of Kalianget, a huge cremation ceremony was enacted in honour of the legendary popular hero Jayaprana.[2] There were some attempts to turn the young general, who had been murdered at the instruction of his ruler after the latter had become enamoured of his bride, into a 'hero of honour of the resistance', and to interpret Jayaprana as a representative of the struggle of the common man against the thraldom of feudalism. A similar interpretation to the tale has been given by the Dutch novelist Jef Last, who has re-written the drama of Jayaprana, whom he portrays as a symbol of the age-long struggle of the *Bali-aga* people against the Hinduized rulers and against the aristocratic order of society.[3] One could surmise that this is a modern interpretation which attempts to read back into Balinese tradition a modern concept of class strife. But the recent publi-

---

[1] See for example V. E. Korn, *Het adatrecht van Bali* (The adat law of Bali, Second Ed., The Hague, 1932), p. 149, p. 165; Jef Last, *Bali in de kentering* (Bali in transition, Amsterdam, 1955), p. 74.

[2] H. J. Franken, 'The Festival of Jayaprana at Kalianget', in *Bali: Studies in Life, Thought and Ritual* (The Hague/Bandung, 1960), pp. 233 ff.; see also C. Hooykaas, *The Lay of Jayaprana: The Balinese Uriah* (London, 1958), p. 9.

[3] Jef Last, 'Djajaprana', *Indonesië*, Vol. 7 (1953–54), pp. 381 ff.

cation and translation of the original texts of the Jayaprana poem by Dr. Hooykaas provides some indications that the interpretation of the tale as an expression of a social protest may be justified. The poet opens the poem with the words 'The writer is a low-caste man'.[1] And when he describes the family from which Jaya-prana springs, he writes, referring to the father of the hero: 'A *Sudra* comes into the poem'.[2] Apparently, the Balinese people themselves have always been conscious of the anti-aristocratic element inherent in the drama as transmitted from one generation to another. In his study on 'Form and variation in Balinese village structure'[3] Clifford Geertz describes the present-day tensions between the *Sudra* group and the *Triwangsa* within a Balinese village in some detail.

For a further illustration of the 'counterpoint' concept I shall at random take a few examples from other societies. In the foregoing I already mentioned the tales of the *Uylenspiegel* type. This pattern of tales is current and popular in many civilizations and is always to be found as a less conspicuous corollary to the dominant type of tales giving expression to the officially accepted communal values (for example the obligation of the youth to obey and respect their elders even though the prescriptions of these would seem completely unintelligible). The special attraction of the *Uylenspiegel* type of tales for the common people springs from the fact that all the official values are turned upside down and that the popular hero ridicules and denies the formal hierarchy of his society and still gets away with it. Their wide diffusion throughout the world – including the *Nazreddin* tales from the Middle East, or the *Kabayan* stories from Western Java[4] – testify

[1] Hooykaas, *op. cit.*, p. 33.
[2] *Ibidem*, p. 35.
[3] Clifford Geertz, 'Form and Variation in Balinese Village Structure', *American Anthropologist*, Vol. 61 (1959), p. 1008.
[4] Lina M. Coster-Wijsman, *Uylespiegel-verhalen in Indonesia, in het biezonder in de Soendalanden* (Uylenspiegel stories in Indonesia, with special reference to the Sundanese speaking areas of Western Java, doctoral thesis Leiden University, Santpoort, 1929).

to the universality of the human spiritual needs to which this type of stories appeals.

Another popular kind of expression of elements of social protest is to be found in religious movements all over the world. While the dominant system of hierarchy finds expression in religious forms as well, the underground protest against the dominant system equally seeks an outlet in religious forms. Recent analysis of messianic cults all over the world has revealed a wealth of materials on the protest element inherent in many of those movements.[1] Under conditions of colonial rule these religious movements assume the role of rallying forces in opposition to the official hierarchy in a situation where overt opposition would be severely suppressed.

Counterpoint elements have never been absent from Western society either. The mediaeval institution of the royal buffoon has served to mitigate the rigidity of princely etiquette. The counterpoint was used here as a well-devised design by those in power to reduce the protest to futility. Then, the Sunday has always been an institution in which the dominant values were reversed. In the church, the high and the mighty were as likely to be chastised from the pulpit as the common people, even more so. The poor people rejoiced intensely when listening to the damnations thrown at those to whom they had to bow in daily life. Once in a week they could feel themselves the equals of the wealthy people, or even superior to them. For a few hours their inferiority was taken away from them. In the church it was not the hierarchy of this world which was observed, but the hierarchy before God – although even there, in the outward arrangement of the seats, homage was paid to the worldly hierarchy.

And even in the present-day secularized West the Sunday has

---

[1] See for example Emanuel Sarkisyanz, *Russland und der Messianismus des Orients: Sendungsbewusstsein und politischer Chiliasmus des Ostens* (Tübingen, 1955); George Balandier, *op. cit.*: Peter Worsley, *The Trumpet Shall Sound: A Study of 'Cargo' Cults in Melanesia* (London, 1957); A. J. F. Köbben, 'Prophetic Movements as an Expression of Social Protest', *International Archives of Ethnography*, Vol. 59 (1960), p. 117 ff.

kept its character of a counterpoint to the daily order of things. On that day the prominence of the writing-desk aristocracy, who rule on weekdays, is being challenged by the hierarchy of physical valour as symbolized by sports. In this sports Sunday the protest against the intellectual elite of a managerial world is embodied in a temporary revaluation of humanity according to bodily strength.

Some of the foregoing illustrations, such as for example the messianic cults mentioned earlier, could also serve to reveal the role which the dormant protest elements may play in promoting social change. The institutionalization of the protest is used as a temporary expedient for those in power to restrict its disruptive force. But under favourable circumstances the protest may gather force and break through the culturally accepted patterns which kept it within its institutional bounds. In fact, the disguised protest elements may contain the germ of future rebellion or revolution. The dynamic processes of change can never be understood if the opposing value systems within society are not taken into full account.

This point is well illustrated by Margaret Mead's successive experiences in her research of Manus society. During her first visit in 1928–1929, she was struck by the discrepancy between childhood and adulthood, by the seemingly unbridgeable distance between the social roles expected from the children and from adults. She was well aware that the child's world formed a kind of counterpoint to the acquisitive adult world, a more or less separate subculture in the total fabric of Manus culture. But the existence of this set of contrary values did not impair the integrative quality of society. In her opinion the acceptance of the specific values of the child's world did not last beyond the individual's entrance into the adult one. She took 'the triumph of the adults' for granted, and only wondered, 'how these children, permitted a life so at variance with the life of their elders, developed into men like those same elders'.[1]

Her main experience of 1953 was, that as a matter of fact, they

[1] Margaret Mead, *New Lives for Old: Cultural Transformation – Manus 1918–1953* (London, 1956), p. 114.

had not. She discovered that the discrepancy between the values accepted in childhood and in adulthood had been one of the potent factors bringing about social change, though 'the contrapuntal experiences of childhood were not sufficient in themselves to enable Manus adults to throw over the institutions of their culture'.[1] But it is the vigorous impact of the West which released the dynamic forces dormant within Manus society and turned a universal polarity between generations into a true conflict of generations.

If the counterpoint concept (Margaret Mead also used the term 'contrapuntal' without, however, elaborating it further) could help us to a better understanding of dynamic change in the non-Western world, it seems probable that it might equally contribute to our insight in dynamic change within modern Western society. Lloyd Warner's view of social stratification as an objective reality to be established by a strict methodology has been much criticized lately.[2] The concept of the status system as a continuum instead of a fixed pattern of status classes, the 'multi-dimensional' approach proposed by Milton Gordon, the types of 'status instability' studied by Stone and Form, the 'revaluation' phenomenon elaborated already in 1936 by Speier,[3] they all combine to throw doubt upon the viability of Warner's attempt to apply the structural model adopted from the classic interpretation of non-literate society.

However, one could raise the question whether the criticism of the current stratification concept should not be carried much

---

[1] Mead, *op. cit.*, p. 158.
[2] See for example Ruth Rosner Kornhauser, 'The Warner Approach to Social Stratification', in R. Bendix and S. M. Lipset (ed.), *Class, Status, and Power* (Glencoe, 1953), pp. 244 ff.
[3] Gerhard E. Lenski, 'American Social Classes: Statistical Strata or Social Groups?', *American Journal of Sociology*, Vol. 58 (1958), pp. 139 ff.; Milton M. Gordon, *Social Class in American Sociology* (Durham, 1958), pp. 85 ff.; Gregory P. Stone and William H. Form, 'Instabilities in Status: The Problem of Hierarchy in the Community Study of Status Arrangements', *American Sociological Review*, Vol. 18 (1953), pp. 149 ff.; Hans Speier, 'Social Stratification in the Urban Community', *American Sociological Review*, Vol. 1 (1936), p. 201.

farther; whether this concept should not be completely reconsidered. Does social stratification exist anywhere in society, except
in the image of the people themselves?

In fact, in Lloyd Warner's view they are psychical realities;
but he starts from the assumption that within one society the
evaluations converge into one objectively valid hierarchical
system. Therefore, in his view, sociological analysis has the task of
detecting the common system of evaluation accepted by each
individual. But do the communal value systems, profusely utilized
in sociology, really correspond to any objective reality? Is the
idea of a hierarchical system pervading an entire society, a construct which really adds to our insight in society?

I would suggest that value systems have to be interpreted as
psychical realities, accepted in different shades of intensity among
definite segments of society. There may be something like an all-
pervading dominant value-system, to be interpreted in more or
less hierarchical terms. But these subjective realities are balanced
by the existence of equally important sets of subjective value-systems opposed to the dominant one and upheld by different sections of society. In many marginal individuals or sections the competitive sets of values are operative as a source of inner conflict or
insecurity.

It would appear, then, that a structural model of this type
could help us to obtain a better insight into dynamic social change
than the concept of an objectively existing (or throughout a
given community universally accepted) stratification system,
pre-supposing a 'national society' as a separate entity. Perhaps
this view of hierarchical systems and class structures as subjective
interpretations of society by different social layers might even
explain, to some extent, the seeming incompatibility of conflicting
views at the Third World Congress of Sociology (held in Amsterdam). Different theories may reflect a different position towards
the dominant value systems in one's own or an alien society. In
order to be able to cope with the dynamic elements of society, we
have to develop a conceptual framework which does justice to
these fluid elements – in fact a dynamic type of analysis.

A rejection of the structural model used by those who start from the assumption that homogeneous 'national' cultures exist also implies a rejection of the 'plural society' concept as a tool for understanding colonial and post-colonial societies. If any society to be found in the world can be viewed as a composite of conflicting value systems, there seems to be no need for a distinct conceptual model devised especially for societies where the clash between divergent value-systems is more pronounced. Moreover, while there is a tendency to over-estimate the homogeneity of the value systems dominating a 'national' society, there seems to be, on the other hand, a tendency to over-estimate the 'plural' character of colonial or post-colonial societies. Though these societies took their origin in the contact of foreign and mutually conflicting cultures, a common system of values has gradually been developed as a superstructure which keeps colonial society together. The dominating group has called into life a hierarchical system of stratification according to race which it succeeded in imposing upon the social structure, and which has been, to a certain extent, internalized by the members of the dominated groups.[1]

Therefore, the type of plurality and the character of contrapuntal protest forms are not essentially different from the situation within the so-called 'national' society.

Finally I would suggest that the foregoing observations imply the necessity of a new approach to field research. We should not primarily look for the inherent structure of a given society, but for the value systems adopted in different layers of society. We have, in the first place, to learn how members of different segments of society view society as a whole. The division of society might even be based upon a distinction according to the value systems accepted. Instead of searching exclusively for integrative expedients, we should with equal intellectual force try to detect strains and conflicts in society, as possible agents in future change. There-

[1] The present author's criticism of the 'plural society' concept is elaborated in greater detail in the following paper, dealing with minority problems.

fore, a description of the structure of society in purely synchronic terms seems basically inadequate, as conflicting value systems can only be understood in a diachronic perspective.

A good instance of the insoluble inadequacies, into which the one-dimensional approach to society is liable to run, is to be found in Skinner's interesting analysis of leadership among the Chinese community in Thailand.[1] The author has attempted to analyse that community in terms of an evaluation of prestige which is assumed to be generally accepted among the Chinese group. But his own analysis presents sufficient proof that the dominating values as found by the author are not generally accepted. There are several incidents reported in his book which indicate that a large section of the Chinese community does not accept the leadership of those assuming that role, as for example the mass demonstrations for a fee reduction for Chinese,[2] or the chain of events during the period of emergency measures after a heavy fire in Bangkok.[3] And if the trend to further assimilation of those leaders within Thai society, as anticipated by the author, should be forthcoming,[4] it seems all but certain that the majority of the Chinese, who will not be in a position to attain the same kind of integration and gratification, will shift their allegiance to other leaders who give more attention to popular needs and to those values of vital importance for their well-being.

Thus, a different approach to the stratification problem may equally influence the techniques of social research. It appears to me that the following suggestions for the trend of social research might be derived from the foregoing argument:

1. Any fact may be important as a symbol of a social process involving a conflict of value systems within society. Therefore the social anthropologist and sociologist have to develop a keen sense for discovering hidden signs of social discontent and conflicting

[1] G. William Skinner, *Leadership and Power in the Chinese Community of Thailand* (Ithaca, 1958).

[2] Skinner, *op. cit.*, p. 152.

[3] *Ibidem*, p. 158.

[4] *Ibidem*, p. 316.

value systems in the most trivial forms of behaviour, in the same way as the Freudian school of psychology developed the capacity of detecting significant symbols of conflicting norms in such seemingly futile phenomena as lapses or dreams.

2. A great distrust of 'official' informants, such as chieftains, village elders, 'experts' of customary law, is essential for a social anthropologist or sociologist doing field research in the non-Western world. These people are in general only expressing the 'dominant' value system. To detect hidden or overt forms of protest, the attention has to be shifted to how representatives of different layers of society think and feel about the society in which they live, and how they actually behave.

3. If we are still in search of objectively valid elements in the structure of society as a basis for scientific sociological knowledge, they have to be looked for in the way the different systems of subjective value systems interact and keep a precarious balance, rather than in social structures viewed as rigid realities. Refined sociological analysis should be directed at a discovery of what people think and how they feel about society, rather than of how society *is* like. The sociologist should in the first place attempt to gauge the balance of power between conflicting value systems.

According to William H. Whyte,[1] for the Lloyd Warner school 'conflict, change, fluidity – these are the evils from which man should be insulated'. The modern social anthropologist – and sociologist for that matter! – should ask himself whether these very 'evils' should not be viewed as the deepest sources of human progress.

[1] William H. Whyte, *The Organization Man* (New York, Doubleday Anchor Ed., 1956), p. 44.

In March 1962, at the invitation of the *Institut d'Etude des Pays en Développement* of the Catholic University in Louvain (Belgium), the author read a series of lectures on topical problems in Southeast Asia. One of them dealt with 'Het minderhedenvraagstuk in Zuidoost Azië' (The minority problem in Southeast Asia). The lecture has been repeated in Antwerp, in december 1963, and published in Dutch in *De Nieuwe Stem*, vol. 19 (1964) pp. 94–109, with the title 'Ahasverus in de Tropen' (Ahasverus in the tropics).

The present essay is a thoroughly revised and extended version of the lecture, which is being published for the first time in this volume. I am indebted to my assistant Mr. O. D. van den Muijzenberg for his substantial contribution in analysing and clarifying the 'plural society' concept and terminology as current in post-war literature.

The paper is an elaboration of a viewpoint forwarded by the present author about fifteen years earlier in *Het rassenprobleem: De ondergang van een mythe* (The race problem: Decline of a myth; The Hague, n.y.), chapters 5 and 6, dealing with the Indonesian Chinese in Indonesia, and with the minority problems in post-war Indonesia.

THREE

THE TRADING MINORITIES IN SOUTHEAST ASIA

I

Most of the newly independent states of Southeast Asia are confronted with challenging minority problems. There are the regional minorities – such as the Menangkabau or the Menadonese in Indonesia, the Shans or the Karenni in Burma, the Moros in the Philippines – who generally form a distinct majority in their own region but have a minority position within the state, because of its overall territorial and ethnic composition. This position as a political minority in the state may, however, coincide with a social minority position in different parts of the country; on the other hand, the overall majority within the state (such as the Javanese in Indonesia, the Burmese in Burma) may occupy a social minority position in the regions largely inhabited by a regional 'minority'. In either case, the special position of the social minority also depends, apart from the status as a political majority or minority within the total state structure, on the type of functions performed by such a minority group. For example, the position of Menangkabau people in Java is related to their traditional function either as traders or as intellectuals who enjoyed higher education in Java and never returned back to their land of origin. The Menadonese in Java are often to be found working in clerical functions, either for the government or in some private company, owing to the educational advantage they enjoyed, as a Christian group, during the colonial period. The position of the Javanese minority in parts of Sumatra may be influenced by the fact that they have worked there, for a long time, as coolies in Western plantations.

Moreover, we have to keep in mind that the position as a 'regional minority' may disappear when an ethnic group breaks loose from the national state and calls a new state into being in a more restricted area. This has happened in Central Europe several times in modern history, and the menace of such an occurrence is far from imaginary in Southeast Asia, where national boundaries are the result of colonial history rather than of ethnic affinity. Economic motives may combine with psychological and political ones to foster separatism, if for example a regional minority feels that the foreign exchange earned by the products of its territory are not properly used for the benefit of that area.

From an ideological point of view, the new nations, in general, do not recognize the regional minorities as a special problem. The official motto of the Indonesian Republic, *Bhinneka Tunggal Ika* (Unity in Diversity) gives expression to the idea that each regional group should get its proper share within the national state, but that unity should prevail.

Like anywhere else, however, social reality and political practice in Southeast Asia quite often differ from proclaimed principles. Tensions between regional minorities and political majorities have played an important role in the disturbances which have troubled some of the Southeast Asian countries since the end of the war.

A minority position within a state structure, however, does not necessarily proceed from the geographic distribution of its nationals. A factor like religion may also function as a dividing line between a majority and a number of minority groups. In some cases a religious minority coincides with a regional one, as is the case with the Karenni in Burma or the Menadonese in Indonesia, a high proportion of whom are Christians, or with the Moros, who constitute a Moslem minority in the Philippines.

But there are also minorities within the national state which do not possess a definite area where they 'belong' and form a local majority. Not only religious, but also ethnic criteria may set a group apart from the main body of the population in such a way that they constitute a minority in the whole territory over which the state extends its power.

The Eurasians in Indonesia form such an ethnic and, at the same time, religious minority. Colonial history has set them apart from the main body of native society, and as a consequence of the national upsurge with which most of them were not able to iden-tify themselves – in fact many opposed the national revolution in an attempt to defend privileges acquired during the colonial peri-od – their present situation is hardly enviable, since they lost the support of a colonial power.

But this essay is largely concerned with a different group: those of Chinese ancestry, who are equally a 'homeless' ethnic minor-ity within most of the Southeast Asian states, and who, largely as a consequence of their dominant position in trade, to-day present a serious social, economic and political problem in most of the countries of that area. The Indian minorities, found in the parts of Southeast Asia bordering on the Indian Ocean, show similar characteristics and comparable problems. The present discussion, however, is nearly exclusively based on the specific situation of the Chinese minorities.

There is a wealth of descriptive material on the Chinese or Chi-nese-born who have settled in Southeast Asia. Apart from the overall survey by Victor Purcell, covering the whole of the area,[1] there is no lack of monographs dealing with Chinese communities in a single country or a still more limited area.[2] But there has hardly been any attempt to analyse the position of these minor-ities in terms of sociological theory.

[1] Victor Purcell, *The Chinese in Southeast Asia* (London, 1951).
[2] See for example Purcell, *The Chinese in Malaya* (London, 1948); Maurice Freedman, *Chinese Family and Marriage in Singapore* (London, 1957); G. Wil-liam Skinner, *Chinese Society in Thailand: An Analytical History* (Ithaca, 1957); Skinner, *Leadership and Power in the Chinese Community of Thailand* (Ithaca, 1958); Ong Eng Die, *Chineezen in Nederlandsch-Indië: Sociografie van een Indonesische be-volkingsgroep* (Chinese in the Netherlands Indies: A sociography of an Indone-sian population group, doctoral thesis Amsterdam University, Assen, 1943); W. J. Cator, *The Economic Position of the Chinese in the Netherlands Indies* (doctoral thesis Leiden University, Oxford, 1936); Donald E. Willmott, *The Chinese of Semarang: A Changing Minority Community in Indonesia* (Ithaca, 1960); T'ien Ju-k'ang, *The Chinese of Sarawak: A Study of Social Structure* (London, 1953).

In discussions of the so-called 'race-problem', trading minority groups like the Chinese in Southeast Asia, the Indians in Burma, East-Africa and Natal, or the Syrians in West-Africa are generally left out of consideration. In the Fourth World Congress of Sociology (Milan-Stresa, 1959) a special section was devoted to 'Racial Relations'.[1] The discussions in the section meetings centered well-nigh exclusively on the tensions between 'black-and-white' in societies which have gone through a stage characterized by slave plantations or colonial rule; there was also ample discussion of the 'black-and-white' relationships in European countries where, quite recently, immigration of 'coloured' people from former colonies has become a social problem. But an attempt by a few participants in the discussion to draw more attention to the different type of problems presented by the 'brown-and-yellow' relationships in Southeast Asian countries hardly met with any response.[2] Those present at the section meeting made the impression of being so much preoccupied with the world-wide problem of 'black-and-white' relationships, that they were impatient with those who attempted to deflect the attention to a different problem. The argument put forward by the present author in the course of the discussion to the effect that on the one hand white discrimination against 'coloured' people was bound to decrease in the next few decades, despite the many Little Rocks which had still to be removed on the way to a solution, and that on the other hand discrimination against the trading minorities in newly independent countries was on the increase and might, in the future, assume tragic dimensions, was wrongly interpreted by the chair-

[1] 'The Application of Sociological Knowledge to Ethnic and Racial Relations', in *Transactions of the Fourth World Congress of Sociology*, Milan and Stresa, 1959, Vol. 3 (Louvain, 1961); a short report on the discussion is to be found pp. 209 ff.

[2] There were two papers dealing with these problems: Maurice Freedman, 'The Growth of a Plural Society in Malaya', and M. A. Jaspan, 'Ethnic and Racial Relations in Indonesia' (see for the abstracts *op. cit.*, pp. 206–207), but most of the participants in the discussion hardly paid any attention to these papers. A revised text of Freedman's paper has been published in *Pacific Affairs*, Vol. 33 (1960), pp. 158 ff.

man of the section, the late professor E. Franklin Frazier, as a denial of the present sorrowful plight of the blacks in the Southern States of the U.S.A..

In the present article, which forms a cautious attempt to fill the gap, the descriptive part has been kept restricted in order to leave full scope to the discussion of the theoretical aspects and implications of the 'race relations' connected with the presence of alien trading minorities in Southeast Asian countries.

Though the present discussion is concerned with the Chinese of Southeast Asia in their capacity as a trading minority, it should be made clear from the outset that in some parts of the territory a much broader range of occupations is being fulfilled by people of Chinese ancestry. We have to differentiate between those areas where the Chinese migrants settled among a comparatively dense local population engaged in agriculture, rice cultivation on irrigated fields in the first place, and those mostly infertile areas where at the time of their arrival the country was still sparsely populated.[1] In the former areas they mostly found an integrated society, in which they had no access to agriculture nor to other occupations in which sections of the native society were firmly entrenched. As foreigners they were in many cases not allowed to acquire land, and consequently they were relegated to occupations which were not yet filled by the natives, the evident avenue for migrants being trade, which in a predominantly patrimonial[2] or feudal society was a profession despised both by the aristocra-

---

[1] This distinction has been elaborated by H. J. H. Alers, *Dilemma in Zuid-Oost-Azië: Een anthropo-geografische interpretatie van de Chinese penetratie in Zuid-Oost-Azië* (Dilemma in Southeast Asia: An anthropo-geographical interpretation of Chinese penetration in Southeast Asia, Leiden, 1955). Although some of the author's geopolitical tenets are highly debatable and his work would appear to suffer from a certain inaccuracy and lack of scholarly method (there are, for example, no bibliographical references whatever and the bibliography at the end of the book is rather slipshod), some of the basic ideas of his book are original and worthy of serious consideration.

[2] For the term 'patrimonial', which is derived from Max Weber's concept of patrimonial as opposed to modern bureaucracies, see the fifth paper of this volume, devoted to corruption as a sociological phenomenon.

cy and the peasantry. In addition they could engage in all kinds of handicrafts, which also were typically urban occupations. Thus the foreigners had to fill, what Rinder[1] has called 'the status gap', but what could even more correctly be termed an 'occupational gap', in the way the Jews had filled a similar gap in mediaeval Europe or the Armenians in nineteenth-century Turkey. As a consequence, in those areas the Chinese became a functional group; and though, in the course of time, they were admitted to or were able to make headway towards several other occupations, they have still to bear the odium attached to the trading profession by a rural society in which aristocratic and feudal values are still strong.

A situation like that described in the foregoing could develop in most parts of Java, in the fertile deltas of the Menam and Mekong rivers, and in the Tonkin delta.[2]

This situation may be opposed to that which arose in other parts of Southeast Asia where the Chinese settled in a comparatively empty area. This type of migration, in actual history, may have been preceded by the former one, which was attracted by the existence of Southeast Asian harbour principalities entertaining trade connections with China and offering the settlers a market for commodities and crafts. But in later centuries the latter type of Chinese settlement assumed remarkable proportions. The Chinese, many of whom may have been impoverished peasants in their home country, had no specific preference for trade as a living. This is shown by the wide variety of occupations filled by people of Chinese ancestry in such empty areas. Many of them have engaged in agriculture, for example pepper growing in Banka and Western Borneo, sugar and later rice cultivation in the Tanggerang area to the West of Jakarta, gardening in Thailand; in addition large numbers of Chinese, mainly belonging to the Hakka speech group, were employed as indentured labourers on tobacco plantations in the Deli area of East Sumatra. Mining

---

[1] Irwin D. Rinder, 'Strangers in the Land: Social Relations in the Status Gap', *Social Problems*, Vol. 6 (1958–59), pp. 253 ff.

[2] Alers, *op. cit.*, pp. 99 ff., 119 ff.

also attracted large numbers of Chinese, for example tin extraction in Malaya, Banka and Billiton, gold digging in West Borneo, more in particular in the nineteenth century, before they had to shift to agriculture; there were further Chinese lumbermen in the Riau archipelago, and fishermen on Sumatra's East Coast; generally speaking, Chinese flocked to any occupation which promised a living and was not a closed monopoly of any social group.

Whereas in densely populated areas in which the Chinese were largely relegated to trade, their numbers generally did not exceed some ten or twelve per cent, in empty areas they could even attain a distinct majority.[1] The area in which they settled in a great variety of functions centered largely around Singapore, a predominantly Chinese city; it included large parts of Malaya, of Northeast Sumatra, the Riau and Lingga Archipelago, the islands of Banka and Billiton, the Tanggerang area West of Jakarta, large parts of West Borneo and Sarawak, and Cochin China. The position of Chinese in that part of Southeast Asia is essentially different from their situation in areas where they were relegated principally to trade, though stereotypes derived from the latter situation could adversely influence their position in the former areas.

Besides type of settlement, the groups of ethnic Chinese (this term is meant to include both Chinese nationals and those of Chinese ancestry who have acquired local citizenship) also widely differ in their rate of adaptation to the cultural environment of Southeast Asia. In originally empty areas where they have settled as complete communities – for example in the Straits Settlements – it is understandable that they have, to a large extent, retained their Chinese identity and, thus, preserved many elements of

---

[1] See for the rice-growing areas where the Chinese are largely relegated to trade, Alers, *op. cit.*, pp. 99 ff.; in the Tonkin delta and Java the percentage is still lower, according to Alers because the high population densities have brought about a development towards a 'closed rice economy' in which trade is becoming less and less profitable (pp. 102 ff., 123). For the empty areas see *ibidem*, pp. 109 ff., 131 ff.

Chinese culture.[1] On the other hand, in areas where they had to establish themselves as a functional group, a much higher degree of cultural adaptation to the surrounding population is likely, more in particular as far as the children and further descendants of migrants are concerned, born out of mixed marriages or concubinage with local women.[2]

However, in general, complete assimilation could only develop as an individual process, which does not exclude its occurrence on a large scale.[3] In some of the countries of Southeast Asia there were strong factors opposing such a complete assimilation, the most effective one probably being colonial rule.

Complete assimilation, which went as far as the adoption of a native name, was most likely to occur in a situation where such an assimilation could produce, for the individual concerned, a definite rise in social status. This could be the case in independent kingdoms, where the descendant of an immigrant who had become sufficiently adapted to the surrounding culture and had risen to a relatively high status, for example by success in business, could marry into one of the influential local families. This could be the case in Thailand, but also in Java before the establishment of Dutch colonial rule. In either case the individual taking the step to complete assimilation was likely to adopt the religion of the native ruling group. In Buddhist Thailand such a religious conversion was an easier step to accomplish for a Chinese than in

[1] Maurice Freedman, 'The Growth of a Plural Society in Malaya', *loc. cit.*, pp. 159, 164 ff.

[2] This situation is characteristic of the *peranakan* in Java; but even for parts of Malaya this thesis appears to find support from census data. T. E. Smith, *Population Growth in Malaya: An Analysis of Recent Trends* (London/New York, 1952), p. 67, observes that literacy in Malay, although low among the Chinese of Malaya everywhere, 'is highest in such areas as most of Kelantan and Trengganu which have a predominantly Malay population, and in which many of the Chinese are shopkeepers serving the Malay community'. See also Tjoa Soei Hock, *Economic Aspects of Life in Malaya, with Special Reference to the East Coast* (doctoral thesis Utrecht University, Utrecht, 1963), pp. 104 ff.

[3] Such large scale assimilation is suggested, as far as North Borneo is concerned, by Spencer St. John, *Life in the Forests of the Far East*, Vol. 2 (1862), pp. 308 ff.; see in particular pp. 312–313.

Moslem Indonesia or Malaya, and consequently such a complete assimilation is known to have occurred on a comparably high scale throughout Thai history.[1] But even in Java complete assimilation through conversion to Islam seems to have occurred rather frequently, more in particular before the arrival of the Dutch merchant-adventurers.[2]

But in a colonial situation the odds are distinctly against complete assimilation. The higher strata of native society have been removed from actual political power, and their place has largely been occupied by members of the white colonial ruling caste. Inasmuch as a status of inferiority became attached to the position of 'being a native', the attraction of complete assimilation within native society decreased accordingly. Though ethnic Chinese, who were considered as more or less foreign elements, suffered from a good deal of discrimination on the part of the colonial authorities, still their position within the colonial setting, which set them apart from native society, was in general more favourable than it would have become after complete assimilation. For ambitious members of the higher strata of local Chinese society the trend became rather to identify themselves with the colonial upper caste.

The difference between the position of Chinese in Thailand and in pre-war Java illustrates the foregoing observations. In Java there was, during the colonial period, no strong incentive to complete assimilation of Chinese.[3] But this did not preclude a high degree of cultural adaptation to the Javanese environment, which was stimulated by the position of Chinese as a functional

[1] Skinner, *Chinese Society in Thailand* (*op. cit.*), pp. 128–134; Skinner, 'Change and Persistence in Chinese Culture Overseas: A Comparison of Thailand and Java', *Journal of the South Seas Society*, Vol. 16 (1960), pp. 86 ff.

See also L. E. L. Sluimers, *De Delta-landen van Zuidoost Azië* (The Delta lands of Southeast Asia, Meppel, 1961), pp. 107 ff.

[2] F. de Haan, *Oud-Batavia* (Old Batavia, Second Ed., Bandung, 1935), pp. 394 ff. Those Chinese who had been converted to Islam, were called by the Dutch, in the first decades of the seventeenth century, 'shaven Chinese'.

[3] Skinner, 'Change and Persistence in Chinese Culture Overseas', *loc. cit.*, pp. 89 ff.; Sluimers, *op. cit.*, p. 107.

group of traders catering to the needs of the native society. Many Chinese took an Indonesian wife or one of mixed ancestry, and their children or grandchildren adopted several elements of Indonesian culture, including the local speech (Javanese, Sundanese or Batavian Malay). But this cultural adaptation did not imply a complete assimilation and identification with the Indonesians even for those belonging to a second or third generation. The Chinese-born, as a rule, kept their Chinese identity, symbolized by the retention of a Chinese name; in addition they retained quite a number of distinctive traits. As a group of Chinese-born within the colonial society of Java, they remained separate from the main body of Indonesian society and developed, as a group, a solidarity of their own. Though they were clearly differentiated, as *baba* or *peranakan* (the latter term meaning 'children of the country'), from the first generation of immigrants (the so-called *singkeh*), they were still indicated, together with the latter group, as Chinese. And though culturally they may have been nearer to Indonesians or to Europeans living in the colony than to the newly arrived Chinese immigrants, legally and socially they were still counted among the Chinese.

According to Skinner's analysis the situation of the Chinese in Thailand was essentially different. Assimilation with Thai society was prevalent to such an extent that no intermediate group parallelling the *peranakan* from Java has developed there. Those second or third generation ethnic Chinese who found an incentive for a complete transition into Thai society, including the adoption of a Thai name, lost the sense of identity with the local Chinese; there were even quite a few among them who, as true renegades, became strong supporters of discrimination against Chinese. But those who did not take the decisive step remained members of the 'Chinese community' and retained a culture which was predominantly Chinese. Even though many of them had to learn a certain amount of Thai to facilitate their trade relationships with the local people, the general social and cultural orientation remained distinctly Chinese.[1]

Greater still is the variation in modes and rates of adaptation to

be found among ethnic Chinese who have settled in comparatively empty areas. Such an adaptation was not likely to occur at all
where Chinese only came on a temporary basis, to earn, during a
definite period, some money as labourers in a tobacco plantation
or a tin mine with the intention of returning afterwards to their
families left behind in China. Cultural adaptation was also un-
likely to occur in areas where Chinese immigration included a
large number of Chinese women. This situation developed in
parts of Malaya and in Singapore in the course of the first decades of the twentieth century and more in particular after the crisis of 1930, when male immigration was restricted but female immigration, for some time, was still left free.[2] In such a society the
cultural focus, around which both new migrants and those belonging to the second and third generation revolved, was bound
to be predominantly Chinese. This was to remain the case even
though, in a later period, immigration was severely restricted and
the female element became mainly local-born. In a society where
those to whose needs the Chinese traders catered were also Chinese, and where a sex-ratio nearing equality of males and females
strongly diminished the need to take non-Chinese wives, cultural
adaptation was at its lowest.

On the other hand, in areas where Chinese had established rural
settlements in a distant past, but where at that time there was a
dearth of Chinese women, and consequently the descendants were
of mixed ancestry, cultural adaptation could develop farther than
among a largely urban trading community. An extreme case of
such a cultural adaptation is to be found among the *peranakan*
small peasants in the Tanggerang area not far from Jakarta. Go
Gien Tjwan has studied a village in that area, where one third of
the farmer population claimed Chinese ancestry.[3] Dr. Go sug-

[1] Skinner, *Chinese Society in Thailand* (*op. cit.*), p. 129; Richard J. Coughlin,
Double Identity: The Chinese in Modern Thailand (Hongkong, 1960), pp. 190 ff.
[2] Smith, *op. cit.*, pp. 12, 71.
[3] Go Gien Tjwan, *Eenheid en verscheidenheid in een Indonesisch dorp* (Unity and
diversity in an Indonesian village, unpublished doctoral thesis Free University of Brussels, 1962).

gests that in that area Chinese immigrants were the first to reclaim land for the cultivation of sugar; later on they shifted to the cultivation of rice, to gardening and to fish-breeding in ponds. Indonesian fishermen may have been living along the coast at the time when the Chinese arrived; but after the Chinese had reclaimed the land, Indonesian peasants also gradually flocked to the area and ultimately attained a distinct majority. But unlike the situation in other parts of Java, those of Chinese ancestry were allowed to stay on the land as small tenants under the special provision drafted for the large *latifundia* ('private estates') in the Jakarta neighbourhood. In this case the rate of cultural adaptation to the Indonesian environment has been very marked.

For a casual visitor to the Tanggerang area it is hardly possible to distinguish the *peranakan* peasant from the *asli* (purely Indonesian) one. In this rural community studied by Dr. Go, the tensions prevalent in those parts of Java where ethnic Chinese have been relegated to non-rural occupations appear to be almost absent, social intercourse and intermarriage being comparatively frequent. Still, the overall position of Chinese in Java under colonial rule has influenced the community in setting even these Chinese-born small peasants apart from the natives and in developing among them a sense of Chinese identity and mutual solidarity to the point of preventing their formal conversion to Islam. When anti-Chinese riots started in the town of Tanggerang during the revolution (1946) the disturbances also spread to the rural communities in the neighbourhood. Culturally these *peranakan* peasants are still distinguishable from the Moslem *asli*, though any contact with China has been practically absent for at least two centuries.

The wide variety in the rate of assimilation or cultural adaptation, to which we may add the complication caused by legal definitions, accounts for some difficulties in the statistical assessment of the numbers of Chinese in the different countries of Southeast Asia and of their demographic characteristics. The actual numbers largely depend on the criteria used. In the past, definition by ancestry in the male line would largely coincide with a definition according to the citizenship act passed in 1929 in China, which had reaffirmed the *ius sanguinis* principle. Those who had undergone a complete assimilation by adopting, for example, a Thai name and Thai nationality, would no longer be recognizable as ethnic Chinese; but those who had become Dutch or British subjects by birth in one of the colonies, but still retained a Chinese name, would automatically be included in statistics dealing with overseas Chinese, and rightly so, even though their Chinese 'nationality' would no longer have any effect in their actual life. For example, according to the census held in 1930 in the Netherlands Indies, both the *singkeh*, most of whom possessed no other nationality than Chinese, and the *peranakan*, who were most likely to be Dutch subjects in addition, were counted as Chinese. This was quite reasonable, as the 'Chinese' occupied a special position as 'Foreign Orientals' in the Netherlands East Indies legislation, even though their Chinese 'nationality' was without any legal effect, the Chinese consulary officers not being allowed to interfere when ethnic Chinese who were Dutch subjects were concerned. In the 1930 census, complications only arose so far as Indonesian women married to 'Chinese', or 'Chinese' individuals who had obtained the legal status of 'European', were concerned (both groups were counted as Chinese in the census).

But since Indonesian independence, and more particularly since the implementation of the Sino-Indonesian dual citizenship Treaty concluded in 1955, the decision to be taken by statisticians has become less obvious. A high percentage of *peranakan* have acquired Indonesian citizenship (the status of *warga nagara*), forsaking their claim to the status of Chinese nationals. Though they are still clearly distinguishable as ethnic Chinese, most of all through their name, and though their legal position may still, in some respects, be different from the status of *asli* as a result of some remnants of colonial law which have been kept intact, they could still rightly object to being included within the category of 'Chinese'. They could resent such a procedure as conducive to discrimination; as far as I am aware, they were not separately counted at the 1961 census.

As a matter of fact, discrimination against ethnic Chinese, both socially and legally, is rife in most of the Southeast Asian countries.

Apart from the great variety in the situation of Chinese minorities according to geographical area, the historical factor is also highly relevant, as is apparent from several instances in the foregoing observations. The Chinese have experienced many vicissitudes during their stay in Southeast Asia.

Discrimination against Chinese is not a new phenomenon in Southeast Asian history. But the kind and amount of discrimination underwent significant changes in the course of centuries.

Before the arrival of West European merchant-adventurers, the colonies of Chinese traders were mainly to be found in the Southeast Asian harbour principalities, described by Van Leur.[1] The traders' and artisans' colonies, grouped together in separate quarters according to the nation and the place they came from, were subject to princely authority, but they enjoyed a certain amount of internal autonomy, since each colony's quarter was left under the immediate rule of its own chieftain appointed by the harbour prince, who kept the supreme power.

It is difficult to deduce from the scarce source materials available a general picture of the treatment which the Chinese traders' colonies received at the hands of the Southeast Asian harbour princes and their officials. About 1600, in Bantam, an important sea-port in West Java where the ruling dynasty at that time was Moslem, the Chinese traders enjoyed a favourable position. Edmund Scot, who visited Bantam in 1602, was impressed by their economic position.

> This China Towne, is for the most part built of Brick, every house square, and flat over-head, some of them having Boords, and small Timbers, or split Canes over-crosse, on which are laid Bricks and Sand, to defend them from fire. Over these Bricke Ware-houses is set a shed, being built up with great Canes, and Thatched, and some are built up with small Timber, but the greatest number with Canes onely. Of late years, since we came thither,

[1] J. C. van Leur, *Indonesian Trade and Society: Essays in Asian Social and Economic History* (The Hague/Bandung, 1955), pp. 98 ff., 130 ff., 137 ff., 197 ff.

many men of wealth have built their houses to the top, all fire free, of the which sort of houses, at our first comming, there was no more but the Sabindars house and the rich Chyna Merchants house.

Further on, Scot writes that the Chinese 'who like Jewes live crooching under them', 'sucke away all the wealth of the Land, by reason that the Javans are so idle.'[1]

Though it is possible to conclude from such descriptions by European travellers that the Chinese colonies enjoyed much economic power, and though one could easily assume that their position might have evoked much envy on the part of their non-Chinese competitors (Scot writes, that the Javanese 'doe much rejoyce when they see a Chynese goe to execution: as also the Chynois doe when they see a Javan goe to his death'), it also appears that some harbour princes generally encouraged Chinese trade since they could derive distinct advantages from it. John Jourdain writes in 1614:

> ...there is greate scarcitie of money, by reason that the China junckes carrie itt yearlie for China; which the Kinge doth suffer because the China marchannts doe bribe him, which hee is content to take although itt be the overthrowe of his commons.[2]

Concrete cases of anti-Chinese moves by princely authorities in Southeast Asia are not unknown, but these may have been mainly occasioned by political motives, connected with a fear of China as a mighty power. There is also a lack of evidence on the way the Chinese were internally organized. They may have created protective organizations such as guilds or secret societies, but there is, as far as I am aware, no reference to them in the historical accounts for the period under discussion.

Under conditions of colonial rule, the position of the Chinese

[1] Master Edmund Scot, 'A Discourse of Java, and of the first English Factorie There, with Divers Indian, English and Dutch Occurrents', in: *Hakluytus Posthumus or Purchas His Pilgrimes: Containing a History of the World in Sea Voyages and Land Travels by English and Others*, Vol. 2 (Glasgow, 1905), pp. 439–443.

[2] Scot, *loc. cit.*, p. 467; *The Journal of John Jourdain 1608–1617: Describing His Experiences in Arabia, India, and the Malay Archipelago* (Cambridge, 1905), p. 316.

changed appreciably. The Dutch East India Company, which tried to get a foothold in Jakarta, was much in favour of attracting Chinese people to the newly-built fortress, which they called Batavia. Chinese could be better relied upon than the Moslem natives, who were likely to sympathize with the Moslem rulers of Bantam and Mataram. According to a well-known pronouncement by Governor General Jan Pieterszoon Coen, 'there are no people in the world which serve us better than the Chinese, and which are as easy to get'.[1]

At that time the primary aim was to get a labour force for the construction of fortifications in Batavia. However, getting the Chinese into Batavia did not prove to be as easy as all that. The way Coen succeeded in providing Batavia with a Chinese population was not always conducive to a sympathetic attitude on the part of the Chinese: many of them were simply kidnapped from Chinese junks and shores by the Company's men of war. But Coen's successors put an end to such practices, and for some time voluntary Chinese migration was much favoured by the Dutch. The Chinese were even allowed, in Jakarta and later in the surrounding area, to develop a much wider range of economic activities than trade alone, many of them being occupied as artisans, sugar-planters, arrack-distillers, gardeners, fishermen, lumbermen, water-carriers, and finally as lessees of different government monopolies and tax farms.

But while the Chinese had been brought in as a much-favoured group, in the course of time many shifts in the attitude of colonial powers toward Chinese were bound to occur. The first colonial centre where this happened was probably Manila. The Spanish conquistadores, who had at first welcomed the Chinese as artisans and as labourers for building churches, convents, and forts, soon changed their attitude. In 1603 a terrible massacre occurred, which resulted in the death of over 20,000 Chinese.[2] The fear of China as a mighty power may have played a certain role in that

---

[1] H. T. Colenbrander, *Jan Pietersz. Coen: Levensbeschrijving* (Jan Pieterszoon Coen: A biography, The Hague, 1934), p. 309.

[2] Purcell, *The Chinese in Southeast Asia* (*op. cit.*), pp. 590 ff.

case; but the basic motives must have been different, as might appear from the parallel provided by the massacre of Batavia in 1740.

In the eighteenth century, the Dutch also had altered their attitude toward the Chinese population. The Dutch Company began to fear the power of the Chinese settlers who rapidly grew in numbers, and she attempted to restrict immigration. Tension increased, the Dutch authorities developing an hysterical fear of the Chinese settlers in the rural area around Batavia. The hysteria culminated in a terrible pogrom started in 1740 and resulted in a massacre of a large number of Chinese dwellers of the town who had never been anything but peaceful traders or artisans.[1] The massacre was accompanied by the looting of their stores and houses by the populace, who evidently could be easily incited by playing upon their pent-up feelings of envy and economic rivalry. It is this element of economic competition which also may have been prevalent in the history of the Philippines.

Soon the Dutch authorities discovered, however, that they had slaughtered the goose that laid the golden eggs; consequently they tried to encourage Chinese immigration again. And about the turn of the century the Chinese had, once more, acquired a position which Dirk van Hogendorp described in the following words: 'The Chinese have been made the owners of Java'.[2]

Throughout the nineteenth century colonial rule, as applied by British, Dutch, or Spanish authorities, kept shifting from a certain amount of protection to repression and back again. The Chinese communities could provide great advantages to the colonial economy – but on the other hand they also provided convenient scapegoats for popular discontent in times of stress. Together

---

[1] The best study of the massacre of Batavia (1740) is the one by J. Th. Vermeulen, *De Chineezen te Batavia en de troebelen van 1740* (The Chinese in Batavia and the 1740 riots, doctoral thesis Leiden University, Leiden, 1938).

[2] Dirk van Hogendorp, *Berigt van den tegenwoordigen toestand der Bataafse Bezittingen in Oost-Indië en den Handel op Dezelve* (Report of the present condition of the possessions of the Batavian Republic in the East Indies and of the trade thereon, Second Ed., Delft, 1800), p. 18.

with the growth of a greater concern for native welfare, at least in verbal expressions, it became fashionable to put the blame for the backward state of the native community on the Chinese and their role as intermediaries. In general, even in periods during which a certain amount of encouragement was provided to Chinese, they were also submitted to all kinds of restrictions which were motivated largely by consideration for native welfare. A restriction of utmost importance was imposed upon the movement of Chinese into the countryside and upon their settlement, resulting in the creation of urban *ghettos*. These measures tended to accentuate the position of the Chinese as a functional group relegated to trade and other urban professions and crafts.

The Chinese groups gradually developed organizational forms to counter discriminatory measures taken by colonial authorities. The interests of the *peranakan* of Java were more or less respected by colonial authorities, within the bounds of their special position as 'Foreign Orientals'. The Dutch East India Company had adopted from the Indonesian harbour princes the system of rule over the different groups through their chieftains, and during the nineteenth century the government authorities still dealt with the locally born Chinese largely through the formally appointed 'majors', 'captains' and 'lieutenants' of the Chinese. Much more vulnerable, however, was the position of recent migrants, who formed the *singkeh* communities in Malaya, in Thailand, and in the Outer Islands of Indonesia. These poor migrants sought protection against all kinds of arbitrary power through *kongsi* (district or clan associations) or *hui* (secret societies), which, perhaps, sometimes also fulfilled a function comparable to that of occupational guilds.[1] Similar organizations were also established in relatively empty areas where groups of Chinese settled with the con-

---

[1] Skinner, *Chinese Society in Thailand* (*op. cit.*), p. 140: 'One of the chief functions of the societies was to preserve traditional occupations against intruders'. However, Maurice Freedman, 'Immigrants and Associations: Chinese in Nineteenth-Century Singapore', *Comparative Studies in Society and History*, Vol. 3 (1960–61), pp. 25 ff., draws a clear-cut distinction between secret societies, and voluntary associations including guilds (p. 41).

sent of a local ruler (such as for example the gold miners in West Borneo in the first half of the nineteenth century). It was through the leaders of these largely autonomous organizations (*kongsi*) that the settlers could deal with the local ruler; but the *kongsi* were also able to resist, for many decades, the Dutch colonial authorities, who attempted to establish effective rule in the area.[1]

A new situation arose after 1900, with the advent of what Romein has called 'The Asian Century'.[2] The overseas Chinese were stirred by the revolutionary transformations in their home country. In the past, those who left the ancestral graves were considered deserters; the Chinese dynasties had never shown any real interest in the fate of the emigrants in the *Nan Yang* (the Southern Seas region). But with the growth of Chinese nationalism it became important to the Chinese politicians at home, both official authorities and revolutionaries, to re-establish contacts with the Chinese community abroad, which could provide a source of moral strength and of financial support for political movements or for officially sponsored projects. The Chinese communities in Southeast Asia underwent appreciable changes. Several groups of ethnic Chinese, for example among the *peranakan* of Java, who since a long time had lost contact with their home country, now developed a new interest in Chinese politics and culture and even in the Chinese language, which most of them had never learnt. The discriminations, to which the Chinese were subjected, reinforced the tendency to look to the Chinese mainland for material or moral support.

[1] For a short account in English of the struggle of the Dutch colonial government against the Chinese gold and diamond mining *kongsis* in West Borneo, see Purcell, *The Chinese in Southeast Asia* (*op. cit.*), pp. 489 ff. The best-known study of these *kongsis* is still J. J. M. de Groot, *Het kongsiwezen van Borneo: eene verhandeling over den grondslag en den aard der Chineesche politieke vereenigingen in de Koloniën met eene Chineesche geschiedenis van de kongsi Lanfong* (The *kongsi* institution in Borneo: A treatise of the foundations and character of the Chinese political associations in the colony, supplemented with a Chinese history of Lanfong *kongsi*, The Hague, 1885).

[2] Jan Romein, *The Asian Century: A History of Modern Asian Nationalism* (London, 1962).

Organizational life among the overseas Chinese also underwent the impact of modern Asian nationalism. The secret societies lost much of their former influence, as was shown during the troubles in Thailand about 1910; gradually they were replaced by modern unions and Chambers of Commerce, many of which no longer were restricted to a particular locality or to a separate speech group. The Chinese attempted to establish such unions on the basis of an overall solidarity of all Chinese living in one country of Southeast Asia. In Indonesia, organizational activity in the field of education, assisted by official authorities in China, was especially noteworthy.[1]

This development towards a greater group solidarity, however, was matched, and as a matter of fact more or less provoked, by similar developments within the host countries. Growing nationalism among the peoples of Southeast Asia directed itself not only against the colonial power, but equally against the local Chinese. Consequently, the position of the Chinese minority has been subjected to increasing restrictions, to the point of becoming threatened in several of the countries.

Some of the restrictions were introduced when colonial conditions still prevailed. The 'ethical policy' initiated about 1900 in the Netherlands East Indies, which put the interests of the native population in the forefront, was interpreted by many Dutch officials – according to the Dutch lawyer P. H. Fromberg, who was a great sympathizer with the Chinese and an expert in their laws and customs – in such a way that 'protecting the natives' amounted to 'pestering the Chinese'.[2] A few successive Advisers for Chinese Affairs for the Government in Batavia, who could be compared as far as their function was concerned with the Protector of Chinese in Singapore, were ironically called by the Chinese community in the Indies: 'Protector against Chinese'.

[1] Skinner, *Chinese Society in Thailand* (*op. cit.*), pp. 165 ff., and more in particular pp. 170 ff.; Lea E. Williams, *Overseas Chinese Nationalism: The Genesis of the Pan-Chinese Movement in Indonesia, 1900–1916* (Glencoe, 1960).

[2] P. H. Fromberg, *Verspreide geschriften* (Collected essays, Leiden, 1926), p. 406.

But it was rising nationalism among the peoples of Southeast Asia which in subsequent years began seriously to impair their position. *Sarekat Islam*, established in 1912 in Java, was at first called into life by Javanese *batik* traders and industrialists in an attempt to counter the economic power gradually acquired by the Chinese. In 1918 serious anti-Chinese riots flared up in the town of Kudus in Northern Java, where Moslem traders had considerable influence. In Thailand a pamphlet appeared in 1914, under the title *The Jews of the East*, the authorship of which is generally ascribed to king Vachiravut.[1] After the revolution of 1932, the Thai authorities started an anti-Chinese campaign, which resulted in numerous restrictions on their economic activities. The same happened in the Philippines, after it had become a Commonwealth in 1935.[2] After the end of the Japanese occupation of all of Southeast Asia, anti-Chinese sentiment flared up to unknown heights. Anti-Chinese campaigns were reinforced in Thailand and the Philippines, while they also started in newly independent countries such as Indonesia and, in a much more virulent form, in South Vietnam. The enforced formation of a Federation of Malaysia, which is to include the Borneo areas, is largely intended to offset the Chinese preponderance which would prevail in a territory restricted to Malaya combined with Singapore only.

The acquisition of an Indonesian nationality by most of the *peranakan* does not exempt them from discrimination, for example in the field of higher education, one of the rationalizations being that they lack true solidarity with the national movement and that many of them took an opportunistic attitude during the years of the revolutionary struggle for independence. There also seems to be some doubt whether the slogan *Bhinneka Tunggal Ika* should apply to other than regional minorities, and in particular to the *warga nagara* of Chinese ancestry.

The cold war aggravates the situation, because it facilitates all kinds of measures against distinct groups of Chinese. In the SEATO countries anti-Chinese measures can be rationalized as

[1] Skinner, *Chinese Society in Thailand* (*op. cit.*), pp. 164 ff.
[2] Purcell, *ibidem*, pp. 632 ff.

anti-communist ones; on the other hand, in Indonesia during the Sumatran rebellion of 1958, anti-Chinese measures could be excused as being directed especially against those sympathizing with the Kuomintang, for Taiwan ostensibly supported the rebellion. But there are also other reasons why the cold war may unfavourably affect the position of Chinese: there are some indications that the drive against foreign traders in the countryside of Indonesia, at the end of 1959, was instigated by those who would like to see the relations between Indonesia and the Chinese People's Republic deteriorate.

One of the paradoxical aspects of the present condition of Chinese in Southeast Asian countries is that many of them decided in the past to support China in becoming a strong national state, hoping thus to improve their own position as a minority group in their host country, in the way the Japanese had managed to achieve special treatment as soon as Japan had been recognized as a power to be reckoned with (in the Netherlands East Indies they had acquired a status equal to that of 'Europeans' as early as 1900).[1] At present, China has become one of the great powers. But to the overseas Chinese this seems to be of no avail, except for the possibility, for a number of them, of returning to their home country should the situation in the host country become unbearable. Strong China does not appear to signify much more to the overseas Chinese than Palestine meant for the European Jews during the anti-Jewish campaign in Nazi Germany: a place of refuge.

II

So far for the general outline of basic facts. We have now to try to provide an adequate analysis in terms of sociological theory.

First I should like to discuss a few attempts which have been

[1] This point has been elaborated in more detail in W. F. Wertheim, *Het rassenprobleem: De ondergang van een mythe* (The race problem: Decline of a myth, The Hague, n.y.), pp. 129 ff., 153 ff.

made by other authors to provide a theoretical frame for our problem.

We could consider as such the minority typology developed by Louis Wirth.[1] In addition to classifying the minorities according to such criteria as number and size, the amount of participation in social life and relations with the dominant group, this author has also attempted to elaborate how the position and the characteristics of a minority could be expected to evolve in different settings. He has tried to establish under what conditions a development towards assimilation is likely to occur among minority groups, and under which ones other tendencies ('pluralistic', 'secessionist', or 'militant') will prevail. But unfortunately, as appears from his main distinctions, he has envisaged the minority problem largely as one of political power and cultural identity. His typology does not sufficiently take account of the dynamic change originating from social and economic factors. This may have been the reason why he did not distinguish, in his typology, between the different economic functions which a minority group may fulfil. For example, Wirth did not view the trading minority groups as a separate problem, related to other minority issues but still one which shows some particular characteristics wherever such functional minorities occur. This neglect of the economic factor prevented him from realizing that the assimilation issue may differ from one minority situation to another. For instance, it is not at all probable that the Chinese minorities in Southeast Asia would be allowed by the social environment collectively to assimilate should they prefer to do so. Inasmuch as the traders of native stock want to oust what they call the foreign intruders, their problem will not be solved at all by a massive assimilation of these competitors, whatever rationalization they may verbally express as a reason for their actions against the group labelled a 'foreign' one. This simple example shows that economic factors cannot be left out of consideration in our analysis of the minority issue.

[1] Louis Wirth, 'The Problem of Minority Groups', in Ralph Linton (ed.), *The Science of Man in the World Crisis* (New York, 1945), pp. 347 ff.

Apart from the problems connected with the economic functions of a definite minority, we should also distinguish, as we have done in the first pages of this article, between those minorities which could only be considered as such in a political sense, because of the territorial and ethnic composition of a nation-state, but which form a majority in their own territory, and those which constitute a minority everywhere in the state. In the latter case the minority situation is a clear sequel of a process of immigration; but the type of migration and the kind of functions performed by the descendants of the migrants may differ widely. Wirth's typology and his concern with the assimilation issue does not take sufficient account of this wide variety of minority situations.

From the foregoing it should be clear why I cannot agree with Wirth's attempt to convey a qualitative instead of a quantitative meaning to the terms 'minority' and 'majority'.[1] According to Wirth's definition, it is not numbers, but political power, social status, and economic strength, that count. If we accept this terminology, then, in a colonial setting, the small numbers of European overlords would constitute the 'majority', whereas the many millions of 'natives' would constitute a 'minority'. With the attainment of political independence, according to Wirth's definition, the situation could be reversed overnight. No specific consideration has been paid, in Wirth's system, to the enormous difference between the presumed 'minority' position of the broad mass of those under colonial domination and the true minority position of the small group of former members of a colonial upper caste, who have lost their political power but may still have retained part of their former economic position. It seems to me that this terminology starts from an overestimation of power as a decisive factor and from an underestimation of sociological and economic factors which account for a wide variety of minority

---

[1] Wirth's terminology has been endorsed by Georges Balandier, *Sociologie actuelle de l'Afrique Noire: Dynamique Sociale en Afrique Centrale* (Paris, 1963), pp. 16 ff.; Balandier, 'La situation coloniale: Approche théorique', *Cahiers Internationaux de Sociologie*, Vol. 11 (1951), pp. 63 ff. Otherwise I agree with Balandier's analysis in several essential respects.

characteristics in different settings. I prefer the use of a purely statistical concept, which in the first instance leaves out of consideration the problem of to what extent the 'majority' has actual power.

Therefore the use of the minority concept and typology as developed by Wirth, in my view, do not appear relevant for a deeper insight into the manifold problems concerning the Southeast Asian trading minorities.

Another approach which seems worthy of closer consideration is the 'plural society' concept first elaborated by Furnivall, the more so as the concept was particularly developed with the countries of Southeast Asia in view.[1]

Furnivall opposed the plural society, which he viewed as a product of colonial rule and economic exploitation, to the homogeneous society typical of Western European countries. In contrast with Western societies where, according to Furnivall's analysis, there exists a 'common social will' rooted in identical cultural values, the plural society is broken up into unrelated sections, 'living side by side, yet without mingling'.[2] The members of the different groups only meet in the economic field, or, to use Furnivall's expression: 'in the market-place, in buying and selling'. Social contacts and cultural relations between members of the different sections are fairly absent. According to Furnivall's view, a plural society can be compared with a medley; the elements 'mix but do not combine'. 'Each group holds by its own religion, its own culture and language, its own ideas and ways of life.'[3]

In the colonial setting of the Netherlands East Indies, the separate segments are the different 'racial' groups: Europeans, Chi-

[1] J. S. Furnivall, *Colonial Policy and Practice: A Comparative Study of Burma and Netherlands India* (New York, 1956); Furnivall, 'The Political Economy of the Tropical Far East', *Journal of the Royal Central Asiatic Society*, Vol. 29 (1942), pp. 195–210.

[2] Furnivall, *Netherlands India: A Study of Plural Economy* (Cambridge/New York, 1944), p. 446.

[3] Furnivall, 'The Political Economy of the Tropical Far East', *loc. cit.*, p. 198.

nese, Indonesians. According to Furnivall's analysis, their life in the Indies – which practically amounts to the urban centres, as Europeans and Chinese were predominantly urban groups – is completely segregated.

In Furnivall's view, the tensions and troubles of a colonial society can be largely accounted for by its plural traits. The lack of contact and of common values produces a preponderance of economic motives over all other factors. Not being bound by moral restrictions which would restrain an individual from extreme forms of economic exploitation at home, the individuals pursue their economic aims without any consideration for the basic interests of members of the other racial groups.[1] Only by rebuilding a homogeneous society, that is to say by putting an end to colonial rule, could the social body be restored to a sound organic whole.[2]

Furnivall's use of the plural society concept as a theoretical frame has not found many followers among students of Southeast Asian societies. This is understandable, as some of his basic theses appear to be highly questionable in view of historical facts.

For example, though there is some truth in his view of colonial society as segregated, still social separation was not nearly as complete as Furnivall suggests. The situation in the Netherlands East Indies belies his pronouncement on the absence of cultural interaction. A process of 'creolization' strongly influenced 'European' life in the Indies, and in the nineteenth century a new way of life developed, which I have elsewhere termed a 'mestizo culture'.[3] In particular, the *babu* (nurse), who had the care of the small children, played a very important role in transmitting Indonesian cultural values to members of the European group, thus disproving Furnivall's thesis that the only meeting place is the market. And the *peranakan* also underwent a creolization process,

---

[1] Furnivall, *Colonial Policy and Practice* (*op. cit.*), pp. 308 ff.

[2] *Ibidem*, p. XII: 'Nothing less than independence could transform nationalism from a destructive fever into a creative force'.

[3] Wertheim, *Indonesian Society in Transition: A Study of Social Change* (Second Ed., The Hague/Bandung, 1959), pp. 174 ff., 290 ff.

which went so far as to include the adoption of an Indonesian language.

A further weakness in Furnivall's approach was the use of the 'plural society' concept as a static image. Whereas Furnivall takes full account of economic change as a dynamic factor, the view he takes of the social structure neglects the historical perspective. Hence, as a tool for an analysis of social reality the concept appears to be too rigid.

It is therefore understandable, that as far as Southeast Asia is concerned, the concept of pluralism has never been further developed as a tool for sociological analysis. The term 'plural society' has been used by some authors, but only in a casual way and without any further elaboration.[1] Where still used in a more specific sense, the term is more likely to be applied to a country like Malaya, where cultural separation between Malays and Chinese is rather pronounced, than to Indonesia and Burma, the two countries to which Furnivall had referred in the first instance.[2]

Still, Furnivall's concept has been adopted by a group of scholars; but the main concern of those who have tried to develop the concept was not with the area of Southeast Asia, but with the Caribbean.[3] This is understandable, since the 'medley' picture

---

[1] For example by Skinner, *Chinese Society in Thailand* (*op. cit.*), p. 310, who observes that the concept would appear to be hardly fitting for Thai society (the same point is made by Coughlin, *op. cit.*, p. 193); or by Maurice Zinkin, who, in *Asia and the West* (Second Ed., London, 1953) devoted a chapter to 'Plural Societies' (pp. 145 ff.), without defining the concept any further than by observing that in countries like 'Ceylon and Indo-China and Siam, difficulties between majority and minority, as between one nationality and another, have dominated much of recent history'. He further refers to Indonesia where 'differing economic interests may complicate the integration of differing nationalities into a common state', and finally mentions Malaya, 'the most notable case of all' of a plural society. Tjoa Soei Hock, *op. cit.*, p. 33 and *passim*, uses the term 'multi-racial society' in the same sense without any further theoretical elaboration.

[2] See for example Freedman, 'The Growth of a Plural Society in Malaya', *loc. cit.*, in which article, however, some inadequacies of Furnivall's approach for the Malayan case are pointed out (pp. 166 ff.).

[3] The first scholar to make use of Furnivall's concept in a Caribbean setting

appears to be much more appropriate for most of the Caribbean societies than for countries like Indonesia and Burma. Still, even in the case of the Caribbean societies, I do not find the 'plural' approach promising.

The main difference between the countries of Southeast Asia and those of the Caribbean is that, whereas in the former (with the exception of Malaya and Singapore) one can generally find a native population which is much more numerous than the groups of immigrants (of either European or Asian stock), in the latter countries no numerically overwhelming 'native' majority can be found. The only group which could be considered 'native' in the true sense are the Amerindians, but they are largely outnumbered by different immigrant groups, among them the descendants of the African slaves. Consequently, the picture presented by Caribbean countries is, for the casual observer, one of great diversity of ethnic groups, each clinging to its own cultural heritage and keeping social contacts largely restricted to members of its own group.

From this image it is easy to derive a picture of a 'plural' society

was Rudolf A. J. van Lier, *Samenleving in een grensgebied: Een sociaal-historische studie van de maatschappij in Suriname* (Society in a frontier area: A socio-historical study of Surinam society, doctoral thesis Leiden University, The Hague, 1949), pp. 9 ff., 385 ff.; he further elaborated his views in the following papers: *The Development and Nature of Society in the West Indies* (Amsterdam, 1950); 'Cultuurconflict in de heterogene samenleving' (Conflict of cultures in a heterogeneous society) in: *Sociologisch Jaarboek*, Vol. 8 (1954), pp. 36 ff.

Other important studies embodying a largely pluralistic approach, are the following ones: Vera Rubin (ed.), 'Social and Cultural Pluralism in the Caribbean', *Annals of the New York Academy of Sciences*, Vol. 83 (1960), pp. 763–916; Michael G. Smith, *A Framework for Caribbean Studies* (Jamaica, 1955); H. Hoetink, *De gespleten samenleving in het Caribisch gebied: Bijdrage tot de sociologie der rasrelaties in gesegmenteerde maatschappijen* (The divided society in the Caribbean: A contribution to the sociology of race relations in segmented societies, Assen, 1962); and a series of contributions by Hoetink, J.D. Speckmann and H. C. van Renselaar to the special issue *Anthropologica IV*, of the *Bijdragen tot de Taal-, Land- en Volkenkunde*, Vol. 119 (1963) pp. 56–105. A more general discussion of the plural society concept can be found in H. S. Morris, 'The Plural Society', *Man*, Vol. 57 (1957), pp. 124–125; J. Rex, 'The Plural Society in Sociological Theory', *British Journal of Sociology*, Vol. 10 (1959), pp. 114–124.

held together only by an outward force.[1] 'Cultural borrowing' from alien groups is not excluded in this concept; still, according to the view generally held by those who choose the 'plural' approach, the total structure of society is characterized by lack of integration and by an absence of common social and cultural values.[2]

In my opinion, this approach strongly underrates the degree of integration, distinguishable in most of the Caribbean countries. But in order to appreciate these integrative factors, one has to take into account the historical perspective, as has been aptly pointed out by Hoetink in a critical discussion of Van Lier's and M. G. Smith's views.[3] The West Indian societies could be called 'plural' only in the first moment when the alien groups (the white masters and the black slaves) were brought together. In the course of time, social institutions evolved which included either of the ethnic groups. 'The masters and the slaves', in a plantation setting, came to fulfil complementary roles. Their attitudes were moulded much more by the plantation cum slavery situation than by their original cultural heritages. They developed complementary attitudes which Hoetink, in his doctoral dissertation on Curaçao society, has termed a master's and a slave's pattern of behaviour. Though Hoetink does not draw this conclusion, it appears to me that the mutual acceptance of the two roles points towards an amount of social integration, expressing itself in a certain measure of common social and cultural values.[4]

---

[1] This view, which already found expression in Furnivall's writings, has been elaborated in greater detail by M. G. Smith, 'Social and Cultural Pluralism', in Vera Rubin (ed.), loc. cit., pp. 763 ff.

[2] Van Lier, 'Cultuurconflict in de heterogene samenleving', loc. cit., pp. 45 ff.

[3] Hoetink, op. cit., pp. 154 ff.

[4] Hoetink, Het patroon van de oude Curacaose samenleving (The pattern of early Curaçao society, doctoral thesis Leiden University, Assen, 1958); see also Hoetink, 'Curazao como Sociedad Segmentada', Ciencias Sociales, Vol. 4 (1960), pp. 179 ff.; Hoetink, 'Colonial Psychology and Race', Journal of Economic History, Vol. 21 (1961), pp. 629 ff.; J. D. Speckmann, 'De houding van de Hindostaanse bevolkingsgroep in Suriname ten opzichte van de Creolen'

Not only on the plantations could an integrated way of life evolve;
the urban centres in a still more pronounced way developed a
specific cultural pattern, which has been influenced by the historical situation and by the plantation as a basic institution in
Caribbean society and which shows striking similarities to what I
have termed a 'mestizo culture' in relation to Indonesian society.[1]
It appears to me that both Van Lier in his analysis of Surinam
society and Hoetink in his study of Curaçao have overlooked this
specific Caribbean culture, in paying exclusive attention to the
constituting cultures connected with the distinct ethnic groups,
though from the descriptive part of their studies many of the
characteristics of this syncretic culture could easily be deduced.[2]

This specific Caribbean culture is, in my view, much more significant for future developments in the Caribbean, as a focus towards which these Caribbean societies evolve, than the apparent
plurality inherent in the past.

Flows of new migrants (such as the Indian plantation workers in
Surinam and British Guiana and the Javanese ones in the former
colony) may temporarily have increased the 'plural' traits of
Caribbean societies. But since they occupy definite functions
within the total social structure, they are gradually being integrated into it, though for a long time to come they may keep their
cultural identity and a group solidarity of their own.

Integration should not be mistaken for inner harmony. The
kind of integration which is being achieved in a plantation society, or in a colonial one, does not preclude a large amount of tension
and disharmony. But without a certain degree of acceptance of
mutual roles and a measure of internalization of the values im-

(The attitude of the Hindustani population group in Surinam toward the
Creoles), *Bijdragen tot de Taal-, Land- en Volkenkunde*, Vol. 119 (1963), more in
particular pp. 77 ff.

[1] Hoetink, *De gespleten samenleving in het Caribisch gebied* (*op. cit.*), p. 179, explicitly refers to this concept of a 'mestizo culture'.

[2] Van Lier, *Samenleving in een grensgebied*, (*op. cit.*); Hoetink, *Het patroon der
Curacaose samenleving* (*op. cit.*); however, Hoetink in his later publications has
explicitly recognized the existence in Curaçao of a 'Caribbean variant' of
'Dutch' culture: Curazao como Sociedad Segmentada', *loc. cit.*, p. 185, nt. 12.

posed by the dominant group, the social structure could not last even for one day. A society held together only by force is a rare phenomenon indeed. The secret of any domination is a partial imposition of one's own value system upon the members of the dominated groups.

These integrative factors do not preclude the existence of strong contrapuntal elements within society. In another paper in this volume I have elaborated this counterpoint concept in greater detail.[1]

In my view, the societies which Furnivall considers homogeneous are not at all the harmonious structures this author mistakes them for. Disraeli, it has been reported, said that in any country, including his own, there are two nations, the rich and the poor. The existence of contrapuntal tendencies and tensions is not at all a prerogative of societies labelled 'plural' ones. But it is true that they are more likely to occur in societies based on a plantation economy or on colonial domination. We could, however, ask whether it is really 'cultural plurality' which in such cases lies at the root of social tensions, as those who are using the 'plural' concept appear to suggest.

To me, this seems highly questionable. There are several countries which are, to all intents and purposes, 'plural' in a cultural respect and in which, nevertheless, no remarkable tensions occur. Multilingual Switzerland could be mentioned as an outstanding example. On the other hand, it is very striking that in many historical instances cultural adaptation has increased tension rather than lessening it. The tensions between Indonesians and Eurasians in Indonesia increased when a number of the former, through a spread of education, became culturally more akin to the latter by learning Dutch and by adopting elements from Western culture. The same is the case so far as the tensions between Creoles and Indians in Surinam are concerned.[2] It is not plurali-

[1] See the second paper, dealing with society as a composite of conflicting value systems.

[2] This point is clearly borne out in recent publications on Surinam society: Hoetink, 'Change in Prejudice: Some Notes on the Minority Problem, with

ty which accounts for increasing tension, but the ability to compete in the economic and political field. Else relationships between the Javanese and other ethnic groups in Surinam would not be as frictionless as they actually are.

There is one more approach which we must examine before we can get at the core of our problem: the purely psychological one. In the foregoing pages, there has been some mention of the evident parallel between the position of the Chinese minorities in Southeast Asia and the condition of Jews, especially in Central and Eastern Europe. Though studies of the Chinese minorities problem from the angle of sociological theory have been lacking, there have been quite a few attempts at providing a sociological interpretation of anti-semitism. A well-known approach is the one chosen by Bernstein, between the World Wars.[1] The approach was rather a psychological one insofar as the Jews were viewed exclusively as convenient scapegoats for pent-up aggressive sentiments among the gentiles as a collectivity. This explanation does not sound very convincing, because it does not account for the large amount of variety within the whole range of attitudes towards different groups of minorities, in different types of society, and in different stages of human history. In stressing only one psychological motive, it appears to fall short of the elaboration and refinement which post-war developments in sociological theory would require.

A similar approach to the problem of anti-semitism was used by the American Marxist Oliver C. Cox, who reduced the phenomenon to one single psychological factor: *prejudice*.[2] There is an interesting discrepancy between the way Cox attempts to clarify race relations between 'black-and-white' and the way he deals

References to the West Indies and Latin America', *Bijdragen tot de Taal-, Land- en Volkenkunde*, Vol. 119 (1963), p. 67 ff.; Speckmann, *loc. cit.*, pp. 84 ff.

[1] F. Bernstein, *Der Antisemitismus als Gruppenerscheinung: Versuch einer Soziologie des Judenhasses* (Berlin, 1926).

[2] Oliver C. Cox, *Caste, Class and Race: A Study in Social Dynamics* (New York, 1959), pp. 392 ff.

with anti-semitism. In the former case his approach takes full account of economic factors. He rejects the 'colour caste' approach used by Lloyd Warner and his associates as wrongly suggesting that the imposed domination by whites would be basically accepted by the blacks. His analysis of race relationships of the 'black-and-white' variety is drawn in terms of class struggle. The whites and the blacks are not integrated in one social structure, but they are, in his view, mutually opposed as virtual 'political classes'. The attempt of the dominant whites to relegate the whole coloured group to a low-paid proletariat characterizes the relationship as essentially a 'political class' strife. Different from the country where the 'caste' concept was born (India), in situations like that in the Southern States the 'caste' barrier and the ensuing endogamy are not mutually accepted but imposed by mere force, says Cox, who therefore rejects the 'caste' terminology used by Warner and his associates.[1]

The differences between the 'racial situations' in all kinds of societies – most of them of the colonial type – are explained by Cox as the products of different tactics used by the dominant 'political class', dependent upon the relative numerical strength and the type of economic exploitation.[2]

In contrast with the broadly economic explanation of the 'black-and-white' race relations, however, in the case of anti-semitism Cox completely drops the economic motive as a relevant factor, and takes refuge in the purely psychological concepts of 'prejudice' and 'intolerance'. In his view, the phenomena can be fully explained by the impatience among the majority towards those who are different and who refuse to be assimilated. Anti-semitism and related reactions would spring from intolerance towards those who do not conform to the accepted cultural norms of the majority.

Again, the explanation is too simple since it fails to distinguish between the cases in which this 'intolerance' or 'prejudice' operates, and those in which it does not. Still, one of Cox' observa-

[1] Cox, *op. cit.*, pp. 489 ff.
[2] *Ibidem*, pp. 353 ff.

tions could provide us with a clue to a deeper understanding of the phenomena.

He stresses a basic difference between the 'black-and-white' relationships which he reduces to political class tensions, and the intolerance against minorities rooted in 'prejudice'. In the former case, there is no basic hatred on the part of the dominant whites against the blacks – provided that these 'accept' their role in accordance with the master-servant stereotype. Sharp reactions are only provoked by those who attempt to assimilate themselves, who assume the attributes of the dominant group, who 'do not know their place'.

On the other hand, in the case of intolerance, the aggressive feelings take their root in the fact that the minority group does not want to be assimilated. The hatred against this non-assimilated group may assume such extreme proportions as to induce the majority group to aim at their complete elimination from the society, sometimes even to the point of corporal extermination.[1]

Though the thesis that non-assimilation would be the basic issue is highly questionable, as will be pointed out further on, nevertheless there is some justification for the distinction made by Cox, as far as psychological attitudes are concerned. It is true that in the case of some minorities discrimination may assume the extreme form of a wish for complete elimination, whereas in the case of the general 'black-and-white' tension discrimination is rather instrumental to economic exploitation and may only last as long as such exploitation is viewed as a real possibility. It is precisely this fact which accounts for the present author's mounting worries in connection with the 'intolerance' phenomena, in comparison with the 'black-and-white' race relationships which, in the long run, will tend to lose some of their significance as education and the urge for emancipation are bound to spread to ever broader groups.

It appears to me that Cox is right in stressing the importance of

[1] *Ibidem*, pp. 400 ff.

economic factors dominating race relationships between blacks and whites. But I cannot accept his argument to the effect that those groups only oppose each other in a political class interaction. Not unlike the 'plural society' theorists, he overlooks the integrative qualities inherent even in a plantation society or in a colonial setting. A measure of acceptance of the hierarchical values imposed by the dominant group is a pre-condition to the viability of the social system – and in many cases they have been kept intact for many centuries. This view is not irreconcilable with a realization of the existence of sharp tensions within the social structure which could be basically understood as political class conflicts; neither does it preclude that for a keen observer many protest elements may be distinguishable which escape the consciousness of most members of the dominant group. The two concepts, one starting from a measure of integration, the other one from the existence of basic tension and protest elements, are not mutually exclusive. The counterpoint concept, elaborated elsewhere in this symposium, provides sufficient scope for a combination of both views.

It appears to me that the societies which we have in view should be primarily analysed in terms of social stratification.[1] Despite the omnipresent protest elements, even the so-called 'plural' societies show a hierarchical structure, which derives a certain amount of stability from a dominant value system pervading, in varying intensity, all the segments of society. In my opinion, the caste concept is completely acceptable for societies dominated by so-called 'race relationships', including those under colonial rule. Just as Cox greatly underrates the integrative qualities in a colonial society or in one which has its roots in the slave-plantation economy, he overrates the amount of integration prevalent in Hindu society. Evidently, the Brahmins, who were the only guardians of a literary tradition, had a stake in presenting Hindu society and the acceptance of mutual roles in terms of full harmo-

[1] Lloyd Braithwaite, 'Social Stratification and Cultural Pluralism', in Vera Rubin (ed.), 'Social and Cultural Pluralism in the Caribbean', *loc. cit.*, pp. 816–836.

ny and inner stability. Social reality was, in fact, somewhat different from the official picture. For example, protest elements
against the power of the Brahmins are not at all rare in Hindu
folklore.[1] The stereotyped birth of new, more or less egalitarian
sects, such as in former days Buddhism and Jainism, and later on
the Bhakti movement and the sect of the Sikhs, or the conversion
to more egalitarian religions such as Islam or Christianity, testify
to the existence throughout the ages of contrapuntal elements in
Hindu society.[2]

[1] I owe to Mme Dr. S. C. L. Vreede-de Stuers some striking specimena of folk
protest against the caste structure in India; the following quotations are from
Sir Herbert Risley, *The People of India* (Second Ed., Calcutta/London, 1915):

'Along with sayings affirming... the necessity and inviolability of caste, we
find others which seem to recall an earlier order of ideas when castes were not
so rigidly separated, when members of different castes could intermarry, and
when, within certain limits, caste itself was regarded as a matter of personal
merit rather than of mere heredity' (*op. cit.*, p. 150).

'Love laughs at caste distinctions'.

'Caste springs from actions not from birth'.

'Castes may differ; virtue is everywhere the same'.

'The Vaisyas and Sudras must have come first; and it was from them that
Brahmans and Kshatriyas were made'.

'Every uncle says that his caste is the best'.

Risley also quotes several sayings in which the *Brahmin* is being chided or
ridiculed; I select the following sayings from *Ibidem*, pp. 131, and 305 ff.:

'Blood-suckers three on earth there be: The bug, the Brahman and the flea'.

'Before the Brahman starves the King's larder will be empty; cakes must be
given to him while the children of the house may lick the grindstone for a meal'.

'He will beg with a lakh of rupees in his pocket, and a silver begging-bowl in
his hand'.

'A village with a Brahman in it is like a tank full of crabs; to have him as a
neighbour is worse than leprosy'.

'He washes his sacred thread but does not cleanse his inner man'.

'He defrauds even the Gods; Vishnu gets the barren prayers while the Brahman devours the offerings'.

'A Brahman needs only prophecy; a bullock must plow his furrow'.

These sayings are typical illustrations of my 'counterpoint' notion, elaborated in the second paper of this volume.

[2] Ramkrishna Mukherjee, *Rise and Fall of the East India Company: A Sociological
Appraisal* (Berlin, 1958), pp. 182 ff.; G. S. Ghurye, *Caste, Class and Occupation*
(Bombay, 1961), p. 6, (with special reference to South India); see also p.

The 'colour caste' societies differ from the modern class society in the existence of rigid barriers which severely restrict vertical mobility. One is, to a certain degree, relegated to a definite social position by one's birth. In this respect there is some affinity between the colonial caste society[1] and the mediaeval 'estate' society in Europe. In both cases, vertical social mobility was low. As a general rule a son followed the profession of his father. Ethnic groups were, consequently, attached to a few traditional professions. Popular education did not yet provide a convenient avenue for moving from one occupation to another.

The type of ethnic specialization according to race typical of a colonial society fits without much stress within the general feudal and agrarian pattern prevalent in societies which were subjected to colonial rule.

These factors account for a certain similarity between the position of Jews in mediaeval Europe and the condition of Chinese in colonial Southeast Asia, of Indians in colonial East Africa and Burma, Armenians and Greeks in feudal Turkey, Syrians in West Africa, and a few related cases. As a characterization of the origin of these groups, the 'status gap' concept of Irwin D. Rinder is enlightening, but it does not provide an analysis of the conditions under which tensions tend to increase. In his article on social structure and prejudice,[2] Sheldon Stryker has rightly pointed out that this type of tension in some cases occurs, but not in all of them (the Parsis in India providing a notable exception). But his article does not elaborate any further what these conditions actually are.

11: 'it is not known to many students that the Paraiyans will not permit a Brahmin to pass through their street; so much so that if one happens to enter their quarters they would greet him with cow-dung water'.

[1] As far as I am aware, Raymond Kennedy was the first scholar to elaborate the caste concept in relation to colonial society: 'The Colonial Crisis and the Future', in: Ralph Linton (ed.), *The Science of Man in the World Crisis* (*op. cit.*), pp. 306 ff. I have joined Kennedy in this terminology in *Het Rassenprobleem* (*op. cit.*).

[2] Sheldon Stryker, 'Social Structure and Prejudice', *Social Problems*, Vol. 6 (1959), pp. 340 ff.

It appears to me that the crucial issue is to be found in the economic field. But it is not the 'class struggle' concept, as used by Cox, which plays the main role in these social processes which fundamentally endanger the position of the trading minorities. It is economic competition between adjoining social groups which lies at the root of the tensions, as they present themselves in the actual phase of world history. The present outbursts of violence or organized discrimination on a mass scale are not comparable with the occasional pogroms or riots in past centuries. The basic difference is related to the transitional phase in which newly independent countries find themselves in their attempts to bring about a transformation of the traditional society.

It is not by chance that anti-Chinese campaigns started all over Southeast Asia after 1900. The condition of this development was a gradual breaking down of traditional occupational dividing lines. Raymond Kennedy has rightly pointed out that education 'would be dynamite for the rigid caste systems of colonies'.[1] Once a son is no longer obliged to follow his father's profession, he is free to aspire to other occupations from which he was previously barred. As a consequence, traditional walls start crumbling, and fierce competition can develop in fields which were formerly the preserve of a distinct ethnic or religious group.

But the individuals of the newly competing social stratum soon discover that the way to economic progress and social expansion is barred by the monopolistic position of the group which has a traditional advantage. Consequently, competition on a group basis starts, enabling the new-comers to enlist the support of a much broader following, and a tendency develops to align according to criteria which find their roots in the traditional structure of society. This process is in line with a general tendency, prevalent not only in the non-Western countries but throughout the modern world, to combine forces within more or less organized collectivities.[2]

In countries where a colour caste structure had prevailed in the

[1] Kennedy, *loc. cit.*, p. 311.
[2] Wertheim, *Indonesian Society in Transition* (*op. cit.*), pp. 48 ff.

past, alignments were likely to assume a 'racial' pattern. In other countries where religious communities had formed the base of occupational divisions, group solidarity was more likely to assume a 'communalist' character (as, for example, in India). But in either case the alignment had as its main purpose the pursuit of competition on a collective basis. The fiercest rivalry could be expected where adjoining groups were uniting, each on this principle of a collective struggle.

Therefore, even the interpretation of the usual 'black-and-white' type of racial strife in terms of a class struggle, as developed by Cox, is inadequate, though not essentially wrong. It is true that the new-comers, for example those aspiring to higher functions within the state apparatus, are likely to appeal to class struggle slogans – which may be expressed in terms of nationalism or religious solidarity – in order to rally a large following of proletarians or semi-proletarians (either industrial workers or peasants) in favour of their cause. It is a convenient weapon to brand the opposed group as a foreign exploiter and to appeal to the sentiment of envy and resentment against the high and the mighty. But the leadership of these movements, even though they assume an idealistic terminology by stressing national or proletarian aims, may well be in the hands of groups which fight in the first place to oust and supplant those who, in the traditional structure, had a monopoly of certain prominent functions.

For example, the nationalist movement in Indonesia, for all its idealistic vigour, could also be interpreted to some extent as a drive by Western-educated Indonesians to replace the white and Eurasian upper caste, which had possessed in the past a quasi-monopoly so far as positions of prominence in government were concerned. Rallying the mass of the population behind the leadership by using nationalist catchwords, which at the time when they were launched may have been indisputably genuine, provided this struggle for vertical mobility with a much greater strength. At the same time, we must keep in mind that such rallying of a mass following naturally makes a simple supplanting of the traditional upper caste impossible: those who joined the struggle, would claim a certain reward for the support they provided to the new leaders; the enlisting of their support could not be accomplished without inculcating them with a certain amount of self-reliance and fighting spirit. Therefore any 'nationalist' movement achieves more than a mere replacement of old rulers by new ones. Whereas the stabilized colonial structure could be called a caste society, shifting after the introduction of greater educational facilities and a certain amount of vertical mobility across the former dividing line to a social system which could still be called 'caste-like', in the post-colonial setting a new structural type emerges which gradually sheds the remains of the caste-like set-up. Social stratification, in the post-colonial structure, inevitably becomes less rigid than before, and vertical mobility increases. Still, even in this case, throughout the process of the fight for national liberation, collective competition for rewarding functions remains an important element in any so-called 'race struggle'.

Still more evident is this factor of collective competition in the case of campaigns against the trading minorities. The disruption of traditional 'colour caste' barriers provides opportunities for 'natives' to aspire to functions in trade which they formerly despised. In Indonesia, these aspirations developed first of all among the pious Moslem *santri*, who were more individualistic in their outlook than the common peasantry. Therefore, Islam could easily become the ideology which enabled the small Indonesian traders to fight their strong competitors: the Chinese. The 'national' ideology could serve the same purpose by branding the rivals as 'foreigners'. It was easy to play upon class struggle motives in order to enlist the support of the peasantry against their 'capitalist' oppressors and exploiters. Trade in an undeveloped economy always entails a certain amount of economic exploitation. High rates of interest for loans and sharp commercial practices are often inevitable if a foreigner is to survive in an economy where he is not permitted to acquire the margin of security inherent in the possession of landed estate. Such practices can easily be branded as 'usury', and the 'foreigners' who are accused of such practices as 'blood-suckers'. All kinds of stereotypes about the 'frugal', 'greedy' and 'clannish' foreigners are allowed to develop.

But the campaigns are quite often led by rivals who themselves are compelled to use similar practices if they want to be successful in business in an undeveloped economy. They play upon national or religious sentiments in the first place to further their own interests as a group. The class struggle or nationalist element is rather a rationalization than the real motive force. And again, they attempt to enlist the support of a poor peasantry or urban proletariat, who suffered from the 'usury' or 'malpractices' of which the 'foreign' traders are accused.

From the foregoing it becomes clear that it is not cultural divergence which is at the root of the tensions. The movements become virulent precisely at the moment when the cultural differences are waning to such an extent that competition becomes possible. Lack of assimilation is not the real motive force for the campaign: it is a convenient rationalization. It provides an excuse to select a special group of 'foreigners' as the target. If this group should actually decide to try collectively to assimilate, it would not provide a solution acceptable to the competitors. These do not want their rivals to entrench themselves more firmly by assimilating themselves; their basic aim is to oust them in order to supplant them in their position of economic power. And, though assimilation as a solution for an individual may occur, the minority as a group generally reacts by developing an increasing group solidarity of their own. In order to achieve this, they have to stress certain cultural traits by which they distinguish themselves from the majority group. But in so doing they still more endanger their position as a group.

It appears to me that a similar line of reasoning could be applied if we wish to explain the emergence of anti-semitism and some changing attitudes and inconsistencies throughout European history. Tentatively, I would suggest the following line of inquiry, which has been outlined by the German economist Wilhelm Roscher as early as 1875. In the Middle Ages the Jews had filled the 'status gap' in some countries of Western Europe, England for instance. When an emergent bourgeoisie started to aspire to functions in trade which formerly had been mainly in the hands of Jews, these were ousted and expelled from several West-European countries, France and England first, Spain and Portugal later. To quote Roscher[1]: 'The persecutions of Jews in our late Middle Ages are largely a product of commercial jealousy. They are connected with the first flourishing of a national trading class'.[2] The Jews could, however, fill the occupational gap in Central and Eastern Europe, which were still less developed economically. When a prosperous native bourgeoisie had developed in West European countries, such as Britain or Holland, Jewish traders could be admitted again and easily absorbed by the expanding economic structure – its expansion being largely due, according to Sombart, to the presence of the Jews.[3] But in Central and Eastern Europe a native traders' class only developed as late as the nineteenth century. Formerly, competition took the form of occasional pogroms, the victims of which provided the ruling class with a convenient scapegoat. In the twentieth century, however, nationalism as an ideology proved useful to the native middle class people for starting a competition on a collective basis which, in Nazi Germany, even assumed the shape and proportions of massacre on an unprecedented scale.

It appears to me that, despite the highly abnormal and in certain respects also atypical character of what happened in Nazi Germany, a certain parallel with recent phenomena in Southeast Asia is nonetheless undeniable.

Is there any solution to the problem as it presents itself in con-

[1] Wilhelm Roscher, 'Die Stellung der Juden im Mittelalter, betrachtet vom Standpunkte der allgemeinen Handelspolitik', *Zeitschrift für die gesammte Staatswissenschaft*, Vol. 31 (1875), pp. 503 ff. The author even draws a parallel with the Chinese in Southeast Asia (pp. 524 ff.); see also Werner J. Cahnman, 'Socio-economic Causes of Anti-Semitism', *Social Problems*, Vol. 5 (1957–58), pp. 21 ff.

[2] Roscher, *loc. cit.*, p. 511.

[3] Wilhelm Sombart, *Die Juden und das Wirtschaftsleben* (Leipzig, 1911), pp. 18 ff.

temporary Southeast Asia? Is it possible to avert the terrible menace to many millions of traders branded as 'foreigners' in the different newly independent countries? Or must they prepare to emigrate in large numbers to their home country, in order at least to save their lives or their bare material existence?

According to our analysis, it is economic competition, institutionalized in line with the traditional pattern of group differentiation, which is at the root of our problems. This implies that, even if this type of group rivalry is not necessarily attached to the prevalent economic system, it is nevertheless seriously aggravated by an economy based on private competition. This competition adds to the virulence of the periodical anti-Chinese campaigns. But at the same time it implies that ousting the Chinese will not provide an economic solution to the evils which beset most of the Southeast Asian countries. The exploitative character of the way many Chinese have practised their trade in the past has nothing to do with any special depravity inherent in their national character. It is a characteristic of trade as a profession in an underdeveloped society. The *hajis* and other traders who try to supplant them cannot refrain from similar practices if they have to make a living out of trade. And as far as Java is concerned, such a replacement of Chinese by *asli* would tend to make things worse: in contrast with the Chinese in the past, the latter have always been legally allowed to acquire and possess land; so their actual power over the poor peasantry would, if anything, be greater than in the case of the Chinese trader class.

Pierre Gourou has rightly remarked in one of his pre-war studies on French Indo-China: 'What is the use of eliminating the Chinese intermediary, if in practice it only amounts to his replacement by a native intermediary exactly as rapacious as himself?'[1]

Supplanting of individual traders by cooperatives, especially in the rural sphere, could contribute to a solution. But, in that case, such a measure should not be restricted to 'foreign' traders,

---

[1] Pierre Gourou, *L'utilisation du sol en Indochine française* (Paris, 1940), p. 428.

as was planned in Indonesia in 1959. If cooperatives are prefer-
able to an individual trader, this applies to the native trader as
well.

Still, even in a society which is no longer based on private capitalism, competition for functions on a group basis cannot be excluded. Traditional tensions between different ethnic groups may
express themselves in the shape of competition within the bureaucratic apparatus as well, though the competition may be assuaged
by the elimination of the profit motive.

The only way really to eliminate this type of inter-group strife
in a society which attempts to liberate itself from economic underdevelopment would be a rapidly expanding economy, in
which there are ample economic opportunities for any member of
the society. To quote Raymond Smith: 'It would be ideal if the
rapidity of economic development opened up so many opportunities that the jealousies and fears based on race assumed an insignificant role. If this pace of economic development is not initiated and maintained, then the danger of racial conflict is increased.'[1]

If such countries could really embark upon a process of rapid
planned development, they might discover that full use can be
made of the capacities of all kinds of 'minorities', provided they
are prepared to relinquish their traditional occupations and let
themselves be geared in with overall planned economic development.

[1] Raymond T. Smith, *British Guiana* (London, 1962), p. 143.

'Nationalism and Leadership in Asia' is a revised version of a paper read at the International Sociological Seminar for Students and Postgraduates in Sociology, held in 1960 at Wageningen (Netherlands). The original title of the paper was 'Nationalism and Leadership in the Non-Western World'.

The revised text has been published in *Science and Society*, Vol. 26 (1962), pp. 1–14.

FOUR

NATIONALISM AND LEADERSHIP IN ASIA

Nationalism is a modern phenomenon in world history. The large political structures and movements in existence before the Napoleonic period all over the world were not based on a loyalty of the people to any abstract idea, such as that of a national community sharing the same cultural values. Loyalties were, until the rise to power of a modern bourgeoisie, rather restricted in scope. The loyalties of the peasantry were largely oriented towards local rulers and authorities. Their bonds with the local aristocracy were mostly of a personal and traditional nature.

Consequently at that time the larger political structures could function without any deeper sentimental attachment from the agrarian mass of the polulation. In the patrimonial bureaucracies – this term is adopted from Max Weber's *Wirtschaft und Gesellschaft*[1] and includes regimes generally labelled as 'feudalistic' – existing in the pre-Napoleonic period throughout the Eurasian continent, no dynamic and active loyalty was required from the common people. The stability of the structure rested upon the allegiance of the local rulers or governors to the central royal power. Those local rulers, whether recruited from noble families or appointed by the prince, exacted tithes and services from the peasantry in accordance with established traditions and, in their turn, paid the required tribute to the prince from the revenues. It was the loyalty of the peasantry to the local rulers, combined with the loyalty of the latter to the king, that kept the large patrimo-

[1] For a treatment in greater detail, on the basis of Weber's analysis, of the state structures defined as 'patrimonial bureaucracies' I may refer to the fifth paper included in this volume, which deals with corruption as a field for sociological research.

nial-bureaucratic states together. If only the peasantry delivered their agricultural surpluses, their labour power outside the season of plowing, planting, and harvesting, their beautiful women, and their share in armies raised by the rulers – all according to established customs – this was all the rulers wanted. No dynamic ideological relationship such as allegiance to the nation-state was needed.

Therefore, it was largely a matter of indifference to the stability of a political structure whether the ruler was more or less a stranger to the mass of the population. If a foreign ruler conformed to the imperial and local traditions and adopted the symbols of sanctity and divine favour, the patrimonial state could function as ever, provided that the local rulers, for whatever reason, would shift their allegiance to the new ruler. Still, in times of tension it was always possible for any pretender who wanted to incite the sentiments of the populace to brand his adversary as a foreigner, in order to reinforce his claims. But, in a world in which even people from neighbouring villages or provinces were considered strangers, the difference between an autochthonous and a foreign ruler could be one of degree only.

The foregoing picture does not imply that popular movements directed against more or less foreign rulers were largely absent. On the contrary, rebellions and movements embodying a social protest against the high and the mighty were rife in the pre-modern world. But even if these movements aimed at an overthrow of a foreign ruler, they could hardly be labelled 'national movements' in the modern sense. If there was any ideology from which the rebellion drew its force, it was more likely than not to be expressed in religious terms. Not only did the mediaeval peasant revolts find, in general, a religious sectarian expression – as described for example in Norman Cohn's *The Pursuit of the Millennium*,[1] in Eric Hobsbawm's *Primitive Rebels*,[2] or in Ernst Werner's

---

[1] Norman Cohn, *The Pursuit of the Millennium* (London, 1957).
[2] Eric Hobsbawm, *Primitive Rebels: Studies in Archaic Forms of Social Movement in the Nineteenth and Twentieth Centuries* (Manchester, 1959).

Pauperes Christi[1] – but the rising bourgeoisie of the Western European towns also initially fought their battle against the established powers under the religious banner of Protestantism. At the same time, if part of the aristocracy wanted to enlist the support of broader popular masses against their competitors or against a ruling dynasty, they were also increasingly forced to fly a religious banner. National slogans were much less effective in raising popular sentiments in a world where the ruling aristocracy was more or less international.

The nineteenth century witnessed the rise of modern nation-states, primarily in the Western European countries, and the national ideologies, first mainly affecting the Third Estate, gradually spread to broader layers of society. The dynamic nationally-oriented impulse pervading the Western nation-states enabled their governments to embark upon the foundation of colonial empires beyond their frontiers. The national expansion outside Europe was not restricted to the territories which were turned into political dependencies. Even in non-Western countries which remained nominally free, such as China, Siam and Turkey, the Western states attempted to obtain all kinds of privileges and extra-territorial rights in behalf of their nationals.

Nevertheless, this same nineteenth century of colonialism and imperialism also stimulated, in the long run, the rise within non-Western countries of nationalism as an ideology patterned after the Western model. The colonial or semi-colonial surroundings in which these movements were born inevitably influenced their eventual shape and social content.

In that part of the world, until the end of the eighteenth century, rebellions or movements giving vent to agrarian unrest generally had a character similar to West-European revolts throughout the Middle Ages. Most revolts were led by members of the aristocracy and were part of an eternal struggle for some more power within the ruler's class. The struggle for power could, sometimes, assume a religious cloak, and to that extent a revolt could receive

[1] Ernst Werner, *Pauperes Christi: Studien zu sozial-religiösen Bewegungen im Zeitalter des Reformpapsttums* (Leipzig, 1956).

an ideological underpinning. Religious slogans also could serve
to give expression to peasant discontent against oppressive levies
in excess of established custom. But whether the rulers against
whom the people rose were strangers or not was not of major importance. Even foreign rule as exercised by the Dutch East India
Company in parts of Java did not significantly alter the picture, as
the Dutch adapted themselves to the age-old Javanese pattern of
political relationships. It would be a distortion of historical reality
to call the wars waged by Javanese princes against the Company
national movements. Still, Islam as an ideology could serve to
rally the forces of aristocratic rulers against the Dutch, though the
religious appeal did not always work: the Dutch would never
have succeeded in getting a foothold in the archipelago if they had
not been able to play off the Indonesian rulers against each other.

Only when Islam as a religion had taken deeper roots within the
peasant population, could it become a real threat to the foreign
ruler. Such was the situation in Indonesia in the first half of the
nineteenth century. The so-called Java War (1825–1830) taught
the Dutch that a Javanese prince who flew the banner of Islam
and rallied religious leaders to his cause could secure a huge following from the peasantry and present a tremendous challenge
to their colonial rule. A similar lesson was taught by the Padri
War in West Sumatra, which started in the twenties, and, later
on, by the Acheh War launched in the seventies, both of which
bore out the growing influence of religious leaders over large sections of the peasant population. Islam as a unifier transcending
local or regional loyalties was gradually assuming the role of a
pre-nationalist ideology against foreign rule.[1]

The Dutch learnt the lesson that colonial rule could continue
only if the allegiance of aristocratic rulers could be bought by
granting them a share in the profits earned by colonial exploitation. This is exactly what the so-called Culture System, based on

---

[1] This analysis of Islam as a social force in nineteenth-century Indonesian
history has been further elaborated in W. F. Wertheim, *Indonesian Society in
Transition: A Study of Social Change* (Second Ed., The Hague/Bandung, 1959),
pp. 202 ff.

forced cultivation of market crops and introduced by the Dutch after the end of the Java War, aimed at. In this way the aristocratic class could be disengaged from their potential allies – the religious leaders and the peasantry.

However, throughout the nineteenth century the latter group was easily incited, if colonial rule meant for them increased services and taxes. Consequently, the religious leaders in Java (generally called *kyais*), who increased their influence over the peasantry, became dreaded adversaries of the colonial regime and the special target of all kinds of police measures.

Similar constellations occurred in other non-Western countries as well. The Indian Mutiny in its initial stage evidenced the same kind of alliance between the Moslem aristocracy and the common people as the Dutch had experienced during the Java War. Again Islam proved to function as a pre-nationalist ideology; and again the colonial rulers answered by granting special favours to the aristocratic elite.

And at the time when China had been reduced to a semi-colony of the combined imperialist powers, the Boxer insurrection, accompanied with quasi-religious anti-foreign outbursts, showed a similar alliance between the discontented peasantry and the ruling elite.

But as long as the revolts and rebellions against colonial rule or imperial power were led by the traditional elite groups – the aristocracy or the religious leaders –, the Western governments proved time and again that they were stronger, not only through their modern military equipment, but through better and more efficient organization. Moreover, the Asian aristocracy was seldom ideologically prepared for a struggle to the bitter end; generally, it was possible to disengage them from the mass of the people by granting them some privileges. The national idea was more deeply rooted among the Western colonial powers than among their aristocratic opponents.

About the turn of the century a new situation arose. Gradually in the non-Western world new social groups began to come to the fore and to rival the traditional elite groups of the aristocracy and the clergy. But the composition of the non-Western 'Third Estate' differed significantly from its counterpart in the West. Merchants and people in liberal professions, who had provided the large majority of the Third Estate in the West, formed only a limited part of the new rising class in the East. In a world where governmental institutions increasingly came to dominate, government office was more attractive to those imbued with a modern spirit. As in the West, the new elite based its claims on achievement, not on birth like the traditional aristocratic elite. But contrary to the situation in Western history, trade was only one of the stepping stones to success. In the East, about the turn of the century, modern education was at least as important as wealth acquired by trade as a vehicle for status and prestige. There was in many Eastern countries even a certain scorn for professional trade, not uncommon in countries with an aristocratic tradition. Trade had been largely left to foreign groups, such as Chinese in Southeast Asia, Indians in Burma and East Africa, Armenians and Greeks in Turkey. There was not much attraction for ambitious young Asians to engage in private enterprise. Besides the lack of social prestige attached to trade, there was hard competition with groups enjoying an historical advantage in commerce and consequently firmly entrenched in most trades. Moreover, as large Western concerns had extended their economic activities to non-Western countries and often wielded a near-monopolistic power, the odds in commerce appeared to be distinctly against newcomers.

On the other hand, working in the government's service was quite in harmony with traditional aristocratic values. Modern education was an excellent preparation for such a career. In a period in which the government extended its activities and increasingly came to dominate economic life, the government's service seemed a rewarding outlet for young talented people. In politically independent countries, like Turkey, Siam and China, a distinguished military career was equivalent to working in the civil administration.

Even though the composition of the new elite was different from its counterpart in seventeenth-century Western Europe, the term 'bourgeoisie' seems appropriate to designate the new rising class. Though aristocratic elements were frequent among this group, since they were distinctly privileged as far as educational opportunities were concerned, the new elite also included many members of the petty nobility or even commoners. The outlook and way of life of the whole group was more rational and matter of fact than those cherished by the traditional elite.

This modern outlook lies at the root of the specific role played by the new bourgeoisie in the Asian world. As we have seen before, the nineteenth century had witnessed several protest movements against the colonial supremacy. But these movements were largely ineffective, because both the aristocracies and the peasantry were, in general, fighting against the modern world and for an illusory restoration of their old traditions.

Their struggle had frequently, as in the case of the Boxer insurrection in China, or the Samin movement in Java,[1] the character of a mystical flight from the realities of life. Since a money economy had penetrated the rural areas of Asia, a struggle for a return to a closed village economy was like a yearning for a chimerical Paradise Lost.

Moreover, the rebellious movements under aristocratic or religious leadership generally lacked modern organization on rational lines.

The new Asian bourgeoisie differed from the traditional elite by adopting the modern forms of organization and expression from the West. The first products of modern Western education, such as Ram Mohan Roy and Sir Syed Ahmad Khan in India, Raden Adjeng Kartini and the Djajadiningrats in Java, accepted Western rule in the same way as they adopted Western thought and culture. But when the first serious frustrations were consciously experienced, and the rewards available within a colonial setting appeared to be inadequate, the bourgeoisie took over the leader-

[1] About the turn of the century Samin, a farmer from Blora district (Central Java), became the leader of a peasants' movement which opposed taxes and services claimed by the government and preached a return to the rustic simplicity of pre-capitalist society. See Wertheim, *op. cit.*, p. 318.

ship of the anti-colonial opposition. But this time the protest movements became much more efficient, because the colonial rulers were fought with their own weapons. Both the organization form of modern unions and the Western ideology of nationalism were adopted from the very Western colonial or imperial powers.

At this point the question rises why nationalism as an ideology suited the mental and material requirements of the new elite.

In the first place, there was the colonial or semi-colonial situation, with the concomitant frustrations and grievances. Besides the attraction of nationalism as an emotional outlet for feelings of inferiority and resentment, there were also more rational factors accounting for the appeal of the new ideology. As we have seen before, the claims of the new generation to their elite position were largely based on the modern education they had enjoyed. But the colonial structure prevented most of them from achieving a full gratification of their aspirations. Everywhere in the colonies the whites had built up a kind of upper-caste status safeguarding for the members of their group all positions that were rewarding from a point of view of power, social prestige and profitability. Even in semi-colonial, quasi-independent countries the whites enjoyed preferential treatment. In a changing Asian world, where an individual's status was no longer primarily ascription-based, because noble birth was being replaced by educational achievement, diplomas, and academic titles as a factor conferring high status and esteem, there still remained one important exception to the new stratification principle. The continuation of the colonial structure meant that the highest social and economic rewards were still ascription-based. Belonging by birth to the dominant, white caste was still more important than education, and the possibility of rising on the social ladder by means of achievement was severely restricted by the colonial stratification system based on race and skin-colour. A struggle for national independence would mean a fuller realization of potential capabilities for the rising Asian bourgeoisie.

Furthermore, nationalism could provide a suitable platform for enlisting a broad range of forces equally opposed to the colonial or imperialist powers. The landed aristocracy, whose power had rested primarily upon the peasantry, had never been able to build up an ideology transcending particularistic, local or regional loyalties. The new bourgeoisie, whose mainstay was to be found mainly in the urban centres among the officials in the governments' offices or among an incipient trader class, developed a broader, nation-oriented though not yet universalistic outlook. The first decades of the present century witnessed a gradual extension of all kinds of solidarity on a regional particularistic basis to more-embracing entities. This is true not only for the large anti-colonial political movements, but also for more restricted kinds of group solidarity. For example, the Chinese of Southeast Asia, who had previously known a group solidarity on the basis of dialect groups or secret societies, began to develop organizational forms transcending language groups and including all Chinese living within a given country or colony. For the Indonesian Chinese this process has recently been described by Lea E. Williams.[1] Caste solidarity in India shows a similar trend, modern alignments based on caste increasingly transcending traditional barriers and boundaries which in the past had sub-divided each caste into small, largely local, endogamous groups.[2] Even millenary movements could contribute to an extended solidarity and group loyalty for people who in the past had worshipped tribal deities.[3] Thus, even a spiritual movement which, in certain respects, was a flight from realities, could function as a kind of pre-nationalism by fostering wider and more-embracing loyalties than those inherent in tribal religious traditions.

Nationalism is not a 'universalist' ideology; but it does express

[1] Lea E. Williams, *Overseas Chinese Nationalism: The Genesis of the Pan-Chinese Movement in Indonesia, 1900–1916* (Glencoe, 1960); see also the third paper of this volume, dealing with the trading minorities in Southeast Asia.
[2] See for example G. S. Ghurye, *Caste, Class and Occupation* (Bombay, 1961), pp. 307 ff.
[3] Peter Worsley, *The Trumpet Shall Sound: A Study of 'Cargo' Cults in Melanesia* (London, 1957), pp. 227 ff.

the sense of living in an 'expanding universe' to those whose outlook formerly did not extend beyond the restricted 'universe' of
their tribe or local community. Therefore, it could rightly be
called a 'quasi-universalist' ideology.

Hence, it is understandable that in a colonial situation, in
which the main hindrance to a full development of the potential
energies of the new bourgeois class was the existence of a white
upper caste, nationalism could provide a common platform for
an effective struggle. The potential conflicts of interests between
the dwellers of different urban centres could remain latent behind
the unifying force of nationalism until the attainment of political
independence.

A further extension of the proselytizing power of the new bourgeois class was to be found in a broadening of the nationalist ideology to a more-embracing emancipation movement. The nationalist movement could be interpreted, in its colonial setting, as a
fight for the liberation of oppressed peoples and against racial discrimination. By extending its appeal to other groups subjected to
discrimination in the traditional oriental society, the leaders
could enlist support from those groups. The importance of the
youth element within any Asian nationalist movement is a case in
point. The Young Turks, the Young Persians, the Young China
movement, the Young Java movement, all sprang up within a
few years after the turn of the century and embodied a protest of
the young, modern, educated people against the old defenders of
the traditional, obsolete order. In the second place, the Asian
women, who had been relegated to the background in traditional
Oriental society, played an important role in reinforcing the
nationalist movements. Without personalities like the Soong
sisters in China, Sarojini Naidu in India, Raden Adjeng Kartini in
Java, the national movements would not have been what they
actually were: a rallying of a broad range of talents and energies
neglected under the old aristocratic order.

But there were still other groups for whom emancipation from
traditional bonds and disabilities was an alluring prospect. Unlike the free citizens of seventeenth-century Western Europe, the

new bourgeoisie in Asia was not earmarked for an age-long period of undisputed ascendency. Soon after the rise of the Third
Estate, a Fourth Estate was coming to the fore and raising its
claims. An incipient industrialization in the large Asian cities,
however limited in scope and output, brought the first beginnings
of an industrial proletariat into being. Potentially, the rise of this
group could mean a threat to the position of the new bourgeoisie.
But for the time being, it could also be turned into an asset by
proclaiming, as part of the nationalist ideology, a promise of
emancipation for the urban workers. Still more important as
fellow-fighters in the nationalist struggle were the semi-intellectuals, filling the lower echelons in the government services and in
the offices of the large Western enterprises, for these groups could
easily be won for socialist slogans proclaiming better prospects
for all dependent workers.

To what extent was the nationalist appeal effective in evoking
support from the peasantry – the large majority in Asian countries?

Throughout the nineteenth century peasant revolts had occurred in Asia, and in the first decades of this century agrarian
unrest increased as a consequence of a money economy which penetrated the countryside and upset the economic and social balance. More peasants than ever before were uprooted from their
homes and driven either to the cities or to Western plantations.
Rural bankruptcy and a gradual dispossession of the small
peasantry increased the ranks of the destitute in the countryside.
The famous Indian film, *Two Acres of Land*, gives a trenchant
picture of this process of dispossession and of the ensuing drive to
the cities. This proletarianization was significantly accelerated by
the economic world crisis of the thirties, with its concomitant
rural indebtedness. Thus a rural proletariat began to develop
which was accessible to revolutionary slogans. We in the West
are used to considering the peasantry a stabilizing and conservative factor in society. But in the non-Western world the peasantry
cannot be conservative, simply because it is too poor. As the
British Prime Minister Baldwin once said: 'If you want the

people to be conservative, then give them something to conserve'.

It is not surprising that some important peasant risings, with a nationalist flavour, occurred in Southeast Asia in the crisis years, such as for example the Sakdalista movement in the Philippines,[1] or the Saya San movement in Burma.

Although the loyalties and collective feelings of the rural population had, in the past, been largely restricted to the local sphere, there was a nascent awareness of a broader solidarity. Until the turn of the century this awareness had preponderantly found expression in religious forms and symbols. Therefore, it was not surprising that nationalist movements of the first decades of this century often took a religious shape, for the appeal to a religious solidarity was easier to bring home to the people than an abstract modern idea like nationalism. In this respect the new nationalist movements were able to play upon the element of pre-nationalism inherent in certain religious communities.

In Burma the first nationalist movement was called *The Young Men's Buddhist Association*. In Indonesia the *Sarekat Islam* was the first nationalist movement with a mass appeal. To a certain degree this movement, which was based on Islam as a unifying element, could still be regarded as a pre-nationalist one. But to the extent that it made use of modern organizational devices and operated under the leadership of urban laymen, it was clearly a movement giving expression to the aims of the new bourgeoisie. Islam was, in its Indonesian setting, in the first place an expression of anti-colonial solidarity. The religious appeal was of secondary importance. But it was the religious appeal which enabled the leaders of *Sarekat Islam* to broaden the following to some millions within a few years.

The rapid expansion of *Sarekat Islam* proved, at the same time, that the old-time elites, including both the aristocracy and the religious leadership, were losing their grip upon large sections of

[1] For a thorough analysis of the Sakdalista movement I may refer to David R. Sturtevant, *Philippine Social Structure and its Relation to Agrarian Unrest* (unpublished doctoral thesis Stanford University, 1958).

the population. A new type of leader came to the fore, the urban intellectual who knew how to open avenues to the modern world. Only by joining the broad nationalist movement could the traditional elite-groups retain part of their social prestige. On the other hand, by making use of the religious traditional leaders in the countryside, like the *pongyis* in Burma or the *kyais* in Java, the new bourgeoisie could enormously extend its influence upon the peasant population.

But soon the nationalist ideology was to replace the religious frame of reference. Restriction of the emancipation movement to those sharing the majority's religion excluded many important potential allies from the anti-colonial struggle. For example, among the educated Asians to be found in the forefront of the bourgeois elite there were quite a few Christians who, although they shared the colonial ruler's denomination, still were true nationalists. By abandoning the religious criterion their full cooperation could be secured.

Thus the new elite was able to raise a large popular support for its claims. Whereas both the aristocratic rulers and the colonial regimes had been content with the passive submission of the mass of the population, the national movement drew on its active and dynamic support.

But this was not the only basis of its strength. The new bourgeoisie was sure to win in the long run, because it came to dominate the keys to economic life. Unlike the situation in Western Europe a few centuries ago, economic life is no longer primarily dependent upon small entrepreneurs. At present, economic life is largely dominated by huge concerns and governmental offices issuing all kinds of regulations and directives in the economic field. Without active cooperation of the Western-educated staff of intellectuals and semi-intellectuals, of technicians and civil servants, neither the government apparatus nor the large enterprises can function. That is why the new elite was in a position to disable the apparatus by an attitude of non-cooperation on the basis of a national liberation struggle.

But besides its strength, which made it possible for the nationalists, sooner or later, to win a victory everywhere in Asia, their movement also showed certain weak points. For every group engaged in the liberation struggle, nationalism had a different meaning. For an important section of the new bourgeoisie a nationalist victory meant primarily the taking over of the position of the former colonial rulers. Its aspirations were fulfilled with the attainment of political independence. However sincere its pledge to improve the fate of the small people may have been at the time when it had to enlist their support, it was not genuinely committed to a radical reform of the social structure. On the other hand, for the industrial proletariat and the uprooted peasantry, and possibly also for a part of the urban intellectuals and semi-intellectuals, the attainment of national independence was only a first step on the road to real freedom. Therefore, behind the seeming unity of nationalism there was a latent cleavage which was likely to come to the open after the attainment of the primary aim. Even during the nationalist struggle this conflict between right and left was quite often clearly distinguishable. At present, it is one of the crucial issues in most of the Asian countries which have recently gained their independence.

Apart from such modalities within the national movements, there were still more divergent interpretations of the nationalist ideology. To some sections of the aristocracy, for example, national freedom meant the dream of a return to an idealized feudalistic past; similarly, for many peasants freedom implied a return to an idealized Paradise Lost, without any interference on the part of government agencies. To many religious leaders national freedom means no more than a first step towards the realization of a theocracy, whatever that may mean.

In the same way, other inner conflicts could be hidden behind the appearance of unity. Traditional regional, familial or personal loyalties were strong behind the semblance of a nationalistic or even universalistic ideology. After the main adversary, the colonial power, was eliminated, a fierce competition could start between the urban bourgeoisie from different parts of the young nation. The allies of yesterday could easily become the enemies of tomorrow.

Then there is religious or racial communalism as a potential threat to national unity. In India religious communalism has caused the birth of two nations instead of one. Again competition between different sections of the bourgeoisie was at the root of the split.

In the same way, racial communalism may disrupt the unity of the national bourgeoisie, as is shown in present-day Thailand, the Philippines, Vietnam and Indonesia, where discrimination against people of Chinese ancestry is rife. The anti-Chinese tendencies were already visible in the first beginnings of *Sarekat Islam*, which was primarily founded by Javanese Moslem traders in order to oppose the economic power of the Chinese middle class. Only in its further development did *Sarekat Islam* become a more general anti-colonial movement. But after independence anti-Chinese actions in Indonesia regained force.

The tendency of members of the new Asian bourgeoisie to unite on different lines of mutual solidarity witnesses a new development in Asian countries. After the first phase in which social status was increasingly based on individual achievement, this trend is gradually being overtaken by a new world-wide phenomenon, in which individuals try to achieve their aims by collective effort. Instead of basing their claims to power, prestige and wealth on individual qualities, there is a growing tendency now to use organizations, unions and collectivities as stepping stones to social ascent or to a defense of common interests. As a consequence, the period in which the nationalist movements gain their initial victory is at the same time characterized by a growing struggle between all kinds of collectivities. It is this struggle which comes fully to the open as soon as the primary aim, political independence, is achieved.

Therefore, the leadership of most modern non-Western countries is divided rather than united. The divisions and splits within the leadership spring partially from traditional oppositions and specific loyalties, but they are reinforced by modern aspects of competition on a group basis expressed in terms of group solidarity. Moreover, traditional splits, such as caste divisions in India, or the antithesis between the pious *santri* and the lax *abangan-* Moslems in Java's countryside,[1] are taking on a nation-wide significance in the modern setting, where political and ideological alignments assume nation-wide proportions as well.

The traditional oppositions are becoming all the more virulent as group formation at present assumes modern organizational forms and is able to use all the means of modern propaganda. Thus, the united nationalist movements appear to be only a temporary phase in the history of non-Western peoples.

But anti-imperialist and anti-racialist tendencies are not lost in the new post-colonial setting. While foreign investors, business-men and politicians frequently attempt to play upon regionalist loyalties, in order to prevent strong governments from arising in non-Western countries and from embarking upon a policy of rapid modernization and nationalization, they at the same time tend to reduce those leaders affiliated with their interests to mere puppets. Thus, it becomes easier for popular movements of a more leftist slant to fly the nationalist banner and to brand their adversaries as tools of foreign capitalism. The unifying slogan of nationalism still retains its appeal, for the time being, largely as a rallying force for a struggle of peasants and workers, in alliance with groups of intellectuals and semi-intellectuals, against the remaining power of foreign capitalists and their representatives among the native politicians and businessmen. At present, those unifying trends are even transcending national boundaries and assuming a still more universalistic outlook. Just as Pan-Islamism and Communism were internationalist in outlook from the outset, the erstwhile role of national solidarity is at present being ful-filled, to a certain extent, by the new Asian-African solidarity. Where there is a question of race discrimination on the basis of skin colour or of a continuation of colonialist or imperialist prac-tices, the divided forces can easily be united again in a common action and a common expression of sympathy.

Despite the divisions within the leadership of the present non-

---

[1] Clifford Geertz, *The Religion of Java* (Glencoe, 1960).

Western world, it would be unwise to underestimate the force of the Bandung spirit, in the same way as it was unwise, in the past, to underrate the strength of nationalist sentiments and forces across all the existing inner divisions.

Corruptie als sociologisch studieobject (Corruption as a field for sociological studies) was first read in Dutch at a meeting of the Nederlandse Sociologische Vereniging in January 1960, and published in *Sociologisch Jaarboek*, Vol. 14, Part One (1961), pp. 5–40. The English translation has been kindly prepared after a revised and abridged text by Mrs. Nell Clegg-Bruinwold Riedel and Mr. Arthur Clegg; the author is also indebted to Professor Harry J. Benda and Mr. A. van Marle for their critical remarks and kind assistance in editing the final text. The present text was also read as a lecture in universities and learned societies in the United States, the Soviet Union and India, and has been published in *Sociologia Neerlandica*, Vol. 1, no. 2 (Autumn 1963).

FIVE

SOCIOLOGICAL ASPECTS
OF CORRUPTION IN SOUTHEAST ASIA

There is often a considerable discrepancy between the significance of a social phenomenon and the attention paid to it
by sociology. One greatly neglected phenomenon is that of corruption. Though a favourite subject for club conversation and
newspaper headlines, it has so far received remarkably little
attention from professional sociologists. As a result, the current
concept of 'corruption' is still enmeshed in emotional reactions
and popular notions; it hardly reflects any real understanding of
the historical roots and social significance of the phenomenon.

This explains how it was possible for an experienced sociologist
like Raymond Aron to consider corruption in the state apparatus
to be one of the most important causes of revolution.[1] He could
have asked himself whether the argument should not run the
other way. The truth is, rather, that in a revolutionary situation
the accusation of corruption is raised because it has always proved
to be an effective weapon. Clearly Aron still takes his point of
departure from the popular notion that there must be a necessary
and logical connection between corruption and the fall of a regime or dynasty. However, as early as 25 years ago Van Leur
wrote that corruption does not necessarily impair the efficiency
of an administration. A corrupt regime can be quite viable and
function smoothly, says Van Leur – leaving aside its 'right of
existence': that is not an historical question, but a political and
ethical one, a value judgement.[2] Indeed, world history has known

---

[1] In discussing the problem of rebellion and revolution at the Fourth World
Congress of Sociology, Milan-Stresa, 1959.

[2] J. C. van Leur, *Indonesian Trade and Society: Essays in Asian Social and Economic History* (The Hague/Bandung, 1955), pp. 287–288.

many regimes which have enjoyed periods of stability, and even of prosperity, in spite of practices that would nowadays be called corrupt – or should one even say, because of such practices? One example is the United States at the end of the nineteenth century: the army that waged the 'Comic Opera War' against Cuba exhibited a 'record in bureaucratic corruption, inefficiency and bungling'.[1] But if corruption flourished, so did the United States where the Americans were in the process of realizing Adam Smith's prediction, made as early as 1776, that they would create 'one of the greatest and most formidable (empires) that ever was in the world.'[2]

When therefore corruption in many newly independent non-Western countries hits the headlines, at home and abroad, sociologists should not be content with the shallow judgement that it is a portent of the imminent collapse of these countries, even though the prediction as such may be right. Rather should we analyse the phenomenon within its own historical setting, taking into account the social forces which brand as corruption practices which in the past may not have been experienced as such.

This brings us to the crucial question: What do we mean by corruption? In present-day language we usually associate this concept first and foremost with the readiness of officials to accept bribes. 'In everyday life corruption is taken to mean that a public servant abuses his official power in order to procure for himself an extra income from the public'.[3] It is true that the concept also implies bribery of persons other than public servants, e. g. politicians, trade-union leaders, journalists, members of the liberal professions, electors, and, most important, employees of private industry; it was largely to counteract this last form of corruption

---

[1] Jacob Presser, *Amerika: Van kolonie tot wereldmacht* (America: From colony to world power, Amsterdam, 1949), pp. 399–400.

[2] Adam Smith, *An Inquiry into the Nature and Causes of the Wealth of Nations* (London, 1884), p. 257.

[3] Jacob van Klaveren, 'Die historische Erscheinung der Korruption, in ihrem Zusammenhang mit der Staats- und Gesellschaftsstruktur betrachtet', *Vierteljahrschrift für Sozial- und Wirtschaftsgeschichte*, Vol. 44 (1957), p. 289.

that the British 'Bribery and Secret Commissions Prevention League' was set up. But here I shall for the most part limit myself to a study of corruption of public servants in the countries of Southeast Asia. There, owing to the rapid growth of the administrative apparatus, which sharply contrasts with the under-developed state of private industry, corruption of public officials is of far greater significance than any other form. With the rapid increase of limited liability companies in Western Europe, corruption in private industry became a problem of alarming proportions only from the second half of the nineteenth century onward. Administrative corruption, on the other hand, is an age-old problem which has cropped up wherever an extensive bureaucratic structure of public services has existed. Therefore, although outside the official sphere the problem is not essentially different, corruption can best be studied in its official form, which has its roots in centuries-old traditions.

According to the common usage of the term 'corruption' of officials, we call corrupt a public servant who accepts gifts bestowed by a private person with the object of inducing him to give special consideration to the interests of the donor. Sometimes also the act of offering such gifts or other tempting favours is implied in the concept. Extortion, *i. e.* demanding such gifts or favours in the execution of public duties, too, may be regarded as 'corruption'. Indeed, the term is sometimes also applied to officials who use the public funds they administer for their own benefit; who, in other words, are guilty of embezzlement at the expense of a public body. This problem I prefer to leave outside the scope of the present paper. The specific feature of corruption in its most usual sense is that it involves two or more parties. This is also the fundamental reason why concrete cases of corruption are so difficult to trace; for there is as a rule no sign of it in the accounts of those concerned, and both parties are interested in keeping the transaction secret. Perhaps one might even see in such secrecy – as the Dutch sociologist H. J. Brasz has suggested[1] – a criterion for

[1] H. J. Brasz, 'Some Notes on the Sociology of Corruption', *Sociologia Neerlandica*, Vol. 1, no. 2 (Autumn, 1963), pp. 117 ff.

the 'corrupt' nature of a certain transaction: secrecy shows awareness on the part of those concerned that they are doing something which in the eyes of the society in which they live seems
objectionable, a 'corruption' of morals.

Favours from third parties accepted or demanded by an official
on behalf of members of his family or party, or of other personal
connections, may be referred to as forms of corruption even if he
does not directly benefit either financially or otherwise. In all
these cases the crucial point is the conduct of officials who in-
fringe the principle of keeping their public and private concerns
and accounts strictly separate.

At the same time, however, this definition shows that what is
nowadays meant by corruption cannot possibly serve as a universal sociological concept. For it presupposes a social structure
in which the separation between these two kinds of account-keep-
ing has either been carried through in actual fact, or else has been
generally accepted by society as a criterion for proper conduct on
the part of civil servants. Only then can the acceptance, or demanding, of gifts as a precondition for the bestowal of favours be
regarded as a 'corruption' of the prevailing standards of morality.
Therefore a sociological analysis of corruption ought to be preceded by an historical treatment of the social awareness which brands
certain types of conduct as corrupt.

In the above study Van Leur also wrote: 'A modern, strict
officialdom was only created with the Napoleonic state. Criticism
of the integrity of eighteenth-century officials is thus *ex post facto*
criticism.'[1] Indeed, before the time of Napoleon public and private revenues were not kept separate as a matter of principle
either in Europe or anywhere else in the world.

In the pre-Napoleonic period the predominant type of state,
which in Asia dates back even before the Christian era, was
what Max Weber has called the patrimonial-bureaucratic
state.

> Patrimonial relationships as the basis of political structures have been
> extraordinarily widespread... Princely possessions directly administered as

[1] Van Leur, *op. cit.*, p. 287.

territorial domains have always only constituted part of the ruler's political realm, which in addition embraces other territories which are not
regarded as domains proper, but merely as subject to his political authority. ...Whenever, then, a prince organizes his political authority... on the
basic principles that apply to the exercise of his rule over his own domains,
we speak of a patrimonial state structure. Up to the very threshold of the
modern era and indeed in the modern era itself, the majority of large continental empires bear a rather pronounced patrimonial character.[1]

A particular feature of these patrimonial-bureaucratic empires
is their broad agrarian basis. The peasantry produces primarily
for its own needs, but part of the harvest is claimed by the rulers
for the upkeep of the court and the maintenance of the urban
population living in the environs of the palace. Besides this the
agrarian population is required to render all kinds of services. In
the process of further differentiation of functions and more rational organization involving increased clerical work and a growing
hierarchy, the patrimonial administrative apparatus may take
on certain bureaucratic features.[2] All the same, positions in the
patrimonial structure continue to lack the bureaucratic separation between a 'private' and a 'public' sphere, which distinguish-
es them from modern bureaucracy as a conceptual type. In a
predominantly rural society dominated by a barter economy
officials are not remunerated in money, but with a share in the
produce of the land. This goes together with a far-reaching
decentralization of the patrimonial rule, as the administrative
pattern of the crown domains is copied in the more distant territories. Whereas the domains are subject to the direct control of
the prince, the latter territories are merely under his political
authority. Essentially what is found there is but a repetition of
the same pattern in which the local lord maintains a court of his
own by means of the tithes levied from the peasants and the services rendered by them. The peasants are not *taillables et corvéables
à merci:* their tributary obligation is always largely governed by

[1] Max Weber, *Wirtschaft und Gesellschaft* (Second Ed., Tübingen, 1925),
p. 684.
[2] Weber, *op. cit.*, p. 695.

custom.[1] The local lord, for his part, in recognition of the prince's supreme authority, is obliged to pay a tribute to the latter's court, which has usually to be delivered once a year. At the same time he is required to supply the prince, on request, with manpower for large building operations or for wars. This call for agrarian manpower is usually confined to seasons in which it can be withdrawn from agriculture without much damage. Sultan Agung of Mataram (Java) used to conduct his wars, year after year, during the dry East monsoon. And in all probability the huge temples of Java were also built during a succession of post-harvest periods, as were the Chinese Great Wall and the Egyptian pyramids.

Among the large continental empires this type of conglomerative political structure was as of old the most widely adopted form; though its individual manifestations understandably exhibit a great many variations, there is nonetheless remarkable consistency in basic determinants. Even the Chinese empire, in spite of the uniformity of its officialdom displayed, well into the modern era, these characteristics of a conglomeration of satrapies, some of them only nominally dependent, grouped around the directly governed central provinces. As in the Persian satrapies, also here the local authorities kept the revenues from their provinces in their own hands, defraying local expenditures in advance out of such revenues. The central government received nothing but its lawful tribute, any increase in which could only be effected with great difficulty and in the face of passionate opposition on the part of provincial interest groups.[2]

If the above picture of the early Asian empires, which is largely derived from Max Weber's works, is correct – and its correctness is confirmed not only by Duyvendak's study of China but also by such writers as Vella on Thailand, Schrieke on Java and Leach on Ceylon[3] – then Wittfogel's representation of these ancient

[1] *Ibidem*, p. 685.

[2] *Ibidem*, pp. 710–711.

[3] J. J. L. Duyvendak, *China tegen de Westerkim* (China against the Western Horizon, Third Ed., Haarlem, 1948), pp. 205–206; Walter F. Vella, 'The Impact of the West on Government in Thailand', *University of California Publications in Political Science*, Vol. 4 (1955), pp. 317–410; B. Schrieke, *Indonesian Sociological Studies: Selected Writings*, Part One (The Hague/Bandung, 1955), pp. 184 ff.; Schrieke, *Indonesian Sociological Studies: Selected Writings*, Part Two:

Asian empires as strongly centralized units over which the prince exercised 'total power' would appear to be far removed from historical reality. Insofar as the rulers tried time and again to keep the local lords under control by force, this is not a sign of absolute power, but rather of weakness. Among the means tried to prevent imperial disintegration and to ensure the regular payment of tribute, Weber mentions the following: periodic royal tours; dispatch of confidential agents; demands for 'personal guarantees' (in the form either of hostages or of regular appearances at the court); attaching sons of officials to the court as pages; putting relatives in important positions (which usually proved to be a double-edged sword), or just the reverse: appointing people of inferior class or foreigners as *ministeriales;* brief terms of office; exclusion of public servants from seigniorages over territories where they have landed property or family connections; attaching celibates or eunuchs to the court; having officials supervised by spies or censors.[1] None of these expedients proved to be a panacea, and imperial unity was continually threatened from within by decentralizing tendencies.

This system leaves no room for corruption in the present sense of the term. In principle the local lord collects taxes and levies in kind on behalf of his own court. He does not have to render account of his income or expenditure to anybody. So long as he fulfils his tributary obligation to the satisfaction of the prince and shows no sign of rebelliousness, he is free to dispose of the assets he has collected. The limit to these is determined by tradition, which brands any increase in the charges as abuse. Transgression moreover gives rise to the danger of active resistance from the peasants. Therefore the prince arrogates to himself the right to call the local lord to account whenever he has reason to fear that the latter is

Ruler and Realm in Early Java (The Hague/Bandung, 1957), pp. 217 ff.; E. R. Leach, 'Hydraulic Society in Ceylon', *Past and Present*, no. 15 (April, 1959), pp. 2 ff., containing a thorough criticism of Wittfogel's theory; see *e.g.* on p. 5: 'The investigator looks only for positive evidence which will support his thesis; the negative instance is either evaded or ignored'.

[1] Weber, *op. cit.*, pp. 704–705, 708.

becoming too independent or is endangering the continued obedience of the population by too heavy levies. In that case he will
punish as 'abuse' conduct which in the past may have been generally accepted as ancient custom. 'Anyone who enriched himself
too much and too quickly aroused the envy and hostility of these
overlords. What was considered too much or too quickly is not
always clear. In any case 'too much' was simply what others with
sufficient influence regarded as such'.[1] Thus, although in the absence of any clear distinction between the private and the public
spheres no accurate dividing line between custom and abuse could
be drawn, accusations of corruption were nevertheless conceivable within this structure.

This links up with the fact that even long before the Napoleonic
period certain trends came to the fore which eventually led to the
emergence of new social norms. As early as the fourteenth century,
Philippus of Leiden had tried, in his *Tractatus de cura rei publicae et
sorte principantis*, to impress upon his prince the doctrine that he
held the power bestowed upon him for the benefit of the community, and that he was obliged to exercise this power himself and
not to delegate it arbitrarily to any other persons or groups. To
the practice of exercising seigniorial rights for private purposes
Philippus opposed a theory which boils down to the maxim:
'public right is public duty'. Since then the development of
various European empires has proceeded gradually in the direction of increasing bureaucratization, though in the *ancien régime*
bureaucratic features in the modern sense did not yet predominate.

Similarly, in some Asian empires remarkable experiments were
made in the direction of bureaucratization and defeudalization.
For example, the introduction of the examination system in China, combined with the practice of temporary appointments of
mandarins in the function of magistrate, were steps which strike
us at present as surprisingly advanced. But even the examination
system could not fundamentally alter the patrimonial character

[1] Van Klaveren, *loc. cit.*, p. 322.

of the Chinese administration. Many officials still derived their income primarily from those under their control. In an economic system largely based on barter, with a poorly developed transport system, payment of officials in cash from the imperial treasury was difficult to realize.[1]

However, in the eighteenth century new norms were coming to the fore, particularly in the European world. Increasing complaints of corruption – in France, in the United Dutch Republic, in the Indies of the Dutch East India Company – do in themselves not necessarily imply that the phenomena we call corruption were becoming more widespread. They could equally well indicate that a kind of public conduct hitherto considered normal was now looked at with other, more critical eyes.

The patrimonial-bureaucratic type of state was clearly represented by the eighteenth-century Java of the Dutch East India Company. Though formally a commercial body, the Company bore in its main structure a close resemblance to a state organization. Its Java can in some respects be regarded as the successor to the seventeenth-century Mataramese empire, in which patrimonial-bureaucratic features were also apparent.[2]

In the eighteenth century the patrimonial-bureaucratic charac-

---

[1] Still, from E. A. Kracke Jr., *Civil Service in Early Sung China, 960–1067* (Cambridge, Mass., 1953), one might deduce that in the period discussed by the author there have been serious attempts to introduce a system of salaried officials paid from the treasury (see *e.g.* p. 83). On the other hand, even at that time 'among the most conspicuous complaints concerning officials of this period were low morale and venality, particularly in the lower ranks, traceable in large measure to inadequate pay' (p. 196). The author also admits that 'Many of the duties of local administration in the rural areas were carried out, under the guidance of these officials, by local functionaries who served without pay and who undertook such tasks as tax assessment, police duties, the management of storehouses, local public works, and the settlement of minor litigations' (p. 47). At any rate, it should be noted that according to Kracke, China at an early stage 'pioneered... in applying techniques to maintain honesty, discipline, and initiative – in other words administrative responsibility – among government personnel' (p. 1).

[2] Schrieke, *op. cit.*, Part One, pp. 184 ff.; Part Two, pp. 217 ff.

ter of the Company's rule found a typical expression in the letters of the 'transitional figure', Dirk van Hogendorp to his brother Gijsbert Karel.[1] We owe to Mme Elisabeth du Perron-de Roos both the publication of this correspondence and the term 'transitional figure', which stresses the fact that Dirk van Hogendorp, though himself still fully taking part in the patrimonial-bureaucratic system in the Indies, nevertheless in the course of his career developed a new sense of values, a 'new conscience' which gradually made conditions from which he and others profited seem abuses.[2]

The nominal salary drawn by the employees of the Company was of merely symbolic significance. In the case of Dirk van Hogendorp it was such a trifle (80 guilders per month) that he made it over to his two unmarried sisters in The Hague, by way of pin-money. According to the Company's system employees obtained their rewards in a different way. Dirk's father had perished in a shipwreck on the way from Java to the Netherlands; probably his ship capsized as a result of being overloaded with contraband. According to Dirk's memoirs, this was quite a regular occurrence thanks to 'the corruption common to all branches of the Batavia administration and well-nigh legitimated by the detestable system of the Company to pay its employees badly, thus fostering unlimited cupidity...' Dirk's revenues as Commissioner for the extreme East of Java were also of a dubious nature. He excuses himself for them with the argument that he 'could not live on the wind... Moreover such Charges had been imposed upon me that without Revenues I could not possibly meet them'. Towards the end of the eighteenth century these perquisites of office were con-

---

[1] Gijsbert Karel van Hogendorp became one of the outstanding Dutch statesmen. He played an important role in paving the way for the return of the prince of Orange as King William I of the Netherlands after Napoleon's defeat. His brother Dirk, on the other hand, served as a general under Napoleon, and died in exile.

[2] E. du Perron-de Roos, 'Correspondentie van Dirk van Hogendorp met zijn broeder Gijsbert Karel' (Correspondence between Dirk van Hogendorp and his brother Gijsbert Karel), *Bijdragen tot de Taal-, Land- en Volkenkunde van Nederlandsch Indië*, Vol. 102 (1943), pp. 125–273, see pp. 133, 170–171.

sidered so normal that instead of receiving a nominal salary, an annual 'office charge' had to be paid to the Company (in Van Hogendorp's case this amounted to more than four thousand rixdollars). In addition he had to pay two thousand rixdollars to the Governor of the Northeast Coast of Java 'in accordance with ancient custom', apart from other, similar payments. Legal and police expenditure were chargeable to his own account. All this, including his own upkeep, had to be paid for out of the same revenues that his predecessors had enjoyed, such as proceeds from 'overweight' in the levies of rice, profit from the sale of opium, gifts and fines from Natives and Chinese.

Elsewhere Van Hogendorp mentions the frequency with which such gifts are demanded from the native regents: on the arrival of the new commissioner; on each New Year's day; every time the commissioner's wife expects a baby; upon his periodical embassy to the governor general in Batavia; upon his periodical embassy to the governor in Semarang; on his departure; from each new regent he appoints. No need to ask who in the last resort had to bring in these gifts. No one could contract out of this system. Therefore, when on the basis of his new sense of values the militant 'transitional figure' Van Hogendorp criticized the overlords in Batavia sharply in his 'Address to the Dutch People', they were able to accuse him of the very abuses which under the prevailing system were unavoidable. This power of the central ruler to brand at will a custom as abuse fits in with the patrimonial-bureaucratic system.

After the century of growing awareness the Napoleonic reforms came as a revolutionary innovation. The French act of 17 February, 1800 created the administrative foundation of the great political edifice designed in the stern and symmetrical Empire style. 'With this act', according to Presser[1], 'Bonaparte threw a solid block of granite into the shifting sands of post-revolutionary France – not the only one, but one of the most lasting pieces. It

[1] Presser, *Napoleon: Historie en legende* (Napoleon: History and myth, Amsterdam, 1946), p. 143.

was the well-known division into departments, *arrondissements* and municipalities headed by prefects, sub-prefects, and mayors.' Though certainly not biased in favour of Napoleon, Presser nonetheless speaks appreciatively of the dutiful and sober conduct of the first draft of prefects. 'Corruption under a dictatorship like that of Napoleon', again according to Presser, 'is especially to be found at the top, within the leadership. It is centralized. It may easily go together with a high degree of devotion and disinterestedness among the lower ranks of the hierarchy'[1] – at any rate in the early days, before the rot had also penetrated further down.

The Napoleonic structure was of course not entirely new. It borrowed elements both from the Prussian state and from the reforms which immediately followed the Revolution of 1789. But the Napoleonic reforms were in any case the first to create the prototype of a state structure which Weber has called the 'modern bureaucratic state'. According to him, its main features are: a distribution of authority arranged systematically in accordance with generally applicable rules; a hierarchy of offices with a corresponding fixed order of procedural affairs dealt with in writing and with minutes being kept; special qualifications for offices that presuppose a certain amount of training; the principle that an official's normal daily task should be the fulfilment of his duties, and that these various functions should be exercised according to more or less strict, exhaustive regulations that can be learnt.

As a result of this system tenure of office becomes a profession; the position of a civil servant bestows a certain social distinction; the civil servant is appointed by a higher authority, normally for life; he is remunerated in money, with a fixed salary and the right to a pension; the civil servant counts on a civil-service career with a prospect of promotion according to rules of seniority, subject to the specialized qualifications required for a particular office.[2]

The bureaucratic structure, Weber holds, is everywhere a late development. It is possible only in an advanced money economy;

[1] Presser, *op. cit.*, p. 154.
[2] Weber, *op. cit.*, pp. 650 ff. (translated in H. H. Gerth and C. Wright Mills, ed., *From Max Weber: Essays in Sociology*, London, 1948, pp. 196 ff.).

technically it is more perfect than any other form of organization. The system aims at accuracy, quickness, written records, continuity, discretion, uniformity, strict hierarchy. One of its principles is that all cases are dealt with objectively, according to calculable rules and without respect of persons. Public and private matters are kept strictly apart, Philippus of Leiden's principle that public right is public duty, being carried to its logical conclusion.

It is obvious that the preceding features are characteristic of the ideal-type of a modern bureaucratic state, to which reality corresponds only in very rough outline. Thus the prefects of Napoleon's time were not entitled to a pension; and affairs were dealt with very sluggishly, since the various spheres of authority were not clearly defined, and unimportant matters had to wait for decisions at the highest level. Furthermore, the bureaucratic structure long continued to show a weakness in that the apparatus could function properly only with the safeguard of regular supervision. In the Napoleonic apparatus supervision from above was provided for, but the highest levels themselves were not subject to any supervision, and were thus exposed to the temptation of unbridled pursuit of gain. Even the institution of a supervisory body such as the Audit Chamber was no safeguard in itself, for who should keep the keepers? Not until late in the nineteenth century did the trend toward publicity in state affairs and government responsibility to representative bodies create the necessary preconditions for a serious application of the adage public right is public duty.

Still, the nineteenth century atmosphere of modern bureaucratic government allowed the present concept of 'corruption', as defined in the foregoing, gradually to take shape.

Historical reality, however, never conforms to 'pure types' – it always presents itself, as Max Weber put it, in mixed forms. The Netherlands East Indies government apparatus in the middle of the nineteenth century is a good example of such a mixed form, and an analysis of the situation there is the more interesting as it may lay bare the roots of present-day developments in many Asian countries. In that period once again a 'transitional figure'

played a part: Eduard Douwes Dekker, better known as Multa-
tuli, the author of that famous *document humain, Max Havelaar*.[1] His
difficulties and clashes with the official apparatus were partly due
to the tension between a still predominantly patrimonial-bureaucratic indigenous substructure and a modern-bureaucratic European superstructure imbued with a new sense of values which was
only slowly beginning to permeate that substructure.

Daendels had tried in vain to introduce the Napoleonic concept
of government in Java. The Javanese princes and regents were not
prepared to be demoted to the position of civil servants on the
Western model, and to surrender their traditional privileges as
landed aristocrats. A major rebellion, commonly called the Java
War (1825–1830), compelled the colonial government partly to
restore the regent aristocracy to its old glory. Once more their
offices became hereditary in principle and they retained the right
to all sorts of personal services from the population. Moreover
they were rewarded, as were other groups of civil servants – including Europeans –, by emoluments over and above their salaries. This extra income took the shape of a percentage of the
yield of the crops, grown under a system of forced cultivation on
government plantations in their districts – a typical patrimonial-
bureaucratic form of remuneration. In the Priangan regencies
(Western Java) the so-called Priangan System was even maintained up to 1871; this system allowed the regents to keep their
traditional revenues instead of receiving a salary paid by the
government.

Only in an infertile area like Douwes Dekker's Lebak (Southwest-
ern Java) where government plantations were practically non-
existent, did the regents and the lower-echelon indigenous civil
servants have to make do with their salaries; but this was impossible if they wanted to live 'in accordance with their social status'.
To secure the required income they stepped up the tributes and
services demanded from the population to a level far above the

[1] The best-known English translation is the one to which D. H. Lawrence
wrote an introduction; it was published in New York, 1927. A new translation
is forthcoming.

latter's capacity. No wonder that an idealistic civil servant with a modern outlook like Douwes Dekker, who wanted to take a stand against such 'abuses', could not help hurling himself against the powerful, traditional state apparatus – only to be crushed by it.

Towards the end of the nineteenth century, however, attempts were made gradually to bring the Javanese administrative infrastructure into closer accord with modern Western conceptions of government. The so-called *panchen* duties (domestic services due to native civil servants) were abolished. Henceforth the regents, and the chiefs of districts and sub-districts, were expected to live on their salaries. But this modernization failed to reach down to the foundation of the whole administrative structure, the village: the *desa*[1] headmen received no pay from the treasury and were rewarded for their services with a fixed percentage of the land tax collected by them, and with the proceeds of 'official fields' which were specially allotted to them and worked by the villagers on a rotating basis. No wonder that the principles of modern administration had hardly begun to penetrate the sphere of the village economy, and that nothing was easier for a Chinese *batik*[2] manufacturer or the owner of a cigarette factory than to induce *desa* headmen and *desa* police to round up female workers who had stayed away from work and to return them to the factory – although they had no right to do so and the women often stayed away or absconded because of the abominable treatment they received.[3]

What was the state of affairs as regards corruption in the Netherlands East Indies administration? Towards the end of the nineteenth century in many areas conditions still prevailed which to Dutch ways of thinking were quite shocking, and which various publications have brought to light. Thus for example Opheffer

---

[1] *Desa* – Javanese village.

[2] *Batik* – cotton prints made by a special technique, developed in Java.

[3] P. de Kat Angelino, *Batikrapport: Rapport betreffende eene gehouden enquête naar de arbeidstoestanden in de batikkerijen op Java en Madoera* (*Batik* report: Report on an inquiry into working conditions in the *batik* workshops in Java and Madura, Vol. 2, Central Java, 1931), pp. 28 ff., 310 ff.

mentions in one of his letters the Augean stable in the area of Rembang (Central Java).[1] Dijkstra, himself clearly a somewhat odd character, wrote a pamphlet on the basis of his experiences in the Lampongs (Southern Sumatra), denouncing 'The Corruption among Netherlands East Indies Officials'.[2] In 1902 Van den Brand published a sensational pamphlet with the title *The Millions from Deli*, which dealt with the methods used by the tobacco planters of the East Coast of Sumatra to secure the benevolent cooperation of civil servants. In general, the system was an indirect one:

> When Satan sets out to tempt, he hides his horns and carefully disguises his hooves and tail. A direct attempt at bribery is therefore rare. In the first place such an attempt is risky in itself, but what is more, it's stupid, downright stupid. The money has to reach the party concerned, but he must be able to give a plausible reason for its acceptance. ...It is the general custom for a junior European administrative official who is transferred to another post to put up his belongings for auction. And the proceeds are largely determined by his relationship with the local planter during his – the official's – term of office. Obviously a magistrate who punishes the coolies severely at the slightest provocation, and at the same time deals extremely mildly with any offence committed by a European, is held in high esteem by his white compatriots. To express this esteem and prove his appreciation of the administrator as a person, the wealthy planter gladly pays a hundred or more guilders for the pen with which the harsh sentence of his coolie was entered in the register. A pleasant keepsake, for sure... Look at some of the amounts that were spent some three years ago [*i.e.* in 1899] at the auction held by a civil servant who was leaving government service with a decent pension: five hundred and ten guilders for an ink stand, purchaser the chief manager of the Royal Company for the Exploitation of Oil Wells in the Netherlands East Indies; ...three hundred and fifty guilders for a cigarcutter, purchaser the chief manager of the Deli-Batavia Company; ...six hundred guilders for a globe, purchaser the chief manager of the British Deli and Langkat Tobacco Company.

[1] *Brieven van Opheffer*, (Uplifter's letters, Third Ed., Maastricht, 1944), pp. 339 ff. Opheffer (Uplifter) was a pseudonym of a wellknown civil servant, G. L. Gonggrijp.

[2] J. F. Dijkstra, *De corruptie in de Nederlandsch-Indische ambtenaarswereld, of: Mr. Rhemrev als regeerings-commissaris* (Corruption among Netherlands East Indies officials, or: Mr. Rhemrev as Government Commissioner, Rotterdam, 1906).

The Indonesian princes and Chinese headmen also offered incredible prices at these auctions – the princes, according to Van den Brand, 'so as to be able to continue their oppression and extortion of the people'; the Chinese headmen because they controlled 'the farming out of opium, pawnshops, and gambling leases, not to mention the fact that they owned nearly all the brothels'.[1]

However, the *indirect* form that 'bribery' takes in this case – the high prices paid at such auctions were especially intended to show the successor what he might expect if he took good care of the business interests in his locality[2] – is quite significant in itself. For in the course of the years the incorruptibility of the Indies civil service had come to be regarded as an indisputable fact. In this respect the Netherlands East Indies administration as a whole gained a reputation which closely approached that of the Western European democracies. J. S. Furnivall, a noted authority on the pre-war Indies, wrote that in Java corruption was 'practically unknown'.[3]

He contrasted this with Burma, where during the same period corruption thrived so profusely that he devoted nearly eight pages to it...[4] His facts were primarily derived from a report published on the eve of the Second World War. The commission of inquiry doubted if among the civil servants of the two lower grades more than thirty per cent were honest. It was suggested that no less than two thirds of all police inspectors were corrupt; the excise officers were 'by general consent the most universally corrupt'. In the prisons 'a prisoner could have anything he wanted except women; some said he could even have women'. In the medical department false reports could be obtained for a consider-

---

[1] J. van den Brand, *De millioenen uit Deli* (The millions from Deli, Amsterdam/Pretoria, n.y.), pp. 15–19.

[2] Van den Brand, *Nog eens: de millioenen uit Deli* (Once more: the millions from Deli, Amsterdam/Pretoria, n.y.), p. 41.

[3] J. S. Furnivall, *Colonial Policy and Practice: A Comparative Study of Burma and Netherlands India* (New York, 1956), p. 269.

[4] Furnivall, *op. cit.*, pp. 170–178.

ation; ward servants deliberately treated their patients roughly if they were not paid. And so on throughout his survey of the various public services.

The most important source of corruption was stated to be the multiplication of all sorts of 'welfare' measures which were disliked by the public. People readily made small gifts in order to escape such bothersome measures as vaccination, slaughter of diseased cattle, and building restrictions. The extension of the administrative apparatus created new opportunities for corruption. The general public was still unfamiliar with the difference between private and public interests: 'Even to this day the rural public frequently draws no distinction between payments to government officers which go into the Treasury, and those which do not...'

One may well ask what was the reason for the difference between Furnivall's estimate of the situation in Burma and his opinion of conditions in Java. Was there a real difference? Or was it largely due to the fact that in Burma an official inquiry had been held, whereas in Java there had been none? One should keep in mind that in general not only those who have been corrupted, but also those who do the corrupting have little cause for revealing their practices.

On the other hand it might be argued that such inquiries are the product of pressure on the part of a public that is convinced of the existence of large-scale bribery. In Burma this pressure came from nationalist politicians. No doubt Indonesian nationalists, too, would have used accusations of corruption if there had been the slightest chance of backing them up. The absence of such accusations in the, often violent, publications of the nationalists therefore argues in a certain sense against the existence of corruption on a large scale. Moreover corruption is furthered by a public opinion which takes it for granted that it is ubiquitous. For it is very risky to offer bribes to an official if the chances are that he will refuse them.

All the same there is enough evidence to justify the contention that Furnivall, in describing corruption as 'practically unknown',

idealized the actual conditions prevailing in the pre-war Netherlands East Indies. Patrimonial relationships were not confined
to the *desa* economy: in the official apparatus, too, there were
plenty of remnants of the traditional political structure. Thus the
loyalties of Indonesian officials were still divided between state
and family. To refuse a request from a member of one's family,
whether for financial aid or for a job, was contrary to the moral
code which still held good in Indonesian society. Hence Indonesian officials got into financial difficulties because, owing to their
traditional family obligations, they lived beyond the means provided by their official salaries. The colonial government often had
to overlook financial irregularities in its efforts to maintain its
aristocratic props in their posts. Hence also the recurring complaints about 'nepotism' among the regents.[1] The traditional
Javanese custom of presenting those in high office with small gifts
– a basket of fruit, a few chickens – also made it difficult to draw
any sharp dividing lines. More serious abuses, judged by the
standards of the public ethics of a modern bureaucracy, were not
lacking either. They were found especially in the Outer Regions,
where the Indonesian officials were less well trained and, more
than in Java, entangled in *adat*[2] and family relations; where,
moreover, the European officials, often far removed from the
central authority, had to carry extremely heavy responsibilities.

Particularly in the twenties serious complaints were raised in the
Volksraad (People's Council) about the acceptance of secret commissions – mainly in connection with contractor's agreements, for
example by the State Railways. I quote from an article by D. M.
G. Koch:

> Governor General Dirk Fock, who had gained the impression that corrup-
> tion had deeply corroded the Netherlands East Indies administration usu-
> ally so much praised for its integrity, had started a hunt for fraudulent
> officials and ordered a relentless prosecution of those who accepted secret
> commissions or committed embezzlement at the expense of the treasury.
> Sensational cases of dismissal from the service occurred, which created the

[1] See for an attempt to justify the system P. A. A. Djajadiningrat, *Herinne-
ringen* (Memoirs, Amsterdam/Batavia, 1936), pp. 213–214.

[2] *Adat* – custom, customary law.

impression that untrustworthiness had attained vast proportions and that it was creditable to take part in this hunt and to denounce people.[1]

Nevertheless Koch's statement in the same passage to the effect that the administration had a reputation for integrity is true, provided it is taken in a comparative sense by relating it to an Asian, colonial environment. Public morality was moving in a Western-bureaucratic direction, but many remnants of the traditional political structure were still there; and most important of all: insofar as the civil administration was incorruptible, this was due not so much to its Indonesian branch having been imbued with a new morality of complete loyalty to the colonial government, as to a strict supervision exercised by the European authorities.

But perhaps there was also another reason why, during the first decades of this century, the phenomenon of corruption tended to disappear into the background. In the early days it was still very important for a private person to win the favour of a local administrator. Hence the collusion between planter and official to which Van den Brand drew attention – partly the outcome of solidarity among the whites, partly of the great power of the local authorities.

But the period prior to the Second World War saw an increasing concentration of business interests within large concerns whose claims could better be pressed in Batavia or in The Hague than on the spot. At the same time the influence of these concerns in government circles steadily increased. There was no longer any need for businessmen of importance to have recourse to the tricky method of bribery: they could achieve their ends equally well by legal means. When therefore in the 'twenties critics of Governor General Fock's regime complained that high finance was unduly favoured – the cancellation of a proposal to levy export duty on oil meant an annual loss to the treasury of well over fifty million guilders[2] – this criticism implied that businessmen managed to

[1] D. M. G. Koch, 'De zaak-Baljet' (The Baljet affair), De Nieuwe Stem, Vol. 11 (1956), p. 484.

[2] Koch, Om de vrijheid: De nationalistische beweging in Indonesië (For freedom: The nationalist movement in Indonesia, Jakarta, 1950), p. 76.

obtain their ends by perfectly legal means. The rubber policy during the period of the great depression, which was gravely attacked by Governor Van Suchtelen, also favoured the Western estate owners by 'legal' means.[1]

At most one might speak – or rather whisper – of bribery by indirect means. But this no longer occurred on a small scale, as had been the case with the auctions on the East Coast of Sumatra at the beginning of the century. During the period of the growing power of the big concerns high officials who had served the business world well were rewarded by profitable directorships when they were pensioned off. In the public debates on the so-called Jambi affair, for example, the charge was made that a governor general and certain ministers had, in return for services rendered, been awarded with prominent positions in the Royal Dutch Petroleum Company. In this case Minister De Waal Malefijt denied the imputation of corruption, but added:

> Allow me to say that in general I emphatically disapprove of civil servants, who in their former posts were able to render services to a company, being offered high-salaried positions, and accepting them, even though in fact there is nothing wrong. Such offers create the impression that they are intended as a reward for services rendered, and might encourage slackness in officials who are still on active duty.[2]

So the situation began to develop along the lines described recently by an American sociologist: 'Nobody any longer needs to be bribed. Every member of Eisenhower's cabinet has been a director of large corporations, with the exception of the Secretary of Labor'.[3]

In the pre-war Netherlands East Indies a development could thus be noted which lagged behind nineteenth-century standards insofar as certain traditional elements continued to feature in the

[1] B. C. C. M. M. van Suchtelen, *Nederlands nieuwe Eereschuld aan Indië* (The Netherlands' new debt of honour to the Indies, Hilversum, 1939).

[2] *De waarheid over Djambi* (The truth about Jambi, pamphlet, n.p., 1921), p. 78.

[3] Edwin B. Burgum, 'American Sociology in Transition', *Science and Society*, Vol. 24 (1959), p. 322.

administrative structure; on the other hand we also saw a typically twentieth-century development as a result of which nineteenth-century ethical standards ceased to be entirely adequate
in the changing circumstances.

Against this historical background the problem of present-day
corruption can now be analysed in further detail. Again I will
confine myself mainly to conditions in Southeast Asia. There the
world-wide phenomenon of corruption can be observed in its
purest form as it were.

Smith tells us that under President Quirino in the Philippines
corruption extended from the lowest level of the civil service to the
top, excepting the president himself. One could not enter government service without paying for it – small sums in the lower regions, considerable ones higher up. Criticism became so sharp
that the president was forced to call a meeting to start a 'clean-up
campaign'. But much of its effect was lost because a reporter had
been listening under an open window and had overheard one of
the president's closest advisers exclaim: 'But what's the use of
being the majority party if we can't have a little honest graft?'[1]
This of course was promptly printed in the papers.

In Burma the political tensions within the large government
party, which eventually led to military rule, predominantly
centered around the question of corruption. Furnivall writes: 'U
Nu held that without drastic action to purge the party it would die
a shameful if lingering death from the cancer of corruption. Others
held that the remedy was more dangerous than the disease; it
would entail a major operation and the patient would die under
the surgeon's knife'.[2] About Thailand we read: 'The chief problems of the civil service at the present time are low salaries and

[1] Robert A. Smith, *Philippine Freedom, 1946–1958* (New York, 1958), p. 137
See further for an enlightening discussion of the corruption problem in the
Philippines: Onofre D. Corpuz, *The Bureaucracy in the Philippines* (Manila,
1957), especially pp. 221 ff.
[2] Furnivall, *The Governance of Modern Burma* (Second Ed., New York, 1960),
p. 117.

corrupt practices', and 'Corruption is probably more highly organized in the Police Department than in any other department'.[1]

So if in a certain period of the history of post-war Indonesia corruption occupied the centre of attention, this was by no means exceptional in Southeast Asia. At most one might say that the country's pre-war reputation of being a favourable exception had been lost. But the situation in Indonesia during that period – covering the years from 1951 to 1957 – also makes possible a closer study of the nature of post-war corruption and the form in which it appears. I am not sufficiently familiar with local developments after 1957 (the year in which I visited many parts of Indonesia) to determine to what extent the situation in this respect has been remedied since.

First of all we have to take into account that the post-war forms of so-called corruption still frequently conceal relics of the traditional social structure. Village headmen for example are still unpaid, so that they have to maintain themselves by partly legal, partly illegal levies on the population. The patrimonial-bureaucratic substructure still influences all other sections of society, while traditional family ties continue to clash with modern concepts of morality in public affairs. Even as late as 1957 in several public services in Western Sumatra it could be observed that all the personnel in one particular office belonged to a single family group: that of the office chief.

Besides these relics from an ancient past, however, post-independence corruption in Indonesia also had many typical post-war features. In the first place, under the direct influence of war, Japanese occupation, and revolution, the borderline between legal and illegal had become extremely vague and shifting. But even apart from the direct influence of war and revolution, new factors have been operating since the creation of the Indonesian Republic which promote corruption, or give it a new aspect.

One of these is the continuous extension of the duties of the public authorities. In the crisis years before the war a beginning

[1] Wendell Blanchard and others, *Thailand: Its People, Its Society, Its Culture* (New Haven, 1958), pp. 184, 198.

was made with economic controls. During and after the war this process continued, as nearly everywhere else in the world, at ever-increasing speed. This gave rise to a new official apparatus exerting considerable power over the most varied sectors of the economy. Many of these services are manned by personnel without any schooling in the pre-war civil service ethics. As in other Southeast Asian countries, the number of officials in Indonesia has multiplied: this is one of the many aspects of disguised unemployment. This leads, in turn, to serious underpayment of civil servants, which makes it not only a temptation but for most of them even a necessity to seek all sorts of supplementary remuneration.

In contrast with the extremely low level of living imposed by the salaries paid to officials is the demonstration effect emanating from the luxurious way of life of certain groups, such as foreigners and the new class of Indonesian traders and industrialists. Before the war the Indonesian officials and politicians considered the way of life of the European elite as beyond their reach. But since the Revolution much larger sections have come to regard a life with private cars and weekend bungalows as no more than their due.

Another factor which lends a new aspect to the phenomenon of corruption is that of party politics. During elections officials charged with the issue of numerous licences and permits took it upon themselves to make such favours dependent upon a donation to their party funds. The introduction of party politics has led to a spoils system – as was also shown by that conversation overheard in Manila.

Intervention by the army was regarded by many – in Burma, Pakistan, and Indonesia – as a means of putting an end to the political corruption. But experience soon taught that unlimited power in the hands of the army leadership, after an initial period of improvement, only tended to make matters worse. The regional commanders often start off with the best intentions, their actions being provoked by the fact that the central government does not provide them with sufficient funds for properly discharging their duties. Thus for example it is known that the regional commander in Celebes conducted a large-scale contraband trade in copra with the Philippines in order to obtain the necessary foreign exchange. In 1957, I heard the following story: A Chinese trader from Menado (Northern Celebes) told a friend in Jakarta of his intention to return to Menado. 'But why, I thought you left there after the Revolution because you could do better business over here?' 'Yes, in those days. But you know how it is... Here in Jakarta I have to tip five high officials to get a licence, but in Menado I only have to bribe one lieutenant'.

Besides, in the countries of Southeast Asia business affairs are getting so much tangled up with the state apparatus that many transactions smelling of corruption are conducted by strictly 'legal' methods. When representatives of foreign interests use part of aid funds for the benefit of high officials, for example by offering them expensive trips abroad, this could certainly rate as an attempt at 'corrupting' these officials, though the action does not come strictly under the technical heading of 'corruption'.

The foregoing, mainly historical, survey was necessary because history and sociology, if they can ever be separated at all, are certainly inseparable in this case. We may now attempt to draw from it a number of theoretical conclusions.

In post-war conditions we find various factors which clearly foster the phenomenon of corruption, such as the moral disruption caused by war and revolution, the extension of government intervention in economic life, the low remuneration of officials, and the lure of the way of life of certain groups. Moreover the great publicity given to corruption tends in itself to promote corruption.

However, there are also factors which point in the direction of changing social views and which may be regarded as indications that a new sense of values is breaking through. In the colonial era there could be no question of complete loyalty among indigenous officials in Java to a government which embodied the Western concept of the state. Under certain circumstances obligations towards relatives weighed at least as heavily. And the peasantry knew loyalty only towards their regent, hardly at all towards a central state apparatus of foreign origin.

The nationalist revolution was symptomatic of a new type of solidarity on a national basis. But this sense of unity has not penetrated deeply enough to guarantee strict loyalty from civil servants and citizens also in times of peaceful construction. The traditional particularistic loyalties are now seen to be too narrow; but an extended 'quasi-universalistic' loyalty towards the Indonesian Republic is for many still too wide. Party politics make it possible for an intermediate loyalty to arise, loyalty towards a political party, which frequently overrides loyalty towards the state as a whole. Hence making the grant of licences conditional on the receipt of donations to one's party is not felt as an infringement of public-service morals. In the absence of a fully matured national conscience, loyalties also frequently attach themselves to ethnic entities: one is faithful not primarily to one's national leaders, but rather to those of one's own area or island. This lay at the root of the Nadjamuddin affair, a sensational case in what was the State of East Indonesia during the few years of federal government under Dutch control, when an ex-premier was tried for corruption without losing his prestige among his followers.

Such intermediate loyalty in conflict with loyalty to the Republic can also be due to faithfulness to a military leader under whom one has fought during the Revolution. The regional commander who maintains his own troops on the proceeds of so-called smuggling may be completely accepted by his followers. The way in which he demands levies and services from the population in his area often still bears pronounced patrimonial-bureaucratic features – a relic from the past.

In contrast to these more or less particularistic loyalties a growing national consciousness condemns as 'corruption' actions which those concerned do not feel to be reprehensible. As in Western Europe in the eighteenth century, present-day Southeast Asia is in a period of transition, during which value systems are gradually shifting. Moreover, along with the new set of values that is breaking through, much higher demands are made on the government than formerly. True, in the past many activities which in the Western world were left to private initiative, in the East were performed by the government. But this was largely done on traditional lines. The present world situation requires from the public authorities a dynamic and imaginative activity which is possible only if all loyalties are concentrated on this all-embracing social task. This new sense of values brands as corruption many formally legal instances of collusion between private persons and government officials, so that those most deeply impregnated with the new norms are even inclined to style the whole of Southeast Asian society as 'corrupted'.

It is this discrepancy between norm and reality, between expectations and shortcomings, which draws so much public attention to the phenomenon of corruption. The attempt to inculcate nineteenth-century standards of public behaviour into the civil administration founders on the one hand on the immature sense of loyalty of the public servant himself, and on the other on the multitude of demands made on him, which in a growing welfare state far exceed those which the nineteenth-century bureaucracy had to meet. Thus the lack of stability of the new Asian regimes is due primarily, not to the frequency of corruption, but to the discrepancy between social norm and reality – a permanent tension with a dysfunctional and disintegrating effect.

The foregoing also makes it clear why the fight against corruption in the new Asian states is such a labour of Sisyphus. In 1953 a high Indonesian official saw three possibilities: first, to shoot all corrupt officials – but that he thought too radical a measure; second, to imprison them, but that (and I quote literally) 'would cause work to come to a standstill, as it is mostly minor officials that are involved' (it is interesting to learn that minor officials are more indispensable than higher ones); the third way, according to this 'expert', was the best: 'to introduce a new tax only payabel by corrupt people...'[1] Apparently it did not occur to him that

[1] *Indische Courant voor Nederland*, 24 November, 1953.

this would merely lead to higher tariffs... quite apart from the fact that most corrupt people are not in the habit of advertising their bad practices. But more intelligent experts, seeking a solution for example in stricter supervision are also faced with insurmountable difficulties. Who should keep the keepers? And, as we have seen above, to have recourse to a military dictatorship in the long run only makes matters worse by withdrawing government activities from public control.

All such measures fail because of their negative approach: they merely combat undesirable symptoms. The root of the evil is the lack of a more positive attachment to the government and of a spiritual involvement in its task in society, on the part both of the officials and of the whole community.

That is why the Chinese example is so instructive, for there a serious attempt has been made to encourage such a positive approach in all public servants – through education and propaganda accompanied by sharp measures against any deviations. In 1951 a mass movement was started from above, popularly known as the 'Three Anti's' and directed against the following evils in the public services: corruption, waste, and a bureaucratic outlook. But it is interesting that this action was soon followed by a new mass action, this time among the population and directed against similar activities regarded as harmful to the state: the so-called 'Five Anti's' movement against bribery, tax evasion, fraud, theft of state assets, and leakage of state economic secrets.[1] These mass movements were accompanied by pressure on every citizen, from highest to lowest, to denounce any instance of corruption or similar abuse that had come to his knowledge – criticism and self-criticism in official terms, spying and brainwashing according to Western terminology. These campaigns moreover were conducted in an atmosphere in which Spartan simplicity, thrift, and discipline in private life were being stressed. The breaking off of practically all contact with the outside world and the expulsion of

[1] Theodore Hsi-en Chen and Wen-hui C. Chen, 'The "Three-Anti" and "Five-Anti" Movements in Communist China', *Pacific Affairs*, Vol. 26 (1953), pp. 31 ff.

many wealthy foreign traders helped to eliminate the possible demonstration effect emanating from the way of life among social groups living in luxury.

The Chinese example also teaches us, however, that in an atmosphere of dynamic reconstruction the sharp distinction between public servant and citizen is in the process of disappearing. In the welfare state the public servant is required not only to keep public and private concerns strictly separate, dealing with the first in accordance with the prevailing legal regulations; a positive attitude and a dynamic activity in the interest of the community are also demanded of him. But the private employee, too, is no longer expected to be merely a faithful 'organization man': he has to be conscious all the time of his social task in the community in which he lives, and conflicts may arise between these two loyalties.

This trend, though in many countries still quite weak, is of the utmost importance for the development of the concept of corruption. Just as in the eighteenth century a new sense of values broke through in keeping with the maxim public right is public duty, so now a new sense of values is developing that might be summed up in the adage private right is public duty. The idea of trusteeship which has recently been incorporated in all world religions and which implies that the owner in effect administers his property for the public benefit, is a clear indication that this new sense of values is not confined to Asia alone.

But in this light the situation in these Southeast Asian states, which have so recently won their independence might be summarized as a tension between a past in which patrimonial-bureaucratic and particularist features strongly predominated and a universalist future aimed at socialization of the means of production. In their present condition of tension, these states cannot possibly find a secure foothold in a nineteenth-century official morality which is becoming obsolete.

The author read a short paper in Russian language on religious reform movements in South and Southeast Asia (Reformatorskije tečenija v religijach južnoj i jugo-wostočnoj Azii), at the 25th, International Congress of Orientalists (Moscow, 1960). The Russian text has been published in the transactions of the congress (*Trudy XXV ᵍᵒ Meždunarodnogo Kongressa Vostokovědov*, Vol. 4, Moscow, 1963).

The English translation was read in an extended version at the Oxford Conference on the Sociology of Religion (1961). The present text is nearly similar to the one which has been edited with the kind assistance of Dr. Norman Birnbaum, and published in *Archives de Sociologie des Religions*, no. 12 (1961), pp. 53–62.

A German translation, titled 'Religiöse Reformbewegungen in Süd- und Südost-Asien' has been published in *Probleme der Religions-Soziologie*, a special issue of the *Kölner Zeitschrift für Soziologie und Sozialpsychologie* (1962, Sonderheft 6, pp. 179–190).

SIX

RELIGIOUS REFORM MOVEMENTS
IN SOUTH AND SOUTHEAST ASIA

Contemporary sociologists of religion in the Western world are often mainly interested in the sociology of Christianity. However, they could learn from Max Weber, the founder of the modern sociology of religion, how much the study of Christianity could gain in depth when combined with a thorough scholarly analysis of other world religions. Weber's inquiries encompassed Judaism, Buddhism, Hinduism, Taoism and – if we may also term it a religion – Confucianism. He did not live to extend his studies to Islam, as he had planned; since his death, however, other sociological studies of Islam have appeared (for instance, those of R. Levy and more recently Montgomery Watt[1]).

Most of these sociologists (including Weber himself), when dealing with religions the majority of whose followers are Asian, were largely concerned with these religions in their earlier and traditional forms. The reform movements that have developed within these 'Oriental' religions from the beginning of the nineteenth century have not been given sufficient attention. (Incidentally, all the world religions – including 'Christianity' – were 'Oriental' in origin). This lack of attention is the more surprising, as these Asian reform movements may prove of special interest to the Western sociologist, since they show some striking analogies with the Protestant movements which were the main objects of interest to those founding fathers of the sociology of religion, Weber and Tawney. These analogies are easy to understand: several Asian countries have recently been passing through an

[1] Reuben Levy, *The Social Structure of Islam* (Cambridge, 1957); W. Montgomery Watt, *Islam and the Integration of Society* (London, 1961).

economic process more or less comparable to the rise of capitalism in Western Europe.

An attempt to establish both the parallels and the divergences between these Asian developments and their Western European counterparts struck me as an attractive task. I do not consider this essay as anything but an initial trial, based mainly on my specific knowledge of Islamic movements in Indonesia, combined with a much more superficial notion of developments in the fields of Hinduism and Buddhism.[1]

I propose to begin by simply enumerating the movements I am concerned with.

A remarkable phenomenon within Hinduism in the first half of the nineteenth century was the rise of Ram Mohan Roy's *Brahmo-Samaj* movement, whose followers were mainly members of the Indian bourgeois intelligentsia. In this context the term 'bourgeois' is meant to include officials of a modern type, who are products of the contact of the toplayer of the Asian world with Western capitalism and education, and are living in a Westernized, patrician style.[2] New movements came to the fore in its wake, for example, the *Arya-Samaj* of Dayanand Saraswati, and the schools led by Vivekananda of the *Ramakrishna* movement, Tilak the nationalist, Rabindranath Tagore and Gandhi. All embodied an attempt to renovate Hinduism and, in so doing, to adjust it to the requirements of the modern era. These movements testify to the believers' desire to preserve the basic tenets of their religion, whilst adapting it to the needs of a changing world.[3]

[1] I must acknowledge my debt to Wilfred C. Smith, who was the first scholar to attempt a sociology of Islamic reform during the past century in his stimulating first major work, *Modern Islam in India: A Social Analysis* (London, 1946). An important more recent contribution is Clifford Geertz, *The Religion of Java* (Glencoe, 1960); see also C. A. O. van Nieuwenhuijze, *Aspects of Islam in Post-Colonial Indonesia: Five Essays* (The Hague/Bandung, 1958).

[2] This concept of an Asian 'bourgeoisie' has been further elaborated in the fourth paper included in this volume, dealing with nationalism and leadership in Asia.

[3] One of the best analytical surveys of Hindu reformist and revivalist movements is still the one contained in a Dutch work: D. M. G. Koch, *Herleving:*

A similar trend may be noted within Islam, in Indonesia and Malaya as well as in Pakistan and India. During the earlier decades of the nineteenth century, Moslem movements in both India and Sumatra were under *Wahhabi* influence. From 1850 onwards, however, something like bourgeois modernism may be discerned within Islam – the term 'bourgeois' again being used in the same broadened sense. In India and Pakistan, this trend was reflected in the movements led by Sir Syed Ahmad Khan and Ameer Ali. In a later period, Sir Mahmud Iqbal's teachings and, additionally, the two *Ahmadya* movements (both the Qadian and Lahore branches) continued the development. In Indonesia, the *Sarekat Islam* and *Muhammadyah* movements, both strongly influenced by Mohammed Abduh and the *El-Manar* of Egypt, were aiming at religious reform.[1]

Buddhism in Burma and Siam was not exempt from attempts to adapt religion to the needs of the modern era. As early as the middle of the nineteenth century, the Siamese Prince Mongkut (later King Rama IV) insisted on the necessity of a renewed study of the classical *Pali* texts. The activities of the Christian missions were viewed as a menace to traditional Buddhism and the Buddhists were impelled to meet the challenge of the rapid expansion of the Christian religions. A liberal school of thought within Buddhism grew rapidly in the first decades of the twentieth century, in both Burma and Siam.[2]

The differences between these religions (and countries) are obvious, yet important and essential similarities in the development of the separate religions are striking. The only possible explana-

---

Oorsprong, streven en geschiedenis der nationalistische beweging in Britsch-Indië (Revival: Origin, purpose and history of the nationalist movement in British India, Weltevreden, 1922). See also A. R. Desai, *The Social Background of Indian Nationalism* (London, 1948).

[1] Smith, *op. cit.*; Smith, *Islam in Modern History* (Princeton, 1957); W. F. Wertheim, *Indonesian Society in Transition: A Study of Social Change* (Second Ed., The Hague/Bandung, 1959), pp. 195 ff.

[2] Kenneth P. Landon, *Thailand in Transition: A Brief Survey of Cultural Trends in the Five Years since the Revolution* (Chicago, 1939); Landon, *Southeast Asia: Crossroad of Religions* (Chicago, 1947).

tion of these similarities would appear to be their connection
with parallel phenomena in the social and economic sphere. To
a certain degree, these movements are also comparable with what
happened in Western Europe during the Reformation period.
We should not forget, however, that similar events there occurred
some centuries earlier, on the eve of Modern History with the
birth of the capitalist order.

A comparison of the new trends within the Oriental religions
with the rise of European Protestantism is, therefore, only partially justifiable. If we acknowledge the parallelism, we still have to
consider the important differences occasioned by the great distance in time between developments in the seventeenth and twentieth centuries. Further at present, similar processes take place at
a rate incomparably greater than that prevailing in an earlier
epoch. Moreover, there is another important reservation I wish
to make clear from the outset: in discussing parallels, I do not
deal with the specific values inherent in each separate religion but
rather stress the similarities underlying all the apparent contrasts
and variations. To a theologian, it is mainly the differences that
matter; the sociologist is primarily interested in what different
religions have in common.

We may begin with the situation in a relatively static social
structure.

In a traditional, feudal, or patrimonial social structure, religion
also had – in general – a largely traditional character. Divine
worship followed a prescribed ritual. Exactly as the populace was
accustomed, in worldly matters, to obeying their Princes, they
accepted the spiritual authority of clerics – whether Brahmins,
Muftis, Mullahs or monks.

Social discontent expressed itself in sectarian schools of thought
often of a mystical character, or in messianic – sometimes millenary – movements, which may be interpreted as attempts to flee
oppressive realities. Even as members of these movements, however, the believers generally submitted unconditionally to the will
of their spiritual leaders. In the course of time, such sects gen-

erally lost their original and – more or less – revolutionary character. The spiritual leaders gradually arrived at an accommodation
with the secular authorities; the peasantry, realizing the impossibility of an escape from reality along a messianic or millenary
path, submitted again to those in power.

Religion, in the case of messianic or millenary movements, may
serve as a symbol for a hidden or open social protest. In Java,
periodical local uprisings under the leadership of a fanatic who
assumed the title of *Ratu Adil* (Just Prince) and who promised in-
vulnerability to his followers, typified a common sort of millenary
movement. During the nineteenth century, these gained in
strength, following the deepening influence of Islam upon the
rural Javanese population; they quite often resembled the *Mah-
dist* movements of the Arab world.[1] These *Ratu Adil* uprisings
were generally expressions of discontent with Dutch colonial rule.
As popular movements embodying a social protest, they were
largely ineffective – as messianic movements mainly are – since
they advocated a sudden social change to be achieved by irration-
al and miraculous means.

As with most mediaeval millenary movements, uprisings of this
sort seldom achieve any lasting gains for the mass of the participants. The spiritual leaders are either liquidated, or, if they succeed in constituting a 'heretical' sect and maintaining a measure
of influence they often accommodate to the established order and
submit to those in authority. In the course of human history, a
great variety of sects did arise in this way. (One could even assert
that some of the major world religions originated in precisely this
manner). In the long run, religious protest movements in pre-
capitalist society did not better the lot of the large mass of the
rural population.

---

[1] A few of these movements have been analysed in G. W. J. Drewes, *Drie
Javaansche goeroe's: Hun leven, onderricht en Messiasprediking* (Three Javanese
gurus: Their life, teachings and messianic preaching, doctoral thesis Leiden
University, Leiden, 1925). A more general treatment of this type of movement
in Asia is to be found in E. Sarkisyanz, *Russland und der Messianismus des Orients:
Sendungsbewusstsein und politischer Chiliasmus des Ostens* (Tübingen, 1955).

What occurs, then, when a capitalist development begins in a relatively static society? Amongst the peasantry, the first reaction was usually one of rejection. The growth of commerce, the luxurious style of life developing in the urban merchant class, evoked censure from the common peasants and artisans; they suffered, moreover, from an increase in indebtedness. Their discontent often found expression in religious forms. Those who represented the official religion, having accepted office in the service of the rulers of the world, were accused of perverting the true sources of religion and of deviating from the sober and virtuous behaviour of the early communities of believers.

The social ideal of these movements of rejection aimed, primarily, at restoring the original agrarian order – without any accretions 'born of Satan'. A return to the true Holy Scriptures was the mode of restoration of these primitive communities.

Within European history, the *Lutheran* Reformation may be mentioned as an example of an anti-capitalistic movement upheld by artisans and peasants. Within Islam, the *Wahhabites*, active in the Arabian countries at the end of the eighteenth century and in India a few decades later, fell in the same category. In Indonesia, the so-called *Padri* sect on Sumatra were similar inasfar as they attempted to free the Moslem religion of all accretions and superstitions; their orientation, however, was not anticommercial as *Lutheranism* undoubtedly was.

In India parallel tendencies can be found in connection with what is generally described as the *Bhakti* movement. Artisan castes were prominent in this movement, which opposed the supremacy of the Brahmins, stressed the vernacular languages and held that 'even the lowest caste (*sudras*) may study the philosophy of Brahman'.[1] It is curious, however, that much later – when capitalism had already achieved considerable proportions in India – Mahatma Gandhi again propagated ideas comparable to *Lutheranism*. He, too, opposed economic progress and the growth of an urban industry. He preached a return to a sober rural life in

[1] Ramkrishna Mukherjee, *The Rise and Fall of the East India Company: A Sociological Appraisal* (Berlin, 1958), pp. 182 ff.

which there would be neither luxury nor indigence. He tried
to give a religious basis to his ideal by reinterpreting the Holy
Scriptures, in the first instance the *Bhagavad Gita*.[1]

This was the first stage during the development of capitalism.
Soon afterwards, however, a new trend can be observed and this
may be interpreted as the second stage.

Whereas the artisanry and the peasantry opposed capitalistic
economic development, the rising bourgeoisie experienced a
growing need for a new ideology, more appropriate to an urban
and commercial way of life than that provided by traditional
beliefs. Traditional religion, indeed, had satisfied the requirements of an urban traders' class living and trading in a traditional
way. The modern bourgeois, however, needed a philosophy more
adapted to the rational and scientific views of his time, and one –
moreover – in which he could express his individuality.

Independent study of the Scriptures had been begun by the
anti-capitalistic movements of the artisanry and peasantry. This
now provided the bourgeois with the means to search the Scriptures for truths more consonant with his new social environment.
The study of the Scriptures permitted laymen to approach the
Deity personally and immediately, without having to call upon
the Saints or the priesthood.

Instead of the mediaeval fatalism, the acceptance of poverty and
suffering as inevitable, the self-reliant bourgeois yearned for an
optimistic ideology which would affirm the possibility of increasing the productive forces of mankind.

The new religious convictions were at first impregnated with a
liberal spirit, corresponding to the comfortable way of life and
broadened vision of the *haute Bourgeoisie*. The prosperous merchants, modern administrators and those engaged in liberal
professions asked from their religion only a sanctification of their
endeavours to expand their entreprises and radius of action and
to exist easily, comforted by their own enlightened views. Believ-

[1] T. K. N. Unnithan, *Gandhi and Free India: A Socio-Economic Study* (Gronin-
gen/Bombay, 1956), pp. 245 ff.

ers were required to behave with charity, dignity and honesty in their individual relationships. These were the bourgeois virtues: bourgeois religion did not impose any specific obligations with respect to an individual's relation to society as a whole. The way of life of the *haute Bourgeoisie* was patrician and approached the style of an aristocracy, with whom this section of the bourgeoisie frequently maintained close political and social ties.

Within Christianity, the Dutch *Remonstrants* of the early seventeenth century are an example of a reformist movement of this type. The lawyer Grotius was a famous representative of this liberal sect.[1] In the Islamic society of the Indo-Pakistan subcontinent, the scholar Syed Ahmad Khan emerged as an exponent of liberal bourgeois beliefs. Within Hinduism, the *Brahmo-Samaj* movement played a similar role. In Indonesia an autochthonous bourgeoisie did not develop until the twentieth century; there, throughout the colonial period, trade was largely in the hands of the Chinese. The *Muhammadyah* movement, under Kyai Haji Dahlan's leadership, at first had a liberal character – as did similar movements in other countries. Equally, in Siam, in the course of the twentieth century, new bourgeois interpretations of Buddhism gained ground among the intellectual upper strata of society. Laymen were influential in this development. One of them, Phramaha Khumsaen, asserted in 1933 that education breeds knowledge, knowledge breeds work, work breeds wealth, and wealth breeds happiness.[2] These new truths were sought in the classic Holy Scriptures. Just as the Protestants preached a return to the *Bible*, the Asian reformers preached a return to the *Koran*, to the *Vedas*, or to the *Pali* texts.

With the growth of the merchant class, and as science and rationality take root amongst the petty bourgeoisie, reform movements generally lose their liberal character and become more rigid. This process may be interpreted as a third stage in the development of these religious movements. They promulgate a

[1] For a further discussion of this sect I may refer to the seventh paper of this volume, dealing with religion, bureaucracy and economic growth.

[2] Landon, *Thailand in Transition* (*op. cit.*), pp. 267–268.

more severe individualism, and not only do they allow the amass-
ing of capital but they praise strenuous effort in commerce of
manufacture as in itself pious. The petty bourgeoisie is less than
tolerant, generally, of other denominations. The reinterpretation
of Holy Scriptures leads to a new orthodoxy and even frequently
to a type of 'revivalism' which advocates a renaissance of earlier
beliefs and practices. Outside Europe, the agressivity and intolerance of these movements is often reinforced by the circumstance
that the petty bourgeoisie finds itself in conflict with a foreign,
colonial, power using another religion as an instrument of domination.

These orthodox religious teachings are not imbued with optimism as was the case with the liberals, but rather express discontent with the existing order. This discontent may account for a
'revivalist' tendency and for a belief in a 'Golden Age' – an idealized period in the history of the given religion, when its believers
allegedly observed God's commands for a sober and truthful life.
This 'Golden Age' is usually located in an epoch when religion
was not yet perverted by secular and clerical powers.

Calvinism, under which the Dutch bourgeoisie succeeded in
freeing itself from Spanish Catholic domination, exemplifies this
stage of a more rigid individualism within Christianity. The
'Golden Age' for Calvinism was the period of the early Christian
communities, by contrast with the Catholics for whom the Middle
Ages were a Paradise Lost. As John Knox put it, Geneva was 'the
most perfect school of Christ that ever was on earth since the days
of the Apostles'.[1] In India, the *Arya-Samaj* was decidedly less liberal than the *Brahmo-Samaj;* with its slogan, *Back to the Vedas*, it had
some of the traits sketched above. Many Hindus conceived of the
Vedic and *Epic* Periods, at the time, as a sort of 'Golden Age'.
Equally, Ameer Ali distinguished himself – especially in his later
years – from Syed Ahman Khan by a greater orthodoxy and
intolerance. The 'Golden Age' of Islamic culture for those who
came after Sir Syed was the Abbaside period of flourishing Arab

[1] Quoted from R. H. Tawney, *Religion and the Rise of Capitalism: A Historical
Study* (Pelican Ed., Harmondsworth, 1938), p. 116.

civilization.[1] In Indonesia, the *Muhammadyah* movement in the course of its further development gradually lost some of its original liberalism.

In tracing these parallels, we have to remind ourselves that a strict correspondence between the general sociological typology of development I have given and the empirical examples cannot be expected. I have used what Max Weber terms the method of 'Ideal Types', to which reality corresponds only approximately and which in fact exists in its pure form only in our conceptions. In reality, the different historical movements present far more shades and nuances, and the traits I associate with two distinct stages are often found together.

It is at this point that the parallels with the Reformation cease to apply to further developments in Asia. The Western bourgeoisie, largely recruited from private entrepreneurs, had at its disposal a period of some centuries in which to consolidate its economic, ideological and political position before a 'Fourth Estate' of labourers menaced the power of the third one. In Asian colonial and semi-colonial societies, on the other hand, the native bourgeoisie emerged so late that soon after its crystallization it was challenged by a rising worker and peasant class. Further, in the twentieth century, international capitalism (whose political and economic power extended over large parts of the world) prevented the realization of the Asian bourgeoisie's potential for independent growth. The native trading class, therefore, had only rather restricted possibilities.

Moreover, as I have pointed out elsewhere,[2] the composition of the non-Western 'Third Estate' differed significantly from its counterpart in the West, inasfar as the new bourgeoisie included many government officials, and employees or technicians working in the service of large enterprises.

Worried by the challenge from worker and peasant movements, certain elements among the Asian bourgeoisie began to utilize

[1] Smith, *Modern Islam in India* (*op. cit.*), pp. 12, 57.
[2] I may again refer to the fourth paper in this volume.

religion as a symbol for a collective defense against these. At the same time, the religious unity promulgated by this section of the bourgeoisie was a weapon against intra-bourgeoisie competition from other denominations. Religion now became primarily an instrument for the defense of their common interests. They no longer assigned priority to religious reform; consolidation under the symbol of religion was more important. The religious leaders were, accordingly, obliged to de-emphasize inner divisions and to water their reformist wine in order to win mass support from the community of believers.

All those elements in a religion which seemed likely to stimulate the morale of believers in conflict with unbelievers or those profes- sing a different creed were now stressed. These movements were socially conservative; their leaders declared that any further evolution in a socialist or communist direction was superfluous, as the true religion already contained all the valuable elements con- tained in socialism. The bourgeoisie, of course, affirm private possession of the means of production. In order to satisfy the critics of the capitalist order, the leaders of the different religions hold that the owner administers his property as a trustee on be- half of the interests of society. This doctrine is promulgated not alone by the Catholic Church, but equally by Gandhi's followers, by Moslems and by contemporary Buddhists.

The Indian case demonstrates, clearly, this new sequence in the historical development of religious movements. The *National Congress* at first united different religious denominations. In the next phase, however, 'communalism' emerged – the collective interests of each of the separate religious groups were stressed. Amongst Hindus these separatist tendencies were represented by Tilak; within Islam a similar doctrine was advanced by Mahmud Iqbal. Both of them attempted to formulate an activist attitude towards life, much in contrast with the passivist ideology preached by traditional spiritual leaders. To Tilak, great men were above common prescripts of good and evil; they had to search for a rule of conduct in the purified atmosphere of the *Bhagavad Gita*.[1] And

[1] K och, *op. cit.*, pp. 228 ff., more in particular p. 233.

Iqbal expressed a similar positive attitude in the following verse:
'If thou a Muslim truly art, Thy effort is thy fate'.[1]

But Smith has very well pointed out, that 'Iqbal the progressive' has gradually developed into 'Iqbal the reactionary'[2] – and it
is the conservative and collectivist side of his teachings which has
been taken up by most of his followers. He is still revered as a
founder of the Pakistan nation. To Iqbal, the 'Golden Age' has
again receded to an earlier period: the *Khilāfat al Rāshidah*, the
brief forty years of sober life from the time that the Prophet set up
his rule in Madinah, until the establishment of the 'corrupted'
Damascus empire.[3] On the other hand, to the activist and communalist Indian Moslems the great Moghul ruler was not the
liberal Akbar, nor the builder of brilliant monuments of Moghul
civilization Shah Jehan, but their successor, the narrow fanatic
Aurangzeb.[4] In the same vein, Tilak eulogized Sivaji, the Mahrat-
ta leader who had fought the Moghul rulers, in a distant past,
with questionable means.

In Indonesia collectivist and reactionary tendencies were lately
mainly expressed within the *Masjumi* party which, though at first
continuing the liberal heritage of *Muhammadyah*, in the long run
had departed more and more from its original individualistic
tenets and increasingly came to stress the collective fight against
leftist movements.[5] Such a development, the evolution of a religious movement originally presenting progressive traits into an
instrument in the hands of those in power is a common phenomenon in history.

---

[1] Altaf Husain, *Iqbal's Complaint and Answer: Being Allama Sir Muhammad
Iqbal's Shikwah & Jawab-i-Shikwah done into English Verse* (Third Ed., Lahore,
1954), verse XXXVI.

[2] Smith, *op. cit.*, pp. 101 ff., 132 ff.

[3] *Ibidem*, pp. 12–13, 117 ff.; Smith, *Islam in Modern History* (*op. cit.*), pp. 245–
246.

[4] Smith, *Modern Islam in India* (*op. cit.*), p. 88.

[5] Wertheim, *op. cit.*, pp. 226 ff. After the rebellion in the Outer Islands
(1958), in which several outstanding *Masjumi* leaders were heavily involved,
was crushed by the Indonesian army, *Masjumi* was dissolved by order of President Sukarno.

But whereas those bourgeois elements interested in a defense of the *status quo* attempt to raise the religious banner for a gathering of conservative forces, as a consequence of which the resultant unity may become in fact a source of cleavage between competing religious groups, popular movements of peasants and labourers, reinforced by large numbers of employees in government offices or in large concerns, assemble their forces under the symbol of class unity regardless of religious differences.

This may be one of the main reasons why the impact of religious reform movements upon Asian society is far less intensive than the influence of Protestantism upon Western European society in earlier centuries. Though the present movements in several respects are comparable to the Reformation, their ideas are mainly restricted to a rather insignificant layer of the urban population. Economic and political developments did not allow a consolidation and a deepening of their spiritual influence upon society. Soon after the birth of those ideas, the initiative was taken over by social groups to which the concept of social progress is not necessarily related to religious convictions, or even appears to be incompatible with religion.

Only by readapting their religious tenets and social philosophies to the psychical and material requirements of the broad rural and urban masses of the rising Fourth Estate, could those religions try to retain part of their hold upon the Asian common people.

Reformism in its classical shape has not been able to accomplish such a readaptation, as it has mainly sprung from social layers with a restricted influence and scope of activity, which put a typically urban and bourgeois imprint upon these movements.

If the Oriental religions will fail to readapt themselves to the material and spiritual needs of the common people, who are passing through a process of rapid transition, they will have to yield to other ideologies – Marxist or whatever they may be called.

Religion, Bureaucracy, and Economic Growth is the text of a paper, prepared for the special session on Religion and Development at the Fifth World Congress of Sociology (Washington, 1962). It has been published in the *Transactions of the Fifth World Congress of Sociology*, Vol. 3 (Louvain, 1964), pp. 73–86.

A French translation, titled 'La religion, la bureaucratie et la croissance économique', has been published in *Archives de Sociologie des Religions*, no. 15 (1963), pp. 49–58.

SEVEN

RELIGION, BUREAUCRACY, AND ECONOMIC GROWTH

In Max Weber's otherwise so lucid studies on the Protestant ethic and the spirit of capitalism, the relationship between these elements during the 'Golden Age' of the Dutch United Republic remains in a hazy twilight.

On the one hand, Weber stresses that contemporary foreign observers ascribed the tremendous growth of the Dutch economy in the first half of the seventeenth century to Dutch Calvinism.[1] On the other hand, he appears to have been aware that many of the patrician merchants of Holland were by no means Calvinists, but members or sympathizers of a more liberal branch of Protestantism: the so-called Arminians, followers of Arminius, Professor of Theology in Leiden. Even after the Arminians were ousted from the official Church, in 1619, liberal orientations remained strong among the richer merchants. Weber notes that the Arminians rejected the orthodox doctrine of predestination and had no part in the inner-worldly asceticism considered by him one of the psychological roots of the rise of modern capitalism. Surprisingly enough, as appears from one of his footnotes, Weber considered this aspect, in connection with his thesis, 'without interest' or even of 'negative interest'.[2]

In another footnote[3] – one has quite often to look into his footnotes for Weber's main arguments – he elaborates his view of the Dutch case more explicitly. He acknowledges that Dutch Puritanism showed less expansive power than its British counterpart. But his argument seems to be that the Calvinist ethic and the

---

[1] Max Weber, *The Protestant Ethic and the Spirit of Capitalism* (Fifth Ed., London/New York, 1956), p. 43.

[2] Weber, *op. cit.*, p. 217 (Ch. IV, nt. 1).

[3] *Ibidem*, p. 273 (Ch. V, nt. 67).

ascetic spirit, which had called forward the rising of the Dutch against the Spanish king in the second half of the sixteenth century, began to weaken in Holland as early as the beginning of the seventeenth century. Evidently, in his view, the rapid rise of Dutch economic power was still related to the Protestant ethic, but its force had been somewhat impaired by the ascension to power of the patrician regents, whom Weber calls 'a class of rentiers'.[1]

The inadequacy of Weber's theory for a clarification of the Dutch case has been pointed out by his manifold critics more than once.[2] Tawney has argued that the rise of a positive attitude to economic growth was a comparatively late development within Calvinism.[3] Hyma has shown the role of other denominations and spiritual currents in the process of economic development within the Dutch Republic and, more in particular, the specific contribution provided by the Arminians,[4] generally called 'Remonstrants' in Holland, a term derived from the *Remonstrance* presented in 1610 by the statesman John of Oldenbarnevelt.[5] Robertson has called attention to the importance of the rise of the Renaissance state and to the ascension of merchants to a position of influence in the state.[6]

Whereas Weber, in his assessment of the role of Calvinism with-

[1] *Ibidem*, p. 169.

[2] One of the best surveys of earlier critical appraisals of Weber's thesis has been published in Dutch by R. F. Beerling, *Protestantisme en kapitalisme: Max Weber in de critiek* (Protestantism and capitalism: Max Weber's critics, Groningen, 1946). A more up-to-date survey is to be found in Robert W. Green (ed.), *Protestantism and Capitalism: The Weber Thesis and its Critics* (Boston, 1959).

[3] R. H. Tawney, *Religion and the Rise of Capitalism: A Historical Study* (Pelican Ed., Harmondsworth, 1938).

[4] Albert Hyma, *The Dutch in the Far East: A History of the Dutch Commercial and Colonial Empire* (Ann Arbor, 1942), pp. 10 ff.; Hyma, *Christianity, Capitalism and Communism* (Ann Arbor, 1937), p. 144.

[5] John Lothrop Motley, *The Life and Death of John of Barneveld, Advocate of Holland*, Vol. 1 (The Hague, 1874), pp. 384–385.

[6] H. M. Robertson, *Aspects of the Rise of Economic Individualism* (Cambridge, 1933), pp. 56 ff., and more in particular pp. 86–87.

in Dutch society, appears to perceive a declining influence of this creed in the first half of the seventeenth century, Dutch historians seem to agree that the actual development was rather the other way round. At the end of the sixteenth century a restricted percentage of the population of the Netherlands could be called Calvinist, and the adherents of this creed were not to be counted among the people in the forefront of economic growth, for prosperous merchants were rare among them at that time. In the course of the seventeenth century, however, their number and their power increased. The short period of persecution of the Remonstrants by Stadtholder Maurice, Prince of Orange (culminating in the execution of his rival Oldenbarnevelt in 1619 and lasting until his death in 1625), during which episode the strict Calvinists were dominant within the Republic, was only of minor importance in this respect. Lasting trends were, in the long run, more efficacious than the Calvinists' dramatic but short-lived political victory in 1619. It should be stressed, that though Prince Maurice's successor and younger brother Frederic Henry (1625–1647) pursued a more liberal policy towards Arminian trends, the second quarter of the seventeenth century is still generally viewed as a period of an increasing impact of Calvinism upon social life in the Netherlands.[1] It was the period, during which it became a custom that in each Dutch livingroom two books had pride of place: the Dutch Authorized Version of the Bible, and the collected works of the minor poet Jacob Cats (1577–1660), which have once been called the Second Bible. 'Father' Cats has played a major role in popularizing Calvinism among the Dutch common people.

According to the thorough investigation undertaken by Beins, however, even at that time the economic tenets of Dutch Calvinism could hardly be called conducive to the growth of a capitalist

---

[1] See for example Conrad Busken Huet, *Het land van Rembrand: Studiën over de Noordnederlandsche beschaving in de zeventiende eeuw* (The land of Rembrand: Studies on the civilization of the Northern Netherlands in the seventeenth century, Vol. 2, Fifth Ed., Haarlem, 1920), p. 105; Pieter Geyl, *The Netherlands in the Seventeenth Century*, Vol. 1 (Second Ed., London, 1961), pp. 77 ff.

spirit.[1] Therefore, it is beyond doubt that the economic growth of the Dutch Republic during its Golden Age was largely due to forces other than the Protestant ethic as defined by Max Weber. And the inapplicability of Weber's thesis to the Dutch case has been of some help to those concerned with European religious history in bringing about a more balanced appreciation of the ultimate value of his brilliant conception.

One is tempted to ask to what extent the Dutch case might do more than serve a negative goal only: the disproving of part of Weber's thesis. In view of the fact that an important part of the current discussion regarding Weber's thesis is centered on the problem of its applicability in the modern Asian setting, I have set about to inquire whether a more thorough analysis of Dutch economic growth might contribute towards a better understanding of the relationship between religion and economic development in the Far East. It would appear that recent investigations in that field have carried the problem to a point where such a comparison may be fertile.

In his study of *The Origin of Modern Capitalism in Eastern Asia*, Norman Jacobs has attempted to draw a comparison between two great Far Eastern countries and societies – China and Japan. Jacobs states his central problem in this way: 'Why did modern industrial capitalism arise in one East Asian society (Japan), and not in another (China)'?[2] In accordance with Weber's concept, Jacobs endeavours to detect religious forces comparable with the Protestant ethic, but he is not able to find any: 'there is no positive logical link between Japanese religion and the rising capitalist forces as such'.[3] Still, he clings to the belief that 'Japan developed capitalism spontaneously'.[4] Thus Jacobs arrives at the conclusion that in Japan, 'although no force arose positively to

[1] E. Beins, 'Die Wirtschaftsethik der Calvinistischen Kirche der Niederlande 1565–1650', *Nederlandsch Archief voor Kerkgeschiedenis*, Vol. 24 (1931), pp. 81 ff.
[2] Norman Jacobs, *The Origin of Modern Capitalism in Eastern Asia* (Hongkong, 1958), Preface, p. IX.
[3] Jacobs, *op. cit.*, p. 214.
[4] *Ibidem*, p. 216.

support the cause of modern capitalism',[1] there was at least no dominant ideology opposing its rise. On the other hand, the dominant Confucian ideology in China was definitely inimical to the development of capitalism. Jacobs even goes so far as to label China, in accordance with K. A. Wittfogel's view, as an example of an 'Oriental Society' apparently incapable of independent economic growth.[2]

Much more enlightening is Robert N. Bellah's attempt to clarify the interdependence between religious values and economic growth in his brilliant work *Tokugawa Religion*. Jacobs does not attempt to draw any conclusions from the fact that, as he admits, 'the religious values of Japan in the mid-nineteenth century, if they can be related to non-religious behaviour at all, were concerned with the problem of the establishment of a modern centralized state'.[3] Bellah, on the other hand, uses this striking phenomenon as a starting point for a searching analysis. Japan remains a riddle only to those who view world history from the usual platform occupied by Western observers, to whom there exists but one road to economic progress: the way of private capitalism. To those who share this view, there remains an aura of mystery about the question to what extent capitalism in Japan might be seen as a product of 'spontaneous' growth, in view of the powerful state intervention during the Meiji period.

To Bellah, Japan is not a case apart; it only 'takes on special significance when compared with other non-Western societies'.[4] Whereas industrialization in the West has been the product of a slow process of accumulation, industrialization in the East 'has been government-controlled or government-sponsored, because only the government has been able to marshal the requisite capital'.[5]

---

[1] *Ibidem*, p. 211.
[2] *Ibidem*, p. 217.
[3] *Ibidem*, p. 214.
[4] Robert N. Bellah, *Tokugawa Religion: The Values of Pre-Industrial Japan* (Glencoe, 1957), p. 192.
[5] Bellah, *op. cit.*, p. 193.

Therefore, Bellah is not at all put out of countenance when he finds that religious values in Tokugawa Japan were not as positively correlated with the growth of private capitalism as would be required in order to justify an interpretation of Japanese economic history in Weberian terms. Nor does he feel any need to reverse Weber's basic thesis by stating, as Jacobs does, that the 'absence' of impeding ideological factors would be enough to produce a 'spontaneous' growth of capitalism out of a society with a 'feudal' structure. What Bellah tries to establish is that 'Tokugawa Religion' contained several elements conducive to an ideology which during the Meiji period could bring about a profound government-sponsored economic change. It was the *samurai* class of aristocratic officials, not the merchants, who were the bearers of the new economic spirit. Principles of *samurai* ethics, as applied to the modern industrialized setting, are listed by Bellah as follows:[1]

Art. 1. Do not be preoccupied with small matters but aim at the management of large enterprises.
Art. 2. Once you start an enterprise be sure to succeed in it.
Art. 3. Do not engage in speculative enterprises.
Art. 4. Operate all enterprises with the national interest in mind.
Art. 5. Never forget the pure spirit of public service and *makoto*.
Art. 6. Be hard-working and frugal, and thoughtful to others.
Art. 7. Utilize proper personnel.
Art. 8. Treat your employees well.
Art. 9. Be bold in starting an enterprise but meticulous in its prosecution.

In Bellah's view, then, the correlation between religion and bureaucracy was decisive in Japanese history. Whereas according to Jacobs, apparently, the correlation between bureaucracy and economic growth can only be negative, to Bellah it is precisely 'a strong polity' which has accounted for the astounding growth of the Japanese economy.

Moreover, in Bellah's view there is no basic contrast between the Japanese case and the Chinese. Bellah, who is much more

[1] *Ibidem*, p. 187.

realistic in his assessment of what is happening in China and the Soviet Union, apparently rejects the 'Oriental Society' approach advocated by Wittfogel.

'China... since its shift from the traditional integrative values to the Communist political values has shown a marked spurt in industrialization and can be expected to join Japan and Russia as the third great non-Western society to industrialize'. And Bellah concludes with the observation that 'political values and a strong polity would seem to be a great advantage and perhaps even a pre-requisite for industrialization in the 'backward' areas of today's world'.[1]

Bellah's lucid analysis inspires us to inquire into its wider implications. If economic growth in the present world may be due to factors which can hardly be labelled as 'capitalistic' in the traditional sense, one is easily tempted to reconsider Weber's thesis in the light of recent developments outside Europe. Just as Weber's theory was developed by comparing the Protestant ethic with religious values in the Asian world, recent experiences in the same part of the world may provide an indication of which direction we should look for a revision of Weber's concept.

To put our new problem briefly: if state intervention is a decisive element in producing economic growth in the world of today, it may well be that past developments in the Western world were much less occasioned by 'private' capitalism than has been generally assumed by Western observers grown up in a world which considered private initiative the decisive key to economic growth. In his analysis of the impact of different religious values Max Weber, too, started from the assumption that it was the attitudes of private capitalists that mattered. In this connection he hardly paid any attention to the spirit of bureaucracy, to other aspects of which he devoted some of the best chapters of his major work, *Wirtschaft und Gesellschaft*. To quote Bellah, who also has detected this weak spot in the accepted approach to Western economic history: 'The orthodox view of European economic

[1] *Ibidem*, p. 193.

history has generally considered the 'interference' of the state in the economy as inimical to economic development, though specific policies were often viewed as favorable. A general consideration of the relation of the polity and political values to economic development in the West might significantly alter the traditional view'.[1] As far as I am aware, Dr. Bellah has never elaborated this point.

It appears to me that the Dutch case, as expounded above, might provide a clue for further inquiry in this direction.

In Max Weber's opinion, mercantilism should be viewed as a transfer of the capitalistic ways of profit-seeking to the sphere of government. 'The state is treated as if it consisted exclusively of capitalist entrepreneurs'.[2] In Weber's system, therefore, mercantilism was a phenomenon which could arise only after capitalism as a mode of production had attained its full growth. To Weber, mercantilism was born in Britain, as an alliance between capitalist interests and the state.[3] The British mercantilist policy was primarily directed against Dutch trade. On the other hand, in Weber's time it was still a fashion among German students of economic history to consider the Netherlands of the first half of the seventeenth century as a country cherishing the principle of free trade; Laspeyres has written that in no other country were economic attitudes as far distant from the theories which Adam Smith characterized as 'mercantilistic' as they were in the Netherlands.[4]

A different view is held by Albert Hyma. He recalls that even early in the seventeenth century Walter Raleigh had observed 'that the Dutch government was vitally interested in promoting the welfare of its merchants wherever they might be engaged in

[1] *Ibidem*, p. 192.

[2] Max Weber, *Wirtschaftsgeschichte* (München/Leipzig, 1924), p. 296. (The English translation published in 1927 and 1951 under the title *General Economic History*, was not available to me.)

[3] *Ibidem*, p. 298.

[4] E. Laspeyres, *Geschichte der volkswirtschaftlichen Anschauungen der Niederländer und ihrer Litteratur zur Zeit der Republik* (Leipzig, 1863), p. 134.

commerce'.[1] In Raleigh's view 'the government was exceedingly efficient in supervising all imports, and in negotiating with foreign governments who had molested the Dutch merchants'. (According to Robertson, these remarks are wrongly attributed to Sir Walter Raleigh, since they were actually made by John Keymor.[2]) The French archbishop Huet had also remarked that the States General 'omitted nothing all that time to increase their trade where it was already established, or to establish it where they never had established it before'. Hyma goes on to discuss several instances of state intervention on behalf of Dutch trade in greater detail, such as, for example, stimulation of the importing of vast amounts of raw materials and the assistance provided to the exporting of manufactured goods. He also mentions the measures taken in order to prevent the imposition of any new customs or imposts on the navigation of the five great rivers of Germany and concludes that the Dutch 'perfectly understood the good points of mercantilism'.[3] Moreover, the influence which the statesman Oldenbarnevelt brought to bear to call into life the United East India Company as a monopolistic commercial body (1602) is an outstanding example of official intervention in private capitalistic enterprise.

Who were those officials who played such an active part in the economic growth of the young Republic? They were the very 'regents' whom Max Weber, in the few lines devoted to the Netherlands in his *Protestant Ethic*, dismissed as mere *rentiers*! That is what these patricians became at a much later stage, when the Republic was past its peak. But in the period generally considered decisive for the rise of the Republic, in the first decades of the seventeenth century, they were for the most part vigorous and efficient administrators who were at the same time wealthy merchants actively interested in trade. And even after many of them had retired from active trade and had developed a more aristocratic style of life, in the second quarter of the seventeenth centu-

[1] Hyma, *The Dutch in the Far East* (*op. cit.*), pp. 14 ff.
[2] See Robertson, *op. cit.*, p. 66.
[3] Hyma, *op. cit.*, p. 18.

ry, they remained enterprising gentlemen actively engaged in such pursuits as the reclamation of marsh land.

The great majority of those people who led the young Republic during its flowering, were different indeed from the Puritan type considered by Weber as characteristic of the capitalist pioneer. Some of them were Calvinists, as for example the burgo-master of Amsterdam, Reynier Pauw, Oldenbarnevelt's great ad-versary, though the two of them had together played a prominent part in the foundation of the United East India Company. But the large majority of the regents and wealthy merchants belonged to a different type, as Weber himself acknowledges. Except for a short period after Prince Maurice had switched his allegiance to the Calvinist faction, the moderates and those sympathizing with Arminian trends formed a majority among the leading regents of Amsterdam. The Dutch historian Johan E. Elias, who has written a standard work on the History of the City Fathers of Amsterdam, notes twenty regents, among them six future burgomasters, in a list of those who in 1628 signed a petition to the city council of Amsterdam in behalf of the Remonstrants; most of the other sig-natures were from prosperous and prominent people as well. The same year Calvinist citizens sent a petition to the States of Hol-land complaining of the slack attitude of the Amsterdam author-ities towards the Remonstrants. There was only one regent among the signatories; most of the others were shopkeepers.[1]

Apparently, during the flowering of the Republic, the majority of those who were most active in developing large-scale capitalis-tic enterprise either belonged to the Arminian Remonstrants or were more or less indifferent in religious matters. An outstanding example of this type of administrator was the burgomaster of Amsterdam, Andries Bicker, who in the second quarter of the seventeenth century equalled or even surpassed Prince Frederick Henry in political power and was once ridiculed in a satirical poem as aspiring to become the 'sovereign' of the Netherlands. For example, it was he who brought about Dutch intervention in

[1] Johan E. Elias, *De vroedschap van Amsterdam, 1578–1795* (The City Fathers of Amsterdam, 1578–1795, Vol. 1, Haarlem, 1903), p. LII, nt. 5.

the war between Sweden and Denmark in behalf of the former, in order to enforce free passage through the Sound (1645).

The question arises to what extent the enterprising spirit of the Remonstrant merchants and regents could be attributed to their religious convictions in a positive way similar to the relationship between the Protestant ethic and the spirit of capitalism as elaborated by Weber. Should we attribute the sober and restrained way of life of the Dutch merchants in the early decades of the Golden Age, admittedly one of the prerequisites for capitalistic enterprise, at least to a certain extent, to their religious convictions? Or is it more probable that this way of life can largely be accounted for by the bourgeois origin of this patrician class, the members of which had not yet learnt to enjoy the fruits of their toil in opulence, as more matured aristocracies are accustomed to do?

At first sight, it might appear that the flowering of Dutch enterprise should be attributed to the absence of an all-pervasive conditioning of human actions by religious motivations, rather than to the positive qualities of the dominant religion: several contemporary foreign observers have attributed the prosperity of the Dutch Republic to the liberal attitude towards alien religions. Tawney[1] quotes William Temple, William Petty, and De la Court as having attributed the prosperity of the Dutch to the fact that every man could practise whatever religion he pleased. If this were true, it would be indifference or moderation in religious matters that would account for economic growth, rather than the positive content or spirit of a specific religion. In that case, economic growth should, by and large, be attributed to the general spirit of humanism prevalent since the Renaissance, to the inquisitiveness of the adventurous human mind open to new discoveries and to the absence of inhibitions rooted in religious dogma.[2]

But upon closer scrutiny it appears possible that the positive ideology of the Remonstrants fulfilled a more active role in the young Republic.

[1] Tawney, *op. cit.*, p. 187.
[2] Jan and Annie Romein, *De lage landen bij de zee* (The low lands near the sea, Phoenix Pocket, Fourth Ed., Vol. 2, Zeist, 1961), pp. 133–134.

Whereas the original concept of the *Remonstrance*, drafted by the Arminian theologians after the death of Professor Arminius of Leiden, had the character of a religious credo and of a justification of Arminian exegetics, the final text, as amended by Oldenbarnevelt and presented by him in 1610 on behalf of the 'Remonstrants' to the States of Holland, had a different character.[1] It had become a political document invoking the intervention of the state to guarantee freedom of worship to the Arminians. Thus the relationship between State and Church was brought into play, and there are even indications that Oldenbarnevelt, whose personal convictions may have been nearer to the Calvinists than to the Arminians, was induced to make this move mainly in order to strengthen the position of the state. He represented in essence the regent class who could not bear the interference of dogmatic and narrow-minded clergymen in their worldly affairs. And Grotius, Oldenbarnevelt's famous companion in the struggle between the Remonstrants and the Calvinist Contra-Remonstrants, even went so far as to advocate the imposition of the Arminian religious doctrine as an official theology to be proclaimed by the state. On the other hand, it was also for political reasons that Prince Maurice sided with the fanatical Contra-Remonstrants, in order to defeat his adversary Oldenbarnevelt. There is a story – its authenticity is not beyond doubt – that, before taking his dramatic decision, Maurice said that he really did not know whether predestination was green or blue.[2]

Weber maintains that the dogma of predestination contributed to the Calvinists' determination in worldly affairs. But at the time of the struggle between the Remonstrants and the Contra-Remonstrants, it was precisely the former who, in rejecting predestination, based their position on a belief in the ability of man

[1] H. Y. Groenewegen, 'Arminius en de Remonstrantie' (Arminius and the Remonstrance) in: G. J. Heering (ed.), *De Remonstranten: Gedenkboek bij het 300-jarig bestaan der Remonstrantsche Broederschap* (The Remonstrants: Memorial volume published at the 300th anniversary of the Remonstrant Brotherhood, Leiden, 1919), pp. 68 ff.

[2] Romein, *op. cit.*, Vol. 2, p. 38.

to improve his ways by exerting himself. In this case, such a rejection may have functioned as a stimulus to an energetic pursuit of the tasks with which the Dutch administrators were burdened.

A closer study of the Remonstrant movement and its relation to the bureaucratic ethic still needs to be undertaken. It is evident that there is an enormous distance between the appeal for religious tolerance supported by Oldenbarnevelt on behalf of the Arminian 'libertines' (as they were called by their adversaries) and State Shintoism as developed in Imperial Japan during the Meiji-period. Still, as far as the interplay between religious beliefs and bureaucratic proficiency is concerned, a further inquiry into parallel phenomena might appear to be worth while.

Such a study should include the further role of state intervention in the process of development of modern capitalism. In the nineteenth century, fierce competition from British interests made it impossible for German industry to flourish without strong support from governmental institutions. Werner Sombart has clearly demonstrated the role played by the Deutsche Reichsbank in promoting German industrial development.[1] Though the shares of the Reichsbank were in private hands, the directors of the bank were officials nominated by the Kaiser. Sombart calls the bank a cross-breeding of capitalist entrepreneurship and 'old-Prussian correctness'.[2] This expression may provide an indication that a further inquiry into the ideology and religious beliefs of Prussian bureaucrats would contribute to a better insight into the ideological components of economic growth.[3] The influence of other governmental measures, such as restrictive tariffs upon the expansion of German modern industry throughout the nineteenth century, should also be thoroughly reconsidered without any pre-conceptions about the benefits of economic liberalism.

---

[1] Werner Sombart, *Die deutsche Volkswirtschaft im 19. Jahrhundert und im Anfang des 20. Jahrhunderts* (Fourth Ed., Berlin, 1919), pp. 171 ff.

[2] Sombart, *op. cit.*, p. 175.

[3] See also Sombart *op. cit.*, p. 64, for the role played by the Prussian bureaucracy in promoting economic growth up to the nineteenth century.

The present analysis may throw fresh light upon the parallelism between the role of religious reform in Western Europe and in Far Eastern countries. In my essay on religious reform movements in South- and Southeast Asia,[1] I attempt to distinguish several stages in the development of religious attitudes towards emergent capitalism. I point out that, whereas the first reaction of reformists *vis-à-vis* capitalist developments may be one of rejection, a new trend develops after the self-reliant bourgeois has begun to yearn for an optimistic ideology which would affirm the possibility of increasing the productive forces of mankind. 'The prosperous merchants, modern administrators and those engaged in liberal professions asked from their religion only a sanctification of their endeavours to expand their enterprises and radius of action and to exist easily, comforted by their own enlightened views'. Within Christianity, I mention the Dutch Remonstrants as an early example of a reformist movement of this type and then continue with an enumeration of several parallels in the more recent history of Asia. I also point to a third stage in the development of these religious movements: the stage when they tend to lose their liberal character and become more rigid, after science and rationality have taken root amongst the petty bourgeoisie. Here I have in view the Protestant ethic, as conceived by Weber, which praises strenuous effort in commerce or manufacture as in itself pious. Those who looked for Weberian parallels in modern Asia were, as a rule, primarily concerned with a study of such groups of reformist traders of the latter 'Puritan' type as the most probable agents of future economic growth. For example, Clifford Geertz, who has made a penetrating study of a region in East Java (Indonesia),[2] apparently looks primarily to the stern and pious Moslems, the *santris*, who represent predominantly a petty urban business class of the *bazaar*-type, for the future agents of economic growth in Java.[3] It is a group of shop-keeping trad-

---

[1] Published as the sixth paper in this volume.

[2] Clifford Geertz, *The Religion of Java* (Glencoe, 1960).

[3] See, for example, Geertz, *Peddlers and Princes: Social Development and Economic Change in Two Indonesian Towns* (Chicago/London, 1963), pp. 79 ff. His

ers among whom Islamic reformism has firmly taken root. Geertz, thus, envisages present developments in an Asian country from a Western point of view that might be less appropriate for countries outside the West.

As I pointed out in my essay quoted above, it would appear improbable that in modern Asia the bearers of an ideology appropriate for a petty trading class might be granted sufficient time to imitate the role played by a more rigid Protestantism in Western Europe. The foregoing analysis makes it more likely that the builders of a modern economy should be looked for among efficient administrators taking over some of the qualities and conceptions developed in previous times by the Dutch Remonstrants, and latterly by their aristocratic and bureaucratic counterparts in modern Asia. Still, as economic growth ultimately presupposes a propensity to save, the desire 'to exist easily', as shown by such social groups, should not predominate; the general way of life has to be sober and restrained, lest the effort to raise production be offset by increasing consumption.

In the case of Javanese society, for example, this might mean that in looking for the most propitious breeding ground for modern industrial growth, one should turn to tendencies manifesting themselves outside the class of petty traders representing a pious *santri* civilization. It may well be that the *santri* have no future under present world conditions and will be overwhelmed by groups with a different outlook. I would suggest that an ideology conducive to modern industrial growth in Java is much more likely to be developed, in the long run, among the modern representatives of the aristocratic *priyayi* class, which is more or less comparable with the regent class in the Dutch Republic and with the Japanese *samurai*, and among leaders emerging from the Javanese common people, the so-called *abangan*, whose general attitude towards life Geertz apparently considers incompatible with economic growth because of their collectivism rooted in

view of economic leadership in Bali is, however, different inasfar as the author stresses the importance of aristocratic elements as a dominant entrepreneurial group.

Javanese rural tradition. In my opinion, this tolerant and syncretistic *abangan* collectivism, combined with the administrative qualities fostered among a modernized *priyayi* class, might well provide a basis for the creation of a bureaucratic apparatus and of modern organizational forms, such as cooperatives and unions, institutions which are, in the contemporary setting, much more conducive to industrial growth than old-style capitalism based on individual profit-making.

Max Weber's basic problem was to explain why the modern industrial world was born in the West, and only there. As he could not conceive of a way other than the capitalist, he searched for psychological causes operating in the West which might account for the birth of a capitalist spirit, exclusive to this part of the world, out of comparable social and economic conditions – and these he found in religious values distinguishing the West from all types of Oriental societies.

Since our experience goes beyond that of Weber, we have to shift to a different problem: why has the East tended to follow a way to modern development different from that of the West? To what extent should our account of what happened in the Western world be revised on the basis of more recent experiences in Asia?

To all appearances, the argument I have developed here runs counter to Weber's way of reasoning and, indeed, implies a reversal of his thesis, since the Protestant ethic combined with the spirit of capitalism as main agents of economic progress are replaced, in my hypothesis, by a sober and restrained humanism combined with loyalty to the state. But in its essentials Weber's approach may still have the fecundity to stimulate a more penetrating analysis of the problem. Over against the theoretical Marxists who sustained the thesis that religious ideologies were nothing but the reflections of economic conditions, Weber posited the autonomous significance of the spiritual forces dormant in religion. It may well be that, in the relationship between ideology and bureaucracy as elaborated above, spiritual forces retain their autonomous role. Over against those who would pretend that the spirit of those administrators who foster economic growth is nothing but a reflection of the existing economic forces, I would hazard to put forward the thesis that the practice in countries under Marxist domination has demonstrated the spiritual strength dormant in an ideology. Without their Spartan sobriety and their strict devotion to their cause, the builders of modern industrial states in the East would never have been able to build a counterpart of the imposing edifice of British eighteenth-century industrial society, which, according to Max Weber, was based on the Protestant ethic.

A paper, entitled 'Urban Characteristics in South-east Asia', was prepared as a contribution to the Unesco Seminar on urban-rural differences and relationships with special reference to the role of small towns in planned development, held in Delhi in December, 1962. The paper, which was also read as a lecture in the Institute of the Peoples of Asia, Moscow, and in the Sociological Department of the University of Bombay, is for the first time being published in this volume, in a revised version and with a different title.

EIGHT

URBAN CHARACTERISTICS IN INDONESIA

About the turn of the century, the rapid growth of big cities (from Metropolis via Megalopolis to Parasitopolis) has been a matter of great concern to many Westerners. Oswald Spengler, Patrick Geddes and, somewhat later, Lewis Mumford expressed their misgivings about those unnatural cancerous outgrowths of the natural environment into which man was born. Spengler viewed these 'deserts of stone' as signs of impending doom, in accordance with what had happened earlier in human history to the civilizations of Babylon or Rome. All kinds of evils were attributed to 'Pathopolis', such as utter loneliness of the individual, suicide, vice, prostitution, crime, and gangsterism. Artists like Masereel, Sinclair, and Brecht painted the urban 'jungle' in livid and bleak shades, as the theatre of human tragedy and despair. Mumford called one of the chapters of his book on *The Culture of Cities:* 'A brief outline of Hell'.[1]

In the past decades the cities of the West have lost some of their most abhorrent qualities, thanks, no doubt, to the influence of town planners such as Sir Patrick Geddes. One gets the impression that modern Western man is gradually adapting himself to urban life and regaining a sense of belonging. The prophecies of doom pronounced by preachers of a past generation seem to have been a bit too pessimistic.

But while, of late, concern about urban problems in the West has been subsiding, misgivings about a parallel process in Southern Asia have been on the increase. The rapid growth of million cities in Southern Asia has bred those refuse dumps of human misery known as the slums of Calcutta, Bombay, or Karachi.

[1] Lewis Mumford, *The Culture of Cities* (London, 1946), pp. 272 ff. See also Oswald Spengler, *The Decline of the West* (2 vols., New York, 1928).

Again, the comparison with Dante's Inferno seems appropriate: Dr. Sen, in his study on Calcutta, calls a bustee 'a housing hell'.[1]

Mahatma Gandhi's attitude to urbanization was largely negative. He viewed urban development primarily as a process giving rise to dire poverty and innumerable social problems. He eulogized rural simplicity and reminded how the ancient Indians had been satisfied with small villages and had considered large cities a snare and a useless encumbrance where people would not be happy but would only serve 'the gangs of thieves and robbers, prostitution, and other vices and create opportunities for the rich men to rob the poor'.[2] 'India's salvation lies in the villages, with the Indian farmer', said Gandhi as early as 1916.

According to Roy Turner,[3] the attitude of the present leaders of India towards urban development is still deeply influenced by this bias against urban life inspired by Gandhi's teachings. He suggests that this negative attitude of Indian administrators might be one of the deeper causes of a general neglect of urban problems, in contrast with the much advertised rural uplift activities. 'Not only is there scarcely any support, in India, for the assignment of resource priorities to the cities', says Turner, 'but exactly the opposite is found to be true'. Though Turner, in this statement, may have been exaggerating, his general criticism appears to be basically just.

It is probable that the same predilection against big cities, both in India and elsewhere, accounts for the preference for 'small towns' among certain Western observers. It is at present generally recognized that urban centres are indispensable if planned development is to include industrial growth. But it is still hoped that,

[1] S. N. Sen, *The City of Calcutta: A Socio-Economic Survey, 1954-55 to 1957-58* (Calcutta, 1960), p. 161. For a more imaginative picture of the hell that is Calcutta I may refer to Claude Lévi-Strauss, *Tristes tropiques* (Paris, 1955), pp. 133 ff.

[2] Quoted from T. K. N. Unnithan, *Gandhi and Free India: A Socio-Economic Study* (Groningen/Bombay, 1956), p. 98.

[3] Roy Turner, 'The Future of Indian Cities', *Asian Survey*, Vol. 1 (1961), pp. 51–52; Turner (ed.), *India's Urban Future* (Berkeley/Los Angeles, 1962), pp. 446–447.

by creating smaller centres, the extreme consequences of urbanization can be avoided and that Asia could produce a technical civilization without going through the processes leading through Megalopolis and its concomitant way of life.

It appears to me that such an expectation is based on false assumptions. It is not the size of the city, but its general character, its economic function, and its outward appearance which decide whether it will be a sound habitat of human beings or a refuse-dump of human misery and a breeding-place for vice and crime. A big city is not less likely to fit in with sound economic planning than a small town.

I shall try to clarify this point by discussing a few aspects of urban development in Indonesia. Though urban distress in Indonesia has never attained the extremes known from cities like Calcutta or Karachi, the rapid growth of a city like Jakarta has given rise to serious concern. However, I hope to show that it is not its size but the type of urban development which is largely responsible for its problems and woes and that its difficulties are not intrinsically different from those in towns of a smaller size.

Nathan Keyfitz, in an enlightening article,[1] has painted the problems of a large city like Jakarta.

> The town planner who comes to Djakarta seems to find his services badly needed. A city whose physical structure was designed for half a million is now the home of about six times that number. It shows in particularly intense form the overcrowding common to nearly all the cities of the world: overfull hotels, traffic tie-ups, queues in stores and markets. The post-World War II increment of population lives in thatch and bamboo huts; people queue at water fountains or buy gasoline tins of water for domestic use; they bathe and wash their clothes in the turbid canals.

It is, therefore, beyond doubt that the big cities of Indonesia face big problems. But these problems are, generally speaking, rather different from the ones in Western countries which worried Spengler and Mumford.

[1] Nathan Keyfitz, 'The Ecology of Indonesian cities', *American Journal of Sociology*, Vol. 66 (1960–61), pp. 348 ff.

Indonesian cities are by no means stone deserts where human beings are completely dissociated from their natural environment. In their outward appearance they look rather like outgrown villages. Buildings are generally low, there are many open spaces covered with green overgrowth. The poor quarters look village-like, with their unpaved lanes, narrow alleys, and thatched huts, hidden behind foliage in the coils of some slowly flowing dirty river.

The town-dwellers are not the lonely and frustrated individuals painted by our Western novelists. To quote a student of one of the larger cities of Indonesia: 'Contrary to the traditional theory, we find in many Asian cities that society does not become secularized, the individual does not become isolated, kinship organizations do not break down, nor do social relationships in the urban environment become impersonal, superficial and utilitarian'.[1] The types of social contact between the city dwellers may appreciably differ from the bonds linking village dwellers in the countryside. They tend to be less traditional, and all kinds of organizational forms control the social life of those who migrated to the city. The urban dweller may join labour unions, political parties, neighbourhood organizations or rotating credit associations (arisan).[2] He may experience enormous difficulties in adapting himself to town life, and he may retain for a long time many typically rural habits. But he is not very likely to disappear into the anonymity often associated with town life in the West, though in individual cases psychological stress may produce tragic consequences.

The real problems of a huge city like Jakarta are, however, of a different character. These problems – social and personal – derive, to quote Philip Hauser, 'not so much from 'urbanism as a way of life' but reflect rather the problems of the nation at large,

[1] Edward M. Bruner, 'Urbanization and Ethnic Identity in North Sumatra', American Anthropologist, Vol. 63 (1961), p. 508.
[2] The Siauw Giap, 'Urbanisatieproblemen in Indonesië' (Urbanization problems in Indonesia), Bijdragen tot de Taal-, Land- en Volkenkunde, Vol. 115 (1959), pp. 266 ff.; Clifford Geertz, The Rotating Credit Association: An Instrument for Development (mimeographed paper, M.I.T., Cambridge, Mass., 1956).

problems arising largely from low productivity and mass poverty'.[1]

The demographic characteristics of the cities of Southern Asia
do not, in general, reflect a typically urban set-up. A more
detailed discussion of a few characteristics of migration to Jakarta,
Indonesia's largest city, may illustrate this point.

Population increase in Jakarta has been extremely rapid during
the past few decades. Whereas the total population hardly exceeded half a million at the 1930 census, it has risen to about
three million at the 1961 census. Certainly, one of the causes
is the extension of the municipality border over a rather wide
area. But still, it is beyond doubt that a far greater number of
people have been 'urbanized' in the Jakarta area than before.

The rapid increase should primarily be attributed to migration.
Except for a few interruptions, for example during a definite
period of the Japanese occupation, there has been a continuous
flow of migrants, mainly from the countryside. In an urbanization study of Jakarta, sponsored by Unesco and performed in
1953–1954, it was found that a very large percentage of the urban
dwellers consisted of new migrants, who had moved to Jakarta
during the past few years.[2] The sample investigated by the survey
team appeared to indicate 'that of the total Djakarta population
more than a third [had] arrived within the last four years'. In
some quarters the percentage of new-comers was much higher
still.

This steady flow of new-comers was in itself sufficient to prevent
the creation of a highly urbanized atmosphere.

But the professional structure of the Jakarta population also
contributes to the same effect. It should be kept in mind that it is,
actually, the occupational structure which sets urban society
apart from the countryside, even in Asian countries. Whereas in

[1] Philip M. Hauser (ed.), *Urbanization in Asia and the Far East* (Unesco, Calcutta, 1957), p. 88.
[2] H. J. Heeren (ed.), 'The Urbanisation of Djakarta', *Economics and Finance in
Indonesia*, Vol. 8 (1955), p. 704.

rural areas primary production is the prevalent way of life, in urban centres agriculture is at best practised as a side-line to other dominating occupations. As a consequence, also the stratification system in urban centres is clearly distinguishable from that in the countryside, the higher strata of society being largely represented in the larger cities. And though the usual view of rural society as a broad, undifferentiated basis of the hierarchical structure formed by the national society at large, may rest upon a one-sided, typically urban value system, it remains true that according to any value system worth considering the highest strata of society are, even in Asia, confined to the larger towns.[1]

Still, the professional structure is clearly differentiated from that in the West. As Heeren says in his report, 'Djakarta is not a typically industrial town, though in some *kampongs* nearly everybody works in industry'. In fact, an important part of this industry is practised on a small scale, and has more of a handicraft character. In addition, however, a large proportion of the migrants had to find work in some other sector, for example as street vendor, or as pedicab driver. A comparatively high percentage (six per cent for the men) was registered as 'unemployed'; but Heeren rightly adds that 'streetselling can be equated with hidden unemployment'. Among the female migrants a high percentage (over one third of all household heads) was employed in domestic services.

These few details raise the question why such large numbers continue to flow into a large city like Jakarta, even though opportunities for employment there are far from adequate. If the 'pull factor' which draws the people to the city appears to be rather weak, then why do they move at all?

The statistics provided by Heeren's report indicate that the 'push factor' operating everywhere in Southern Asia is the main cause of the continuing flow to the cities. The great majority simply move from the countryside to the city out of economic necessity. A certain percentage of the migrants declared that

[1] For a theoretical discussion of the divergence of value systems to be found simultaneously within one society, I may refer to the second paper of this volume, dealing with society as a composite of conflicting value systems.

they had left their villages because of the prevailing insecurity (at that time the *Darul Islam* movement was creating unrest in some areas not far from Jakarta). But they were a dwindling minority when compared with those who mentioned economic reasons as the main motive.

Heeren himself appears to draw a somewhat different conclusion from his materials. In his view, it is evidently the 'pull factor' which accounts for the migratory movement. He deduces, from his statistics, that 'migration to the city definitely means a rise on the social ladder for those involved'. This conclusion seems to me highly debatable, the more so since there is reason to challenge the basic tenet of his argument, to wit: his view of 'peasants' as constituting, together with the unemployed people, plantation labourers, pedicab drivers, street vendors, and domestic servants, 'the lower stratum of Indonesian society'.[1] Again, this low appraisal of the peasant's position in the social system of Java is symptomatic of a typically urban view. Rural society in Java, when studied more closely, shows a wide variety in social status, even among those who call themselves peasants (*tani*). There is a world of difference between the independent peasant-landowner and the landless farm hand, as far as their position in village society is concerned.[2] The former would, on the basis of the value system prevalent in his village society, decidedly not view urban industrial labourers as ranking higher than his own group.

But Heeren's low evaluation does hold true for the landless people and those who cannot subsist on the yield of their tiny plot of land. And these groups, constituting a rural proletariat or semi-proletariat, probably provide the large majority of those who drift away from the countryside to the cities.

For an explanation of this phenomenon it would seem hardly enlightening to turn to Heeren's view of urban migration as promising 'a rise on the social ladder'. It is dire necessity which drives

[1] Heeren, *loc. cit.*, p. 707.
[2] H. ten Dam, 'Cooperation and Social Structure in the Village of Chibodas', in *Indonesian Economics: The Concept of Dualism in Theory and Policy* (The Hague/Bandung, 1961), pp. 345–382.

those people to the town, and it is a lasting trend in land tenure relationships within the villages, which accounts for the increasing dispossession and proletarianization of a high proportion of the *tani* population.[1]

The situation in large parts of the Javanese countryside can be characterized as a steadily proceeding fragmentation of land holdings. To quote Clifford Geertz: 'Complicated tenancy, subtenancy, renting and subrenting patterns have developed which allow a greater number of people to claim a small portion of agricultural output from a single piece of land'.[2] In fact, no rise in *per capita* production has occurred, but the rural population has been able to subsist by a more intensive cultivation of the available surface. A pattern of live and let live, called by Geertz a 'shared poverty' system, keeps the people only slightly above subsistence.

However, rural indebtedness and the disguised unemployment typical for all underdeveloped areas drive an increasing number of people out of the villages. And even though the attractions of city life may prove imaginary to a high percentage of the migrants, still large numbers keep moving, hoping for a better fate in their new surroundings, but primarily pushed by conditions in their home environment.

Keyfitz has described in a vivid manner some consequences of the slowly deteriorating rural situation for the city population, in a way which again somewhat contradicts Heeren's assumption of a 'rise on the social ladder' for the majority of the migrants. How have the innumerable new migrants been maintained?

'Since the war the supplies of food to the cities of Java have diminished at the same time as the number of city people to be fed had increased... As the village populations use more and more of the

[1] Ina E. Slamet, *Pokok-pokok pembangunan masjarakat desa: Sebuah pandangan anthropologi budaja* (Basic elements in the structure of village society: A cultural anthropologist's view, Jakarta, 1963).

[2] Geertz, *The Social Context of Economic Change: An Indonesian Case Study* (mimeographed paper, M.I.T., Cambridge, Mass., 1956), p. 13; see also Geertz, 'Religious Belief and Economic Behavior in a Central Javanese Town: Some Preliminary Considerations', *Economic Development and Cultural Change*, Vol. 4 (1956), p. 134.

food they produce, the rice-purchasing power for city products steadily diminishes'. Printing more money and putting an increasing number of urban dwellers as officials on the payroll do not provide a solution to the problem how to feed the swollen urban population. Only by importing large amounts of food grain have the successive Indonesian governments been able to fill the gap between national production and consumption and to feed the urban dwellers. But the use of foreign exchange for food import has a stagnating influence upon economic development, since it prevents the use of the proceeds from current production for industrial equipment or fertilizers. Moreover, the people from Sumatra and Kalimantan, where most of the foreign exchange earning products are raised, may in the long run oppose the use of their proceeds for feeding the city population of Java. This may create, as Keyfitz states, 'centrifugal tendencies in the Republic'.

Keyfitz concludes that at present there exists basically, in countries like Indonesia, a clash of economic interest between city and countryside. 'The process of drawing people into the city is largely irreversible; their village source of food closes up behind them, and they can hardly go back to the village'.[1]

From the foregoing we can conclude, not only that the main cause of the rapid flow of people to the cities is to be found in the prevalent situation in the countryside, but that the general situation in the country also affects the problems of a capital city like Jakarta. The weakness of the industrial sector in the towns and cities of Southern Asia, including Jakarta, drastically restricts the number of jobs available to the new migrants. A serious unemployment problem is not uncommon, even in Western cities. But in the countries of Southern Asia the situation is much more pressing, the more so as social provisions for unemployed are practically absent. If a great proportion of the urban population is not to starve, a much larger number of jobs has to be created than is reconciliable with efficient management.

[1] Keyfitz, *loc. cit.*

I mentioned before that Heeren equated streetselling with hidden unemployment. But in the same way many other occupations in a city like Jakarta could be characterized as such. There are many more pedicab drivers than could be justified on a purely rational basis. And all the attempts of the trade unions of pedicab (*betjak*) drivers to keep the tariffs on a certain level fail, because the new-comers cannot be forcibly prevented from engaging in the same branch and thus bringing the margin between the rent to be paid to the owner of the vehicle and the daily earnings down to a level that is hardly above starvation.[1]

The same phenomenon occurs in all types of employment. The number of employees in any office by far exceeds the need for personnel, if calculated on a basis of efficiency. As a consequence, most employees have hardly enough work for a few hours, and none of them earns enough. The numerous peons in the offices, the large number of domestic servants in well-to-do families – they all testify to the same 'shared poverty' pattern.

The low productivity of the work – caused by retarded industrial development and a low level of mechanization – is one of the main causes of the low consumption level in Asian cities. But this implies that the evils of Asian cities are not primarily caused by the special characteristics of industrial society, but by lack of industrial development. The problems of a city like Jakarta are not caused by urban-rural differences. There may be a clash between urban and rural interests – but this clash springs from the fact that the urban and the rural set-up are essentially similar. The urban problems have the same basis as the rural ones: a low level of labour productivity and a high occurrence of hidden unemployment. Therefore their mutual position is not complementary, but competitive: both have to fight for their share in the produce of the land. And for the time being it is the villagers who win, because they are closer to the food-source. As Keyfitz states it, 'to increase land taxes has seemed impossible to a national government which depends on votes'. Indirect methods of taxation have

[1] Jef Last, *Zo zag ik Indonesië* (This is how I saw Indonesia, The Hague/Bandung, 1956), pp. 110 ff.

been tried, such as for example enforced purchase of rice at reduced rates, but their success was far from sufficient to feed the
urban population.

But this means that the urban problems of Southern Asia are a
mere continuation, in a condensed and aggravated form, of those
of the countryside. Even the evils generally associated with urban
life show, inasfar as they do exist in a city like Jakarta, a different
character from what they stand for in the West. Slums may be as
bad as anywhere in the world, owing to terrible overcrowding and
to lack of sanitation and hygienic provisions – but in a city like
Jakarta they still tend to show the aspect of deteriorated villages
rather than of dilapidated urban quarters. Their woes mainly
spring from economic reasons. The same applies for crime and
prostitution as features of the big cities of Southern Asia. In contrast with the present situation in some Western countries, where
both phenomena are considered largely attributable to distinct
personality traits which block the way to adaptation to normal
society, they are in Indonesia and in other South Asian countries
more often than not merely a consequence of economic distress.
The Unesco Report on urbanization in Asia, edited by Hauser,
points out that 'women and girls coming from the rural areas to
work as maid servants in cities are often forced into prostitution
when they could not adjust themselves to the families of the em-
ployers'. Both in the Philippines and in Burma, 'women are often
recruited from the rural areas for prostitution under the false
guise of domestic work or the promise of marriage. Once involved,
it is virtually impossible for them to escape'.[1]

In general, I can fully subscribe to the analysis of urban problems in Southern Asia as set forth in the Unesco volume.

Other demographic characteristics of the cities of Southern
Asia tend to confirm the absence of basic urban-rural differences.
Both birth and death rates in Indonesian cities are not very different from those in the countryside. Birth control is either non-
existent or restricted to small groups of the urban population.

[1] Hauser (ed.), *op. cit.*, pp. 238 ff.

And as far as mortality rates are concerned, there are indications that the bad hygienic conditions in several of the *kampongs* may be compensated for by better urban facilities for medical and preventive care.

This general character of urban problems in countries like Indonesia sheds a new light on the quite often heard call for small towns as nuclei of planned development. For, if urban problems are not basically different from rural ones, then why should there be a basic difference between a city and a smaller town? If the shared poverty pattern, with its implications of low efficiency and hidden unemployment, are part and parcel of the urban scene, there is no reason why the pattern in a smaller town should be different.

This is exactly what is borne out by a few sociological investigations in smaller towns. Clifford Geertz has demonstrated the pattern of 'shared poverty' as it prevails in a small town in the Eastern part of Java, called in his publications *Modjokuto*. He points out how this pattern operates both in the market and in small-scale industry.[1]

> Once the goods enter the wholly Javanese market complex they do not go directly to the ultimate consumer, but circulate among the professional traders, each transaction nibling away at the profit margin; the economic return for passing the goods form the large Chinese distributors to the ultimate consumers, small enough in the first place, gets divided among several people... The Javanese trader keeps a running debt balance with the Chinese trader, a balance carefully managed on both sides not to grow so large as to encourage flight on the part of the Javanese and not to shrink so small as to leave the Javanese without any control over the Chinese. In sum, the complexity of economic structure for a fairly simple economic function is surprisingly great.
>
> In a sense the same subcontracting pattern which fractionates the returns from land operates here to fractionate the return from retail distribution... The goods pass from hand to hand, their course regulated by debt manipulations, leaving only a very small profit behind at any point along that

[1] Geertz, 'Religious Beliefs etc.', *loc. cit.*, pp. 134 ff. I also refer briefly to the shared poverty pattern in small towns in the first paper of this volume, dealing with a sociological approach to problems of underdevelopment, and in the ninth paper dealing with inter-island migration in Indonesia.

course. Again, the moral obligation upon the Javanese trader to cut others in on a good deal shows that this response is not wholly rational, wholly economic, but is supported by a motivational pattern rather deeply ingrained in many Javanese individuals. It is in fact, the commercial interpretation of an ethic originally created as a response to purely agricultural demands...

One of my informants set up a cigarette factory in a shed behind his house. He began with two workers – girls rolling the cigarettes by hand, in corn sheathes provided by the workers themselves. The factory grew to employ a work force of twenty girls, the number being determined not by economic considerations but by the entrepreneur's and the girls' notions of the number which should be employed given the amount of work involved. The result was an extremely uneconomically operated factory. Unable to accumulate enough capital to provide sufficient tobacco to keep twenty girls working even six hours a day at full capacityt the entrepreneur merely apportioned out regulated quantities of the available tobacco to each girl each day and the girls worked at a very slow speed, producing only 1000 cigarettes in a working day where they might easily have produced 1500– 2000...

The outcome was typical: twenty workers and an entrepreneur made a semi-adequate living and no one made a good one, with the added consideration in this case that this economically inefficient operation reduced even further the opportunities for the entrepreneur to amass enough capital to increase output and hire more workers.

A report on a small Javanese town by another observer[1] stresses the handicraft character of most of the industrial activities. There is a continuous flow of migrants from villages in an ever widening radius, and it is not only the landless agricultural labourers who are 'pushed' from their *desa*, 'but the share-holder who is squeezed between the controlled price at which the government purchases part of his rice harvest and the rising prices of such commodities as textiles'.

Housing shortage is a characteristic of the small towns as well. 'Formerly the recruit from the village tended to move into the town, but the extreme housing shortage at present prohibits this type of migration'. The people now tend to work in the small town while residing in their village.

[1] Ann Ruth Willner, 'Social Change in Javanese Town-Village Life', *Economic Development and Cultural Change*, Vol. 6 (1957–58), pp. 229–242.

That the situation in the small towns is far from satisfactory to many new migrants could even, with some reservations, be inferred from Heeren's data on the frequency of migration to Jakarta in a few stages. Though about eighty five per cent of all rural migrants moved directly to the capital (most of them came from the neighbourhood of Jakarta, by the way) there was still a substantial number of migrants who had first moved from the countryside to a smaller town;[1] and it is to be questioned if a substantial proportion of them has been actually induced to move in order to provide their children with better educational opportunities, or because they were transferred by a government agency or a private company.[2] Again, lack of economic opportunities in the smaller towns may have been a major cause for migration in several stages.

It seems, therefore, that the widespread bias against large cities is illogical and even not devoid of danger. It is beyond doubt that the large cities of Southern Asia are, in their present state, not too conducive to planned development. But this is largely due to the fact that those cities have gone through a colonial stage. Professor Hauser, in his report, has clearly depicted the effects of this 'colonial heritage'.[3] He establishes that, with the exception of Indonesia, the 'primate cities' of Southeast Asia tend to be from five to ten times as large as the next largest city in the country. They owe their origin and growth to their function as a 'headlink' between the West, typically the mother colonial power, and the indigenous economy. They were likely 'to be parasitic in the sense that they tended to obstruct economic growth in their coun-

[1] Heeren, *loc. cit.*, p. 704, table 7.

[2] *Ibidem*, p. 729, table 13 on reasons for migration: items 6 (continue study) and 8 (official transfer).

[3] Hauser (ed.), *op. cit.*, pp. 86 ff.; see also D. W. Fryer, 'The Million City in Southeast Asia', *The Geographical Review*, Vol. 43 (1953), pp. 474 ff.; W. F. Wertheim and The Siauw Giap, 'Social Change in Java: 1900–1930', *Pacific Affairs*, Vol. 35 (1962), more in particular pp. 231 ff.; *The Indonesian Town: Studies in Urban Sociology* (The Hague/Bandung, 1958), more in particular pp. 63 ff.

try of location by retarding the development of other cities in the nation, by contributing little to the development of their own hinterland, by being oriented primarily toward the contribution of services to the colonial power abroad or the colonial or indigenous élite in the great city itself'. Industrialization has been deliberately retarded by the colonial powers, and the cities have been predominantly constituted as seaports for the export of commercial crops and minerals and for the import of ready-made industrial goods from the West.

Moreover, the colonial setting has contributed to the 'colour caste' pattern of urban settlement, with the concomitant racial segregation. This segregation, again, is responsible for an utter ignorance and general neglect as far as the interests of the native quarters' dwellers are concerned.

If, therefore, there still exists in some of the countries an atmosphere of aversion to large cities with their parasitic character, this is quite understandable. But it should be realized that the real target of this aversion should not be the city as such, but the colonial past.

In the process of planning for sound development, neither the big city nor the small town could be dispensed with. It would be as illogical to concentrate upon the countryside and small towns and neglect the big city as it is to neglect the countryside in favour of the big cities (which seems to occur in some Latin American countries). The foregoing analysis shows that the root of the evils of Asian towns is to be found in the general distress and underdevelopment in the countryside. Therefore rural development is of primary importance. But, on the other hand, the situation in the cities is largely due to the underdeveloped state of the urban economy. Moreover, large flows of migrants into the cities are to be expected for a long time to come. And if rural development gets underway, the number of migrants will, for the time being, tend to increase rather than to decrease, as rural development necessarily implies an increase of *per capita* production, a relative decrease of the number of hands needed in agriculture, and fuller employment for those who remain active in agriculture. Therefore, the number of urban centres, including small towns, should be considerably enlarged. But in order to be able to absorb the continuing flow of migrants, the urban centres, both large and small, have to undergo a process of rapid industrialization. Otherwise a shared poverty pattern will keep urban economy at its present low level.

The main problem of planned development is integration of the urban and rural economies. The distortion of urban growth, inherited from the colonial period, should be remedied by establishing a national economy that is no longer oriented on export and import, but on an integrated interaction of the different sectors of the national economy. A logical net of communications should mutually connect the urban centres, large and small, and at the same time draw the countryside out of its relative isolation.

This integration could only be achieved by an impulse originating primarily in the urban sphere. Though urban life in the cities of Southern Asia differs less from rural life than in the West, yet it has undergone the influence of modern ideas and modern technique. It is from the urban centres that new cultural values, oriented toward achievement, should spring. It is from there that the countryside can be stimulated to launch a comprehensive array of basic innovations. If the cities of Southern Asia are truly urbanized, this could produce an atmosphere from which rural development, too, could draw its inspiration. The integration between town and countryside could be attained only if the countryside gradually loses some of its traditional, typically 'rural' characteristics.

In order to avoid a process from Megalopolis through Parasitopolis to Pathopolis, however, urban development should be a planned development which requires a lot of attention. There is no need for Asian cities to go through all the dismal stages of urban growth in the West. According to the principle of 'dialectics of progress', formulated by Romein,[1] the backwardness of Asian cities can be a starting point for a more rapid and more

---

[1] I may refer to the first paper of this volume, pp. 16 ff.

healthy development; backwardness can often prove to be an advantage.

I wish to conclude with a few quotations from a recent inaugural lecture by a newly appointed Professor of Town and Country Planning and Demography in the University of Amsterdam:[1]

> Our generation will witness and participate in one of the most absorbing social spectacles in history of mankind. On the one hand, a further systematic urbanization of the Western world, on the other an unprecedentedly rapid transformation of agrarian into urban industrial social patterns in the Asian and African world...
>
> However much urbanization presses itself upon us, as an unequivocal and inevitable social phenomenon, there is probably no other phenomenon which is being skipped over so systematically as precisely this problem. A romantic and irrationally founded conservatism urges humanity to seek escape from the spatial effects of population increase, and of the operation of those manifold economic and technological forces which, at present, accelerate the process of urbanization. We dodge the question how in the future urbanized society will or should look like. We attempt to get away from the consequences of social development by nursing a distorted picture of the countryside and the small town.

This pronouncement seems to me highly relevant to the problem of the role of the small town in planned economic development.

Fear has never been a reliable loadstar. If the small town is considered an alternative to the much feared big city, its advancement will prove completely inadequate as a means to solve the problems of urban development. Only if the small town is fully integrated in a totality in which also the big city plays its essential role, can a sound urban development be expected to emerge.

---

[1] W. Steigenga, *Van sociale analyse naar sociaal-ruimtelijke konstruktie* (From social analysis to spatial construction in a social field, inaugural address, University of Amsterdam, 1962), p. 4.

'Inter-Island Migration in Indonesia' is a slightly revised version of two University of London lectures in Sociology, delivered at the London School of Economics in 1958.

It has been published under the title 'Sociological Aspects of Inter-Island Migration in Indonesia' in *Population Studies*, Vol. 12 (1959), pp. 184–201.

Lampong (South Sumatra) Resettlement Areas

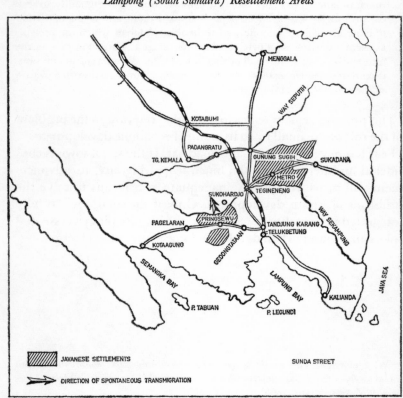

NINE

INTER-ISLAND MIGRATION IN INDONESIA

I

According to general opinion, population distribution within Indonesia is such that the island of Java is overpopulated and the so-called Outer Islands are underpopulated. As far as Java is concerned, the existence of overpopulation is undeniable. The island has a density of about 1,200 persons per square mile. The total population is over 60 millions on a surface smaller than that of the British Isles. According to official estimates which were current about 1957, the annual rate of increase was about 17 per thousand,[1] but the true figure must have been even at that time above rather than below the 20 per thousand level, the average birth rate being constantly well above 40 per thousand, while the average death rate is fairly consistently fluctuating around 20.[2] In official circles there was at that time a tendency to underestimate the extent to which mortality has declined during the post-war years as a result of intensified rural hygiene and preventive medical work and of an increased awareness of hygienic requirements among both the rural and the urban population. If my estimate is correct, the natural rate of increase would amount to at least $1\frac{1}{4}$ millions each year.

[1] *Garis-garis besar rentjana pembangunan lima tahun 1956–1960: Lampiran dari rantjangan undang-undang tentang rentjana pembangunan lima tahun 1956–1960* (Broad outline of a five years' reconstruction plan, 1956–1960: Annex to a bill on a five years' reconstruction plan 1956–1960, Jakarta, 1956), p. 6.

[2] 'The Population of Indonesia: Joint Statement prepared by the Indonesian participants to the United Nations Seminar on Population in Asia and the Far East, Bandung, November 21st - December 3rd, 1955', *Economics and Finance in Indonesia*, Vol. 9 (1956), pp. 92–93. The same estimate is made on p. 11 of *Garis-garis besar* (*op. cit.*), which seems to run counter to the official estimate on p. 6 of the same report.

Unlike the densely populated areas of Western Europe, the population of Java is still preponderantly agrarian, over 80% of them living in the countryside. Unlike Western Europe, the high density is not caused by a high degree of industrialization, but by a highly intensive pattern of land cultivation, largely based on an extensive net of irrigation works. There are ricefield areas where an average family of five or six persons is forced to live on an acre of land or even less.

Symptoms of overpopulation are to be found not only in the low average level of living, but also in the social system itself, rightly described by Clifford Geertz as one of 'shared poverty'.[1] There is a general attitude, both in the villages and in the towns of Java, of 'live and let live'. The cutthroat competition of modern Western society is largely absent. If the harvest in a field has to be gathered, every woman or child of the village is entitled to come to work for the owner and take their shares home. At four in the morning the women already appear on the field to take their places, often less than a square yard in extent. The sight of such a ricefield where harvesting is in process, gives a visual impression of the concept of overpopulation. The rice-stalks are, in accordance with tradition, cut one by one with a wooden rice-knife, the *ani-ani*, a rather slow procedure. But if the *ani-ani* were replaced by a scythe, many a poor woman would be robbed of an essential part of her living. What has at present the character of disguised unemployment, would develop into open unemployment, with disastrous consequences for the majority of the population, considering the present level of production per head. A grasping landowner who attempted to introduce the scythe and prevent the poorer women from working and getting their share, would be liable to become an outcast in his village.

The same system of shared poverty is prevalent in urban Java. A fruit grower in the outskirts of Bogor, declared that he was not willing to take his produce to the market of Bogor himself, in spite

[1] Clifford Geertz, 'Religious Belief and Economic Behavior in a Central Javanese Town: Some Preliminary Considerations', *Economic Development and Cultural Change*, Vol. 4 (1956), pp. 134 ff.

of the profit he would derive, as the pedlar who took his fruits to the market also had to live. Similar situations occur in the large towns where the offices are crowded with low-ranking employees whose work could be easily and perhaps more efficiently performed by a fraction of the existing staff. They have to work for salaries which leave them on the border of destitution. This is bad enough, but a thorough rationalization of human resources would involve unemployment and outright misery for the majority of them.[1]

Another symptom of overpopulation is the new restiveness of the rural inhabitants of Java. They are increasingly abandoning their traditional attitude of resignation and are beginning to move. Radical ideologies find ready acceptance among them, as is shown by the elections held in 1955 and in 1957, and their hunger for more land often brings them into open conflict with the authorities, as for instance when they squat on forbidden government-owned woodlands. They are, in addition, becoming more mobile, and beside the ever increasing *trek* to the towns, about 1957 applications for migration as small farmers to the Outer Islands, mostly to South Sumatra, by far exceeded the vacancies provided by the official Transmigration Service.

Despite the obvious overpopulation of Java many Indonesians, at the time when I visited the country (1956–57), still refused to take the problem really seriously, because of the huge empty spaces of the Outer Islands. In their opinion there was still plenty of space for the surplus people of Java in the underpopulated areas beyond, and the only problem was to organize migration in such a way as to realize the potential absorptive capacity of the Outer Islands. It was estimated that many millions of Javanese could easily be moved to Sumatra or Kalimantan (Borneo), and the population pressure in Java thus be relieved. Admonitions to practise birth control were also often lightly dismissed by Indonesians with smiling reference to the empty spaces in the large islands. This attitude is exemplified by the following statement

[1] The way the 'shared poverty' pattern works in an urban environment has been further elaborated in the eighth paper included in this volume, dealing with urban characteristics in Indonesia.

from an Indonesian Moslem scholar quoted in the Press Bureau *Antara* News Bulletin of October 9th, 1958:

'Dr. Akbar stated that in spite of the average annual increase in the population of approximately 1.2 million, Indonesia did not necessarily adopt family planning because there is still a favourable proportion of unopened and uncultivated land for the total population of Indonesia which is now approximately 85 million.

We can avoid family planning by implementing transmigration, exploiting the virgin lands and woods which still abound in this country, and by many other endeavours'.

I had the opportunity to test this assumption when I visited Indonesia at the invitation of the Indonesian government in 1956–57.

II

In 1931, I went to Indonesia for the first time. My first post as a young assistant in the judicial service was in the Lampong Districts, at the Southern end of Sumatra. I remember travelling for scores of miles by car inland through jungle. Here and there, at great intervals, the bush was interspersed with small hamlets consisting of a row of pile-dwellings where crowds of nice, but untidy Lampong children were playing, alternating with burnt-down clearings used by shifting cultivators. They were, apart from the asphalt road, the only signs of the human hand having made its imprint on the natural landscape.

But while driving from my post, the provincial town of Tanjong Karang, fifteen miles to the West, after a turn of the road, I found the usual landscape suddenly interrupted by a surprising view. Irrigated ricefields were stretching at our feet, fenced off by a chain of mountains far away. It was a typical Javanese landscape, amidst the inhospitable Sumatran wilderness. And it was migrants from Java who, under a government scheme, had settled in the Gedong Tataan area and built a new life in accordance with the pattern of their homeland. About 30,000 Javanese were, at the time, concentrated in that area and formed a kind of Javanese enclave of settled farmers amidst a jungle superficially exploited by Lampongese shifting cultivators.

Twenty-five years later, in December, 1956, I returned to the Lampong region. This time I was there on a short-term mission, to supervise a social research programme undertaken by a group of students from the agricultural faculty in Bogor where I was teaching as a visiting professor on a one-year's term.

My first great shock, when back in the Lampongs, came when I drove inland along the same asphalt road that I knew so well from my first stay. Where there had formerly been an endless growth of bush at either side of the road, now to the right and to the left, wide *alang* grassfields extended as far as I could see. Mountains and hills, also largerly denuded, appeared where the bush had completely hidden them twenty-five years earlier. Even a large rubber plantation I had visited during my first stay had practically disappeared without leaving a trace. It was as if a swarm of locusts had come upon the country and left it barren and forbidding.

According to information which I received, the deforestation had mainly occurred during the Japanese occupation and after, when hunger had driven both the Lampong native population and the Javanese immigrants to the indiscriminate felling of the woods and to the practice of shifting cultivation. The Lampongese had for centuries been shifting cultivators, accustomed to cutting and burning down tracts of forest land in order to provide for their livelihood. When the population was sparse this system could persist, for the forests were given sufficient time to grow again. But as soon as the native Lampongese and an ever-increasing number of Javanese immigrants started competing for the available land, the cycle was interrupted. As a result, the process ended in a victory for the tough *alang* grass and ensuing serious soil erosion.

A turn of the road to the East led us, along a newly dug canal, to the large transmigration centre of Metro. When during the economic crisis of the thirties the transmigration scheme from over-populated Java to the empty lands of Sumatra had to be speeded up, a new settlement area further inland, much larger than the original Western one near Gedong Tataan, had to be opened up. At the outbreak of the Second World War a vast irrigated area had been populated with newly-arrived Javanese, who became small rice-growers, as they had been in their land of origin.

The size of the plot assigned to each family was reasonable – two and a half acres as against an average of one in Java – provided the land was irrigated and the peasants were contented with remaining subsistence farmers forever. But difficulties were bound to arise as soon as irrigation facilities did not keep pace with new clearing, particularly as additional space had to be found both for the increasing number of new migrants and for the second generation of old settlers. As the extension and repair of irrigation facilities was stopped by the Japanese occupation, the consequences made themselves felt much earlier than even a critic like Professor Karl Pelzer had expected.[1] In the irrigated ricefields area around Metro the signs of population pressure are clear. Conditions are already approaching those in Java – for instance, rural indebtedness is increasing rapidly. There are some districts where the peasants, during a great part of the year, have to eat *gaplek*, dried cassava, as they have to in Java. But the greatest difficulties were to arise on the fringe of the settlement area, where new lands have been opened up for several years, and new migrants have been allotted a plot of land larger than before the war, for since 1950, each family was allotted some additional land for the cultivation of commercial crops. The average plot allotted to each family would certainly be sufficient if it were irrigated but unfortunately, irrigation works were lagging behind. After a few harvests the soil was exhausted and the settlers were driven to look for other land. Thus, the process of deforestation progressively

---

[1] Karl J. Pelzer, *Pioneer Settlement in the Asiatic Tropics: Studies of Land Utilization and Agricultural Colonization in Southern Asia* (New York, 1945), pp. 230–231, concluded his analysis of the pre-war system with the following forecast: 'In as short a period as a generation such a colony will already be faced with a scarcity of land, and some members of the new generation will have to look for free land outside'.

extended to other areas, and *alang* grass covered the relinquished land.

For the civil officers in charge of the transmigration area, there existed only one solution to the problem: speeding up the building of irrigation works in order to make the Metro area inhabitable for an additional one and a half million migrants. But agricultural experts were beginning to doubt whether there would be sufficient water in the two large rivers of the Lampongs to provide for the areas already opened up or still to be cleared in the future. Moreover, progressive deforestation in the highlands robs the rivers of their silt. And finally, it is a rather gloomy prospect for Indonesia to continue to move hundreds of thousands of Javanese to Sumatra if the result is a repetition in parts of Sumatra of the same conditions and hardships as a result of which the migrants had left their homeland.

If, however, the irrigation works were not completed within a couple of years the fate of the settlement would become still worse. It would show the usual picture of a hopeless fight against the tenacious *alang* grass, and many of the settlers would have to move as 'local migrants' to other places.

Such an area, where 'local migrants' from the large settlements were moving in large numbers appeared to exist in the Western region, on the outskirts of the Gedong Tataan region, the first transmigration centre in the Lampongs which I had visited in 1931. North of that area all kinds of people were reclaiming forest-land – groups of demobilized soldiers, disbanded guerrilla troops – each with their own official organization –, local migrants and, finally, so-called 'spontaneous migrants' – people moving from Java, without governmental help, at their own expense. Coming from Java by ship we had met a crowd of such 'spontaneous migrants', who, in Jakarta, had been forced to buy 'black' tickets for crossing the Strait of Sunda, at twice the official fare. One of my research associates, who had visited the area before, estimated that there were already about 35,000 settlers in the region, and every week scores of new immigrants arrived.

The village of Sukoharjo, which was already in existence in

1938, formed a link between the old settlement area around Gedong Tataan and the new clearings. The village had first accepted groups of demobilized soldiers who, incidentally, proved to be a troublesome and trigger-happy crowd. In later years Sukoharjo became a reception centre, a kind of transit camp for local and spontaneous migrants intending to reclaim forest land in the interior. The migrants were allowed to work with one of the older settlers and to earn enough to be able to live on during the difficult period of forest clearing and sowing. By 1956 the total number of inhabitants of the village of Sukoharjo had risen to over 10,000.

We began our research by visiting settlers and interviewing them, gathered around the usual glasses of tea, fruits and sweets. We knew from our experience in Java, that the village chief would accompany us during the first days, not so much from suspicion, but rather as a sign of courtesy. Thus, if there was any friction between the common villagers and the leadership, they were not likely to speak openly about it in the presence of the chief. But a group which could be more easily relied upon to speak out freely were the ex-soldiers, as they were still officially embodied in their original organization under military supervision, and were excluded from interference on the part of the civil authorities. Our friend, the village chief, appeared to be rather pleased if the ex-soldiers were asked about their grievances.

The ex-soldiers' complaints were always the same: they felt cheated and left in the lurch by their superiors. When they had left Java they were not told they were expected to become agriculturalists. Many of them were not of peasant origin. They had to give up their arms in Java, as they were told they would receive new arms at their destination, whither they were being sent on a new, honourable mission. As the boxes of new arms, when unloaded at their arrival in Southern Sumatra, proved to contain agricultural implements, it is not surprising that the boxes, implements and all, were flung in fury into the river.

Still, the ex-soldiers were forced to carry on and to clear forestland. They were entitled to many kinds of government help –

much more than normal migrants had ever received. But the general complaint was that part of the amount the government owed them had never been actually paid. Some of the officers had been convicted of corruption or embezzlement. Several others had gone back to Java, without bothering further about the fate of their subordinates. The ex-soldiers still had the attitude of people dependent on outside help, and generally resented their situation. Recently some of them had moved a resolution demanding payment of the debt the authorities still owed to them. One of my more sophisticated hosts assured me: 'Yes, we have made a resolution – not yet a revolution'.

Some of them, mostly former peasants, had shown a fair measure of success. The fields of the majority, however, did not seem very promising. *Alang* grass was making headway, and the fight against it looked like a losing battle. That was not entirely their fault. When the Sukoharjo area was being opened up around 1938, no soil survey had been conducted. A Dutch agricultural expert, in an official report in 1940, considered the area generally unfit for wet agriculture. Still, the older settlers had succeeded in occupying the lower lands which could be used as *sawahs* dependent on rain. But the newcomers were relegated to still uncleared lands farther to the North, which were situated too high to be usable for wet ricefield cultivation. And mixed farming was out of the question, if only because cattle were very difficult to obtain for this out-of-the-way corner, generally neglected and often completely ignored by government agencies. The whole village of Sukoharjo had no more than some forty *carabaos*.

After the soil was exhausted some settlers tried to change over to commercial tree-crops, especially coffee. But the amount of land allotted to each of them – four or five acres – was much too small for making a living out of coffee-growing. They had to look for additional forest-land to be cleared, somewhere in the interior, and the coffee gardens were being neglected, which again facilitated the overgrowth of their original plots with *alang* grass, a sign of serious soil erosion. There were, no doubt, coffee gardens and other tree plantations near Sukoharjo which looked much more prosperous. They were largely owned by native Lampong people, who had some dispersed settlements in this region. They kept rather aloof from the Javanese immigrants and went on with the kind of farming to which they had been accustomed for decades. They had a great advantage in their type of farming in that they still had reserves of forest-land in their far-off family settlements, on which they could rely for food during the years needed for their coffee or pepper gardens to mature. Thus, they were able to devote themselves to tending these gardens according to tradition. To them the Javanese were apparently poor intruders, grabbing land and having no social status. The Lampong people could afford to live, amidst their gardens, in an extremely sober way. They knew that their real riches were far away, where their carved wooden family houses stood. After their coffee and pepper harvests they would sell the land – they themselves would call it, sell the *trees* – to the Javanese and add to their riches at home.

It was still Lampong *marga* chiefs to whom the Javanese had to apply if they wanted access to virgin forest-land. On the other hand, the Javanese felt prosperous compared with their situation at home, and were prone to show off by building nice houses or buying good clothes, as soon as they had secured one or two good harvests. They had to show the Lampongese that they were no paupers either. But they lacked the land reserves needed to imitate the pattern of land-use prevalent among the autochthonous population. The Lampong people were, in general, little inclined to abandon their extensive form of agriculture for the intensive form practised by the Javanese, even though shortage of land made itself badly felt. The use of the *changkul*, the common tool in Java for preparing ricefields for cultivation, was rejected by them with the rationalization that the work was too heavy – which earned them a reputation of laziness among the Javanese, though when using the chopping-knife in the jungle they did not shrink from heavy work.

Social intercourse between Lampongese and Javanese was infrequent, except for some mixing of children in the schools built by the Javanese settlers. There was even some latent friction between both population groups. In particular, the rather unruly ex-soldiers and guerrilla fighters who boasted of their contribution to the national revolution and claimed at least equal rights with the Sumatrans in this part of their country, caused some uneasiness. Shortly after their arrival there had even been some open clashes. But also the arrival in large numbers of the unobtrusive and inoffensive plain Javanese migrants provoked some reaction. A Lampong shopkeeper complained to me, that though the government-sponsored official transmigration was acceptable to his people, as the movement was kept within bounds, it was spontaneous transmigration which spoiled everything.

It was clear that the real cause of these frictions was competition for the land. The system of shifting cultivation as practised by the Javanese threatened to exhaust within a few decades the land reserve available to the Lampong population. Yet, the immediate gain to be secured by the Lampong chiefs for granting to Javanese settlers the right of reclaiming forest-land free induced them, time and again, to forsake the future of their people for a handful of money.

In order to assess the effects of the spontaneous migration on Sumatran society it was necessary to proceed from Sukoharjo to the recent clearings deeper inland, where man and elephant were still neighbours. Most of the research on that area has been done by my research associate Kampto Utomo, who made it the subject of an excellent doctoral thesis.[1] My comments on the area beyond Sukoharjo are based largely on the observations made by him with a group of our students. However, during a short visit I had the opportunity of obtaining a superficial impression of what was going on there.

First, I must express my great admiration for the tremendous efforts made by the settlers to begin a new life far away from home. The spontaneous migrants in general belong to the more

[1] Kampto Utomo, *Masjarakat Transmigran Spontan Didaerah W. Sekampung* (*Lampung*) (Spontaneous transmigrants' settlements in the Way Sekampong department of the Lampong area, doctoral thesis Bogor Faculty of Agriculture, University of Indonesia, Jakarta, 1957).

energetic Javanese. They are unwilling to wait for years until
they reach the top of the list of official migrants, whose journey
and initial settlement is subsidized by the government. They sell
all their possessions and travel to Sumatra at their own risk,
though they often follow a relative who went earlier. Not all of
them pass through the Sukoharjo transit centre. Some of them go
straight to the jungle and assist a relative in clearing forest-land.
These spontaneous migrants do not receive any government aid.
The officials in Jakarta, and even in the provincial capital, often
ignore their existence. The medical services at least give some
help by spraying the houses, built in the malaria-infested bush,
with D.D.T. But more often than not the occupants are already
there before the medical service has heard of their existence.

Despite all hardships, the original frontier society evolves into a
settlement, in the shape of a typically Javanese village. The outline
of roads follows the general pattern, a somewhat larger building
is destined for a town hall, and almost without exception a school
building is provided for. The settlers choose a provisional village
board and then try to have their settlement recognized by the
district chief as an established village.

There was a tendency in the capital to consider spontaneous
migration as an ideal means for fulfilling the government scheme,
as it is incomparably cheaper than the official system practised in
the Metro area.[1] But the advocates of a switch to the spontaneous
migration system overlook some intrinsic weaknesses which may
seriously impair the superficial aspect of prosperity presented by
the new settlements. What appears to be a success at first sight has
in it the germs of a catastrophe.

The new settlements, containing several ten thousands of migrants have arisen without any central planning. The settlers
were able to build, with great energy, a counterpart of a Javanese *desa* (village), according to the pattern familiar to them from
their homeland. But their abilities and efficiency stop at this stage.
Problems arise which call for a more integrated policy, for close

[1] *Garis-garis besar* (*op. cit.*), p. 260.

supervision, for a clear vision of future possibilities and impossibil-
ities. The efforts and the funds to be directed towards the project
have to be at least as large as those earmarked for the Metro area.
Moreover, the central planning and coordination required for
this purpose presuppose a close co-operation between the political parties, which, too often, merely competed with each other, by
inciting new squatters to occupy forest-lands and even granting
them 'land rights', thus trying to win their allegiance in coming
elections. A study of latent conflicts in Sukoharjo society pro-
jecting themselves into the newly reclaimed areas made it clear to
me that it was split into factions largely coinciding with political
party affiliations, thus also preclucing coordinated effort in any
sphere exceeding the village jurisdiction.

The basic weakness of the whole scheme was that the forest-
lands beyond Sukoharjo appear to be, in general, unfit for irrigation. This does not mean that there are no other alternatives.
There are, as for instance a larger scale application of mixed
farming, green manure, or artificial fertilizers, or a much more
efficient application of tree cultivation. But all this would require
an enormous amount of planning, research, pilot surveys, and of
the testing of promising methods — in fact, a replacement of the
traditional irrigation pattern by new expedients.

If a great effort is not made in the very near future, the soil,
which provides high yields during the early years, will soon become exhausted, and the usual *alang* grass will force the settlers
to look for new land. The forests of South Sumatra will dwindle
and the Land of Promise will soon turn into a Land of Despair.

III

After having provided the reader with a descriptive analysis of
inter-island migration in Indonesia, based on my personal experiences in December, 1956, I shall now try to draw some general
and more or less theoretical conclusions from my observations.

First, developments in South Sumatra may provide us with a

clearer insight into population theory, and more particularly may add to our understanding of concepts like 'overpopulation' and 'underpopulation'.

It seems to me that the main fallacy behind the lighthearted attitude prevalent among many intellectuals in Indonesia with respect to population problems lies in the erroneous assumption that the so-called Outer Islands are underpopulated. It is not only numbers of people and areas that count. Other factors have to be taken into account as well. Among the most important are the type of land use and the overall economic structure.

The pattern of land use prevalent in most parts of Java is intensive cultivation of rice on irrigated fields. This agricultural system requires fairly high population densities, for otherwise there would be an evident shortage of manpower. Under this system areas with a density considerably below 300 persons per square mile may be said to suffer from underpopulation. At the other extreme, densities say in excess of 600 per square mile are likely to show the first signs of overpopulation, which may cause a surplus of available hands expressing itself in a *shared poverty* system.

On the other hand a population practising a shifting cultivation attains its marginal density at a much earlier stage. The system is based on a cycle which permits the forest to restore itself, after one or two harvests have been secured from the burnt-down clearing. If the number of people who have to live on the available forest-land increases, less and less time is left to the soil to regain its original layer of vegetable mould. Soil erosion becomes evident and the inhabitants are finally forced to look for other cultivable land.

Sumatrans have for centuries been aware of this situation. William Marsden wrote in his *History of Sumatra*, as early as the eighteenth century: 'On account of the fertility it occasions, the natives do not look upon the abundance of wood in the country as an inconvenience, but the contrary. In few parts of the island do they ever sow grains on land that has been long cleared, and there, more from necessity than choice. I have heard a prince of the country complain of a settlement made by some strangers in the inland part of his dominions, whom he should be under an obligation to expel from thence, to prevent the waste of his old woods. This seemed a superfluous act of precaution in an island which strikes the eye as one general, impervious and inexhaustible forest'.[1]

Thus, areas where shifting cultivation is common can be said to suffer from *overpopulation*, strange as this may sound, at a density of 50 or 60 persons per square mile. Outward signs of this state of overpopulation are clearly discernible. They are the broad *alang* fields covering large tracts of the Outer Islands. They are the barren hills and mountain slopes visible from the aeroplane in large parts of Central and Northern Sumatra. This process explains the increasing protests of Sumatrans, at the time of my visit, against the settlement of Javanese in their island, reiterating the attitude of the Sumatran prince mentioned by Marsden.

Under- and overpopulation can, therefore, be conceived in relative terms only. A given area may be overpopulated in relation to the prevalent mode of land use and the dominant economic structure. It may, in its turn, become underpopulated if a new pattern of land use or a new system of economic exploitation is introduced.

If Java is overpopulated, this does not necessarily mean that absolute numbers per available area are too high. It only means that the prevalent mode of production is no longer capable of utilizing the available manpower to the full. A low average output per head coincides with an agricultural system which leaves an appreciable number of available man-hours unused. The remedy for this situation would not be to drain off the population excess, as a constant removal of a yearly surplus of over one million would be a superhuman task. Neither would birth control in itself be sufficient to remedy the situation, as it would not deal with the roots of the evil. Both remedies, emigration and birth

[1] William Marsden, *The History of Sumatra: Containing an Account of the Government, Laws, Customs and Manners of the Native Inhabitants, with a Description of the Natural Productions and a Relation of the Ancient Political State of that Island* (Second Ed., London, 1784), pp. 61–62.

control, will be helpful, indeed indispensable, only if they are accompanied by a thorough change in the economic structure.

In other words, only industrialization on a large scale could transform Javanese society in such a way that a more balanced relation between available space and manpower could be achieved.

As far as the Outer Islands are concerned, the relativistic interpretation of the concept of overpopulation also has its consequences, though the solution is not as rigidly fixed as in the case of Java.

In theory one could suggest a transformation of the shifting cultivation prevalent in the Outer Islands into a wet ricefield cultivation as practised in Java. Such a development might conceivably transform the 'overpopulation' expressing itself in *alang* grassfields to an underpopulation as soon as the irrigation works are in operation, thus providing room for millions of newcomers. In this manner, the Outer Islands could first pass through the Java stage before approaching a new limit at which the overpopulation factors operating in Java at present would make themselves felt.

But such a conception, which about 1957 appeared to coincide with the aim of the Indonesian authorities, would imply tremendous consequences. First it would call for a complete change from shifting cultivation to intensive agriculture, not only for the Javanese settlers, but also for the local population. At present the trend is the other way round, as could be seen in South Sumatra. Further, a shift to wet agriculture is very much dependent on natural conditions, such as the situation of the land and the easy availability of water. Moreover, experts are doubtful whether the soil in most parts of the Outer Islands is nearly as fertile as are large parts of Java. Again, construction of the irrigation works needed for such a large-scale transformation would call for enormous investment. In Java the network of irrigation has been gradually built up in the course of many centuries. In order to provide room for the yearly surplus population of Java the extension of irrigation works woud have to proceed at an unbelievable pace, in an environment much less accessible owing to very great

distances and poor communications. Thus it goes without saying
that the project tentatively suggested above would be quite im-
practicable. It would be based on a dangerous overestimation of
the absorptive capacity of the soil of the Outer Islands. And it
would come up against that all-important bottleneck in Indonesia, shortage of shipping transport, which even at the peak of
transmigration efforts has limited yearly resettlement to a figure
of 50,000 to 100,000, a number far below one-tenth of the yearly
population surplus of Java.

But the project for the transformation of the shifting cultivation
pattern into a wet agriculture pattern is also highly unrealistic
because it does not take account of sociological and psychological
factors. The absorptive capacity of a society is not measured in
spatial and technical terms only – human motives also come into
play.

Before the war Dutch resettlement policy was directed towards
the creation of typical Javanese enclaves in a purely Sumatran
environment. As the willingness to move to 'the land beyond' had
not yet developed very greatly at that time, the Dutch tried to
make settlement attractive, by reshaping conditions as nearly as
possible to resemble those in the homeland. The land allotted to
each family was limited to two and a half acres – perhaps in order to induce the settlers to look for additional work in the Western
plantations suffering from shortage of labour.

After independence, the Indonesian government adopted a different view. The strict separation of Javanese and Lampongese
was deemed out of date, as a relic of colonial policy. Such a system would not fit into the new ideology of Indonesia as a unitary
state. Javanese and Sumatrans were equally Indonesians, who
had to live together and mix on an equal footing. Both population
groups would have to develop into modern Indonesians, and
work together in building a new society in the melting pot of Sumatra, the Land of Promise.

In particular, the dynamic and sophisticated ex-guerrilla fighters
were envisaged as the prototypes of the new Indonesian, who
would ferment the life in the new settlement, bridge the cleavage

and bring the two population groups together. To be able to achieve a higher standard than at home, they were allotted larger plots of land than the pre-war settlers, so that they could cultivate commercial crops in addition to their food production. In the case of other groups of settlers this system of larger plots has also been applied, though shortage of available land and shortage of manpower often reduced the average plot in practice.

But if the authorities had expected that the new, more dynamic type of settler would more easily accommodate himself to Suma-tran society, they were wrong. If anything, the Sumatrans found the Javanese enclaves which were separated from their own com-munities, more acceptable than the more dynamic type of post-war settlers. Whereas in pre-war conditions they could live side by side and now and then profit from the cheap labour force avail-able in the settlements to tend their coffee or pepper gardens, the post-war migratory movement made much greater inroads in their way of life, by seriously reducing the available reserve of forest-lands and thus endangering their future. And if the com-mercial crops grown by the new settlers competed with those cultivated by Sumatrans in their own gardens, competition for land was sharpened by competition on the market.

The reaction of the great majority of native Lampongese was by no means to adopt the wet agriculture system practised among the Javanese settlers. They did not see why they should abandon their way of life for one of harder work and smaller returns. Their aloofness from the poor Javanese settlers increased, and they resented the pressure exerted on the foundations of their life by people whom they felt to be, in a certain sense, aliens. Their reaction to the influx of Javanese was either one of retreating deeper into the interior, as for instance in the Southern district of the Lampongs where the Javanese now form a distinct majority, or a growing opposition to the transmigration scheme.

The division between the groups was also apparent in party affil-iations, the Northern regions mainly inhabited by Lampongese voting by a large majority for the Moslem party of *Masjumi*, while in the largely Javanese Southern districts the vote was fairly evenly divided between the nationalist and the communist parties, which were dominant in Central Java and the Western part of Eastern Java.

Again, there was a fallacy behind the 'melting pot' ideology: the assumption that in migratory situations the *assimilation* of groups within a society, considered as a whole, is possible. A closer study of several migration situations leads to the conclusion that 'assimilation' is a much more complicated process than is generally understood. In reality, if *groups* move from one environment to another, as in the case of farmer settlements, they more often than not keep together and try to preserve as much as possible of their common cultural heritage. They will try to achieve a kind of integration in the new society, but without losing a certain identity as a group. In the totality of the receiving society they will occupy a special position in accordance with their economic status and potential strength.

If such a group of migrants already exists, new settlers from the same cultural area, whether they move as individuals or in groups, will try to conform as nearly as possible to the patterns of life prevailing in the old settlement. To that extent the term *assimilation* would seem appropriate. The settlers would look for a way of life as nearly as possible resembling their cultural heritage, and find such a focus in the earlier settlements. Every new individual arriving from the same cultural area will become more or less assimilated, not into the whole society but into that segment of it to which he feels attracted both by his cultural heritage and his social and economic status. But even assimilation of individuals migrating separately into an existing society is less simple than suggested in current literature.

Recently an extensive study has been made of the Eurasians, who have left Indonesia since the war to settle in Holland. It was found that though many of them seriously wished to become 'assimilated' in Netherlands society, in fact they tended to associate with groups of previous immigrants whom the newcomers considered nearest in sharing common memories and common interests. They wanted to be incorporated within *definite layers* of

Dutch society, with people among whom they could feel 'at home'.[1] This seems to me the normal situation for an *individual*, at least as far as the *first* generation of immigrants is concerned.

In the case of migration to a technically more advanced society, like Holland or the United States of America, the *wish* of the majority of individuals to assimilate can at least be taken for granted. But it would be completely unrealistic to expect that Javanese would aspire to be assimilated into Sumatran society. The migration situation, in which the invading culture was more dynamic and forceful than the receiving one, excluded such a possibility, the more so as the pre-war enclave policy had already created a focus towards which the new settlers would tend to orient themselves.

Assimilation of Javanese migrants was proceeding, neither to a Sumatran nor to a general Indonesian society, but to a Javanese society somewhat modified by a Sumatran environment. This situation led to an increasing resistance of Sumatrans to the way in which resettlement had been carried on. Such resistance seriously hampered further transmigration efforts. Thus, it can be stated that the *absorptive capacity* of the Outer Islands is not only restricted by spatial and technical but by social factors as well.[2]

But it would be equally erroneous to dismiss the idea of large scale resettlement to the Outer Islands as unrealizable. One has only to disengage oneself from the notion that there is but one possible way: shifting from the extensive land use to the wet ricefield cultivation as practised in Java. This scheme is not only impractical but illogical. Why repeat a pattern which has produced a scarcely enviable situation in Java? Why should a solution of the population problems of the Outer Islands be exclusively

---

[1] *De repatriëring uit Indonesië: Een onderzoek naar de integratie van de gerepatrieerden uit Indonesië in de Nederlandse samenleving* (The repatriation from Indonesia: An inquiry into the process of integration of repatriates from Indonesia into Dutch society, n.p., n.y.).

[2] H. J. Heeren, 'Some Problems of Rural Collective Settlements in Indonesia', *Transactions of the Third World Congres of Sociology, Amsterdam*, Vol. 2 (London, 1956), pp. 302 ff.

sought in the agrarian sector, which inevitably leads to increasing competition for land? Why not try, in this early stage of development, an industrial development which would attract workers both from Java and Sumatra with appreciably less friction?

If the 'melting pot' theory is to be made a reality, a true melting pot should be created. This is only possible in a largely industrial environment. Only in that atmosphere could competition, in the long run, be replaced by cooperation, as there would then seem to be no basic conflict of interest.

Thus, industrial development, which is needed to solve over-population problems in Java, should also be extended to the Outer Islands.[1]

As far as agricultural development is concerned, there is no reason why this should be confined to the traditional wet rice cultivation pattern known from Java. I have already pointed to possibilities in the direction of mixed farming or other means of fertilizing dry fields. Tree cultivation might also be profitable. In this direction Sumatrans have achieved a remarkable level of intensification, for instance, with their rubber plantations, without having to resort to wet rice cultivation. Such kinds of intensification would probably require less investment than a stereotyped construction of new irrigation works.

No doubt, these forms of intensification would not provide enough land for the innumerable applicants coming from Java. But in my opinion the bulk of the Javanese migrants should not be directed towards agriculture, but towards industrial projects. At present there is already a large percentage of Javanese in the Lampongs who are finally settling in the towns or at least in occupations other than agriculture. If industrial and professional sectors are expanded considerably, the average peasant holding can

---

[1] Warnings against a too ambitious industrialization program aiming at quick results on a mass scale, have been expressed by one of J. H. Boeke's students: C. B. van der Leeden, *Het aspect van landbouwkolonisatie in het bevolkingsprobleem van Java* (Pioneer settlement of Javanese peasants outside Java as an aspect of the population problem in Java, doctoral thesis Leiden University, Leiden, 1952), pp. 195 ff.

be larger and more promising for those newcomers from Java who crave for a better life than they had in Java, not only for themselves but for their children.

Such a comprehensive plan would, however, call for much more careful planning and much more efficient management than have thus far been achieved in the fulfilment of the transmigration project. However capable and energetic many individual officials may be, and however industrious and dynamic the pioneers show themselves, in the long run their tremendous efforts threaten to be useless if their activities are not co-ordinated in an overall plan conceived with the necessary foresight and carried out with efficiency.

The problems facing the young national states of Asia are immense, in fact much harder to tackle than the problems which their colonial predecessors had to solve in pre-war times. Whereas pre-war governments could content themselves with a more or less static approach, and were able to deal with their problems largely on traditional lines, the new Asian administrations have to be much more dynamic, if only because the populations have become dynamic and demanding. On the other hand, it is a common experience that the new governments are not equal to the task of developing dynamic policies and the kind of efficiency which is more than a faithful copy of traditionally accepted practices.

It seems to me appropriate to devote some attention to this basic problem, for my experiences in South Sumatra may provide some clue to a better understanding of the sociological sources of this general phenomenon.

The Lampong experiment indicates clearly where the new Indonesian administration succeeds and where it fails. It succeeds in fields in which the people, whether they are plain settlers or officials, are able to follow a set pattern. The pioneers prove equal to the task of creating out of nothing a full-grown Javanese village, complete with secondary roads, market places, playing grounds and schools. But at that point their inventive capacity stops. They lack both the educational level and the financial means needed to provide for more embracing projects safeguarding the future of the constructed village. Their way of building new communities resembles the ways of colonies of ants who by instinct know how to construct new communities, but ignore the outward factors which may endanger the existence of the community.

On a higher level the same phenomenon occurs in the regional administration of the established settlement areas. The district chiefs of the Metro area were quite equal to the task of administering that typically Javanese society. They could rely upon their experience of ruling over similar areas in Java. Some of them were devoting much energy to the task of co-ordinating the different welfare agencies operating within the area.

But the crucial problems of the whole transmigration project seemed in some way to escape them. They were only able to interpret the requirements of their area in terms of more and still more irrigation works. That was the way the civil service in Java had been fulfilling its task, and they seemed unable to conceive of a different solution.

On the other hand, in all instances where the transmigration project called for a co-ordinated dynamic approach involving activity on other than traditional lines, the weaknesses of the system became evident. I have to refer to the complete lack of regional planning in the newly opened Sukoharjo areas; to the failure of the central and regional administration to provide the badly needed guidance and supervision to the spontaneous transmigrants arriving there on a very large scale; to the lack of foresight of Sumatran local chiefs who farmed out large tracts of forest-land for gain without considering the future of their people; to the anomalies of a Forestry Service only interested in chasing squatters from prohibited areas – without any success incidentally – but not at all interested in what happens in the much larger and more vital areas which have not been designated as their particular sphere of action; to the complete lack of co-ordination between military and civil organizations engaged in settlement projects; to a rampant corruption, especially in military or para-military organizations, diverting part of the available funds from their original destination into the pockets of a few; to the competition between political parties and peasant organizations affiliated with them, which preclude a common effort for constructive purposes in fields that exceed the powers of simple village officials.

The primary source of these weaknesses is, in my opinion, the fact that Indonesia, like other Asian states which have recently achieved independence, are still in a stage of transition from a patrimonial to a modern bureaucracy.

The term 'patrimonial bureaucracy' was coined by Max Weber, in his significant study, *Typen der Herrschaft*,[1] unfortunately largely unknown in the Anglo-Saxon world, for only a minor portion of it has been translated into English. The term denotes the kind of bureaucratic states which were prevalent both in Asia and in Europe before the Napoleonic reforms. Their common characteristic was not 'centralism' and 'total power', as assumed by Karl Wittfogel in his study *Oriental Despotism*, but, on the contrary, a high degree of decentralization and a power essentially restricted by tradition.[2] Though the system did not coincide with 'feudalism' in the strict sense, the difference was decidedly less fundamental than Wittfogel and his followers maintain. The decentralization resulted from the need of the central ruler, if only because of poor communications, to leave both the profit and the burden of administration largely to provincial governors, local princes or semi-independent satraps. He was content if the local ruler paid the due tribute once a year and sent his contribution in human labour for military service or public works regularly. The spies frequently sent out by the central rulers had as their main

---

[1] Included in Max Weber, *Wirtschaft und Gesellschaft* (Second Ed., Tübingen, 1925), pp. 603–817. The concept of 'patrimonial bureaucratic' structures has been further elaborated, on the basis of Weber's analysis, in the fifth paper included in this volume, dealing with corruption in Southeast Asia.

[2] This criticism of Karl A. Wittfogel, *Oriental Despotism: A Comparative Study of Total Power* (New Haven, 1957), has been further elaborated in the fifth paper of this volume, dealing with corruption.

task to ensure that the provincial ruler did not neglect his contribution to the central court. Payment of salaries in cash to the provincial rulers was an exception rather than the rule. As in the feudal system, in patrimonial bureaucracies there was no dividing line between private and public interests, between private and public funds. On the other hand, the power of the local ruler was largely restricted to the raising of taxes and services in accordance with traditional practices. Serious deviations were likely to be opposed by strong resistances from the village communities made responsible for the payments and deliveries.

The loyalties of the rural population were largely confined to family groups, village communities or members of the local gentry. A dynamic activation of the rural population for extra-traditional purposes was out of the question because of a lack of conscious participation of the peasantry in affairs above the village level. Hence, the local rulers themselves were not trained in activities outside the scope of their traditional fields of action. Their loyalties were equally devided between their large families and the suzerain.

The upshot of the colonial interregna of the nineteenth century was, in general, that a modern bureaucratic structure was superimposed upon a largely patrimonial bureaucratic organism. That was more especially the case in an area like the Netherlands Indies where indirect rule was generally practised. Though, in the course of time, local rulers received a certain amount of training in Western administration and were more or less imbued with modern bureaucratic ideas, the way in which they performed their task continued to be largely static and traditional. The loyalties of the rural population remained mainly attached to local leaders, as the colonial structure prevented the growth of a loyalty to the state, seen as an entity.

Anti-colonial sentiments were, in the first half of the present century, strong enough to allow the rise of a unified national movement. But the achievement of independence has created several national states in which the inner cohesion, so badly needed for a modern bureaucratic administration, is rather weak.

The main problems facing the newly independent states of Asia, are the need to transform patrimonial bureaucratic forms of administration, especially at the regional level, into modern bureaucratic forms; and the need to transform the diffused loyalties centered on the traditional clusters of the patrimonial bureaucratic type, into an all-pervading loyalty to the national state.

It is in particular this lack of positive mental integration of the majority of the population with modern nationhood, which prevents a dynamic and co-ordinated approach to the major tasks lying before the new administrations. The ancient loyalties towards large families or village communities, are gradually breaking down. New loyalties are born, not yet to the national state but to intermediate organizations like army units, groups of local leaders or political parties. These intermediate loyalties conflict with a slowly emerging new mentality which is nation-centered and which considers such particularistic loyalties out of place. Practices which are called corrupt out of this new sense of national values, may appear fully justified to those who are still adhering to these particularistic norms. Corruption in an Asian country is, frequently, not so much a sign of selfishness and moral depravity as of conflicting loyalties.

The conclusion to be derived from the foregoing is that in such newly independent states a multi-party-system on the West European pattern cannot work. Such a system presupposes a national unity which guarantees a preponderance of considerations of common national welfare over strict party considerations and a willingness to cooperate with the government even if a party is in a minority position. In a society in which loyalty to the national ideals is not firmly rooted party divisions tend to be disruptive and opposed to common efforts. This is the more serious, as these newly-born nations need a dynamic co-ordinated approach at least as badly as states more technically developed. That is why President Sukarno of Indonesia and several others in his country have come to doubt the applicability of the multi-party-system. And that is probably why, in search of a more dynamic and efficient government, most of the Asian states are tempted to experiment with other systems – however unsympathetic they may appear to us Westerners, brought up in a democratic tradition.

Whatever their weaknesses and failures, the newly awakened peoples of Asia will in the long run achieve their aim: economic development and a richer life for the majority of the people. But it would be quite wrong to assume that there is only one possible way towards that end: the Western one. By trial and error the peoples of Asia are feeling their way towards new solutions, better adapted to their circumstances and to their present stage of development. The Western sociologist has not only to teach Asians how to run their administrations. He has at least as much to learn from the experiments conducted by Asians. Sociology cannot stop at the borders of the Western world.

'Social Change in Java, 1900–1930' was prepared as a discussion paper for students in the Java Seminar at the Institute of Social Studies (The Hague), held during the period 1958–1960. The seminar formed part of a larger research program on problems of rapid social change in underdeveloped countries. One of the primary aims of the project was to study processes of social change in terms of the initial program formulated by the innovators at the start of the period of guided accelerated change.

The present paper has, subsequently, been read as a lecture in different universities in the United States and India; it was also read as a paper in a Symposium on Tradition and Economic Development in Southeast Asia, organized by the Centre du Sud-Est Asiatique, Institut de Sociologie, at the Free University of Brussels (December, 1962). It has been published in *La Tradition et le développement économique dans l'Asie du Sud-Est* (1964), pp. 169-190.

Previously, a much extended text had been published under the same title, with the co-authorship of Mr. The Siauw Giap, in *Pacific Affairs*, Vol. 35 (1962), pp. 223–247. The extended text formed a combination of the present paper, and one on 'Urban Development, 1900–1930', prepared by the co-author for the Java Seminar at the Institute of Social Studies.

TEN

Social Change in Java, 1900–1930

1. The Ethical Policy – 1900

The choice of 1900 as a starting point for the study of subsequent developments in Java has a certain significance. It singles out a definite turn in Dutch policy concerning the Netherlands East Indies for a special consideration of its ultimate effects on Javanese society. In Dutch colonial history, the turn of the century stands as a symbol for a shift from a 'liberal' toward an 'ethical' policy. The Dutch liberal politicians whose ideas gained ascendancy in the Netherlands about 1870, had assumed that a system of free enterprise would result in a free economic development of the population of Java. The example of efficient management given by European plantation-owners was expected to be followed by Javanese farmers, who were supposed to be as susceptible to economic stimuli as Europeans once the legal barriers to economic freedom were removed. About 1900, however, there was widespread disappointment since the Javanese peasantry appeared not to have responded to the spur of economic freedom. If anything, economic welfare had declined rather than increased since the inauguration of a liberal policy. As a reaction, a new ethical policy was conceived which placed the interests of the native population in the forefront and was intended to protect them against the onslaught of Western enterprise. Dutch industrialists, who wished to see the market for their textile products expanded, were strongly in favour of a policy which would increase the purchasing power of the Javanese.[1]

The character of ethical policy as a reaction to the period of

[1] J. S. Furnivall, *Netherlands India: A Study of Plural Economy* (Cambridge/ New York, 1944), p. 247.

liberal free enterprise was decisive for its eventual shape and content. It was not meant as a radical departure from the economic
principles adopted during the liberal period. Capital investment
in commercial crop plantations was still considered of primary
importance for the promotion of general welfare. Any deliberate
attempt to bring about a more radical transformation of the
overall economic structure, as for instance by means of the development of industries, was still out of the question. The change
aimed at by Dutch politicians was mainly one of emphasis.
Whereas formerly the accent had been upon Western enterprise,
while native farming was largely left to itself, there was now a
greater awareness of the need to protect the native farmers against
the impact of Western capitalism and to foster native production
in order to promote general welfare. It was understood better
than previously that economic development among the Javanese
population would not ensue automatically from formal freedom.
But there was still a common belief among the ethical policy-
makers that a number of rather simple coordinated devices introduced by government agencies would suffice to set in motion the
economic forces needed to bring about the intended development,
with improved general welfare in its wake.

The devices advocated by one of the main initiators of the
ethical policy, the lawyer C. Th. van Deventer, included irrigation, reforestation, education, an improved credit system, provisions for public health and resettlement of peasants from densely
populated Java in the open spaces of the Outer Islands. What was
needed to effectuate the new policy, according to Van Deventer,
was, above all, *money*. 'Money! That is the indispensable oil with
which the Indies machine will have to be lubricated before it can
be got over the dead point'.[1] As a device for getting the money
needed for the new policy, Van Deventer proposed to use a substantial portion of the wealth earned in the Indies, which in the
past had been transferred largely to the mother country.

[1] C. Th. van Deventer, 'A Welfare Policy for the Indies', in *Indonesian Economics: The Concept of Dualism in Theory and Policy* (The Hague, 1961), pp. 261–
262.

To the contemporaries the new policy, which propagated a kind of 'welfare state', seemed radical and to a certain extent even revolutionary. It was inaugurated in the Netherlands, not as a bone of contention in the political party strife, but as a common program of parties politically rather distant from each other. It was formulated in terms of a new era to be introduced in the Eastern colony and in subsequent years fulfilled with a measure of energy and consistency.

A certain doubt as to the appropriateness of designating this period as one of rapid development only rises when one surveys the results of the ethical policy at the end of the period which was entered in an atmosphere of high hopes and optimism.

2. Results of the Ethical Policy – 1930

a. Inertia of the mass of the rural population

The welfare policy, inaugurated about 1900, aimed at an improvement of the material condition of the Javanese villagers. In order to achieve such improvements, the Netherlands East Indian government had to rely upon the traditional pillar of official policy, the Civil Service. The usual way of handling village affairs by the Javanese officials in the lower rungs of the civil service hierarchy, the heads of districts and sub-districts (*wedanas* and assistant-*wedanas*), had some autocratic traits. The villagers had acquired, in the course of an age-long history of authoritarian rule, a habit of unquestioning obedience to the numerous demands made by the representatives of a colonial government or the Javanese princes. At the village meetings where the *wedana* or assistant-*wedana* was present, the official transmitted the commands of higher authorities. The villagers were expected to approve all he said, answering back being considered a sign of bad taste.

When, about the turn of the century, a new welfare policy was initiated, the same lower officials had to be relied upon for introducing all kinds of innovations into the Javanese village communities. It was not surprising that these innovations were largely introduced in the same aloof, authoritarian way those officials had been accustomed to in transmitting new regulations on taxes or services. *Perintah halus* (gentle commands) became the usual method for promoting welfare.

Whatever new device was to be introduced – an improved irrigation system, better village roads, new planting methods or fertilizers, innovations in the field of sanitation, the construction of village schools – the easiest way to get things done proved to be the use of the 'gentle command'. The villagers nodded approvingly when the officials came and proposed that the village community should adopt a certain innovation. The village chief understood that he had to comply with the *perintah halus* received from above. The burden of implementing the innovation had to be shouldered by the common villagers in the traditional form of communal work to be executed in behalf of the *desa*.

In 1927, Professor J. H. Boeke argued in an epoch-making lecture that the ethical policy had met with failure. The Reports on the Economic Inquiries of 1924 led him to conclude that 'the cultivator eats a bit more than before the [first World] War, but food of somewhat lower quality, and with its production surplus is able to buy slightly fewer imported goods than before the war'.[1] This situation had arisen despite the spending of over 158 million guilders in the course of a quarter of a century on irrigation works alone. According to Boeke, the main weakness of the ethical policy consisted in the stress it laid upon definite objects to be achieved by the welfare measures. This 'objective' welfare policy could only be pursued by making use of the traditional authority of the Civil Service. *Perintah halus* had to be used to induce the villagers to comply with the official projects. As they did not understand the aims and the significance of the innovations, they

[1] J. H. Boeke, 'Objective and Personal Elements in Colonial Welfare Policy', *Indonesian Economics, op. cit.*, pp. 265 ff.; H. Fievez de Malines van Ginkel (ed.), *Verslag van den economischen toestand der Inlandsche bevolking, 1924* (Report on the economic situation of the Native population, 1924, Two Vols., Weltevreden, 1926).

responded to the gentle pressure passively, in their customary way. Insofar as the pressure lasted, the project was duly fulfilled. But since the villagers did not feel actively engaged in the project, there was no sense of responsibility, needed for lasting results. Often the innovation was due to a hobby or a whim of some enthusiastic Dutch civil officer. As soon as he was transferred to another district, which was likely to happen within a few years, the temporary advance was bound to go to waste.

Boeke attributed these failures to the fact that the ethical policy aimed at achieving quick results for the mass of the population. In his opinion any improvement not properly understood by the people concerned was bound to fail. Real successes could be achieved only by a 'personal approach' based on patient education and persuasion. Such a system, however, could not work on a mass scale, but should be directed toward those individuals who showed themselves, for example by better farming methods, more susceptible to rational advice. In this 'personal approach' the welfare officers, according to Boeke, should bypass the Civil Service which was accustomed to working in an authoritarian way. But, in his opinion, such a policy could never hope to attain quick results. Therefore, the welfare policy should not aim primarily at achieving definite 'objects' but at slowly changing the mentality of the rural population.

There was certainly some exaggeration in Boeke's analysis of the situation in Java at the end of the ethical period. There is moreover, on the basis of our experiences since the time when Boeke expressed these pessimistic ideas, sufficient reason to question his view that changing the mentality of the rural population should necessarily be a slow process, inappropriate to be carried out on a mass scale. But in concluding that many Javanese villagers were not actively participating in the welfare measures undertaken in their behalf he was fundamentally right. The ethical policy had not evoked any real change in the mentality of the mass of Javanese villagers. They were generally distrustful of the measures introduced from above and not explained to them in the proper way. Even in the field of education the well-intended measures were, at first, little appreciated by the mass of the people. 'Gentle command' had, again, to be used to induce the parents to send their children to the village school.

In general, all well-intended measures were bound to fail if they were not based on an already existing, consciously felt need of those concerned. Where such a need was lacking, the response of the population gave the impression of a general inertia.

b. Static expansion

Another cause of stagnation was the prevalent pattern of population growth. Since 1800 the population of Java has grown at an amazing rate, from some six million at the start of the nineteenth century to about twenty eight million in 1900. During the period 1900–1930 the population continued to increase: at the 1930 census over forty million were counted in Java and Madura. However, the population increase did not imply a structural change in Javanese society. Even before 1800 the typical Javanese landscape showed the familiar picture of densely populated valleys where rice was cultivated on irrigated fields, alternating with mountainous regions covered with forest. Throughout the nineteenth century population growth had not led to an essential change in the type of agriculture, except for the opening up of large tracts of mountainous waste land for tree-crop cultivation under Western management. The fabulous population increase, however, was largely absorbed by extending the traditional *sawah* cultivation to many more regions and by further intensification of the type of agriculture practised from times immemorial. Thus, the *sawah* pattern prevalent mainly in Central Java gradually spread to large areas in East and West Java, including mountainous areas such as the Priangan plateaus in West Java. Regions such as the Kediri and Malang Residencies were densely populated between 1875 and 1885. Large irrigation works built by the Netherlands East Indian government stimulated the spread of the usual type of Javanese settlements over ever wider areas. The new villages were modelled after the familiar pattern known from the land of origin, and the village structure as such did not appreciably change. Nor did agricultural technique alter significantly, *per capita* production remaining approximately the same.

In areas where *sawah* lands were leased by sugar plantations from individual peasants or village communities, under a system which periodically left the land free for rice cultivation by the original Javanese occupant, intrinsic change in traditional agriculture was not any more evident. The impact of the Western plantation, which hardly provided any other employment for the peasants than as unskilled manual labourers, made the traditional type of agriculture, if anything, more rigid than before, because of the ensuing scarcity of land.

During the period 1900–1930 the process described above was still clearly in evidence. The ethical policy did not produce an intrinsic change in the village structure, since it continued to lay stress upon the plantation economy as the mainstay of economic welfare. Irrigation works, often mainly undertaken in the interest of sugar plantations, promoted a further spread of the *sawah* pattern to the Eastern and Western extremities of Java. For example, the Krawang region, not far from Jakarta, became a rice granary during that period. Boeke has rightly termed this process one of 'static expansion'; the methods of production had not technically developed, but had been extended over an ever-widening territory. 'Java is filling up; and when it is full to the brim, this static expansion will still continue, only it will be transferred to the adjacent islands by means of colonization'.[1]

c. Shared poverty

Rural overpopulation and a continuing fragmentation of land holdings have equally affected the social structure of the Javanese village. Karl Pelzer has summarized the findings of a few Dutch investigators as follows:

[1] J. H. Boeke, *The Structure of Netherlands Indian Economy* (New York, 1942), p. 163.

In 1903 . . . of all those holding land in individual hereditary possession or having fixed shares of communal land, 70.8 percent had less than 0.7 hectare, another 18.2 percent from 0.7 to 1.4 hectares, 7 percent from 1.4 to 2.8 hectares, and only 3.9 percent had more than 2.8 hectares.[1]

But around 1930 the parcelling of land had proceeded much further.

According to a study by Burger comparing conditions in 1868 and 1928, in the *desa* of Pekalongan, regency of Pati, residency of Djapara-Rembang, the average peasant-proprietor had from about 0.7 to 1.1 hectares of *sawah* in 1868 but only 0.5 hectare in 1928.

Burger gives the following distribution of *sawah* area, for 1929, in the *desa* of Ngablak, also in the regency of Pati, where 63 per cent of all *sawah* owners possessed less than about 0.7 hectare and 37 per cent less than about 0.3 hectare:

Less than 0.142 hectare	22	owners
0.142 or more but less than 0.284 hectare	76	,,
0.284 ,, ,, ,, ,, ,, 0.426 ,,	27	,,
0.426 ,, ,, ,, ,, ,, 0.568 ,,	19	,,
0.568 ,, ,, ,, ,, ,, 0.709 ,,	23	,,
0.709 ,, ,, ,, ,, ,, 1,42 hectares	46	,,
1.42 ,, ,, ,, ,, ,, 2.13 ,,	18	,,
2.13 ,, ,, ,, ,, ,, 2.84 ,,	13	,,
2.84 ,, ,, ,, ,, ,, 4.26 ,,	11	,,
4.26 ,, ,, ,, ,, ,, 7.09 ,,	7	,,
7.09 ,, more	1	,,
	263	owners[2]

An increasing number of mouths had to be fed from the produce of a given territory. Partially this difficulty could be met by further intensification of the traditional forms of agriculture. Plots of land previously yielding one crop a year were made to yield two; where two crops were usual a third was added. But as the average

[1] Karl J. Pelzer, *Pioneer Settlement in the Asiatic Tropics: Studies in Land Utilization and Agricultural Colonization in Southeastern Asia* (New York, 1948), p. 166, based on an official report of an inquiry held in 1904–1905, the results of which have been published in 1914.

[2] Pelzer, *op. cit.*, pp. 166–167, based on the studies by D. H. Burger quoted on p. 230 of the present volume, note. 3

landholding diminished, production per man remained at the same level. Increasing the productivity *per capita* by the introduction of new tools would have caused insuperable difficulties to those who did not possess enough land to live from its yield. Additional work had to be performed for the richer landowners – for example at harvest time, when all the women from the village were entitled to join in reaping the harvest by cutting the rice stalks, in order to get their share in the produce. A landowner who replaced the traditional rice knife (*ani-ani*, with which the stalks are cut ear by ear) by a scythe in order to save labour would have placed himself outside the village community.

Thus, the social system prevalent in the villages could be termed one of disguised unemployment. The generally accepted value-system resisted any innovation or technical improvements, as they would mean misery and distress for a significant proportion of the villagers. Clifford Geertz has termed this social system one of 'shared poverty'.

> Rather than a concentration of land holdings and a disenfranchized proletariat, there has occurred a fractionization of both the land tenure and labor rights side of the equation so that the structure can contain more people...; thus complicated tenancy, subtenancy, renting and subrenting patterns have developed which allow a greater number of people to claim a small portion of agricultural output from a single piece of land. Such a social structure, its agricultural base growing more and more labor intensive, holds an increasing number of people on the land through a pattern I have called elsewhere 'shared poverty', a kind of supersaturated solution of land and people sustained at a level of living only slightly above subsistence.[1]

Owing to their general character, the welfare policies of the Netherlands Indian Government during the period under review increased the rigidity of the traditional *desa* structure instead of contributing to a dynamization of Javanese village society.

[1] Clifford Geertz, *The Social Context of Economic Change: An Indonesian Case Study* (mimeographed paper, M.I.T., Cambridge, Mass., 1956), p. 13. For this 'shared poverty' concept as elaborated by Geertz, I may refer more in particular to the first paper of this volume dealing with the sociological aspects of underdevelopment.

The heavy emphasis on irrigation at the expense of other kinds of capital improvement in agriculture – e.g. those concerned with stimulating a medium scale mixed farming pattern of wet and dry crop cultivation plus animal husbandry – encouraged the development in Modjokuto of the classical Central Javanese pattern by recreating the environment to which it is adaptive. By utilizing native-owned land in a monocultural manner and reserving diversification of capital intensive commercial agriculture to 'waste' land where peasant living patterns were not directly involved, the plantation companies encouraged an essentially anti-developmental, self-defeating form of land use on the part of the Javanese. It was (and is) anti-developmental despite – particularly after the disappearance of the planta-tions – the great diversification of native crops, because it implied a steady increase in labor intensification (and so of population density) up to some high and probably still unreached limit and maintenance of the largely uncapitalized (except for irrigation), two and a half to five acre 'Lilliput-ian' farm characteristic of so much of Java. Like the Culture System before them, which they so much resembled, the sugar plantations brought on a rise in population and in food production which so nearly matched one another that *per capita* income was probably virtually constant.[1]

d. Social stratification according to skin colour

A further factor adding to the rigidity of the traditional social structure is to be found in the colonial type of social stratification. In the course of the nineteenth century a class structure had devel-oped in Java which could be termed a 'colour caste' system.[2] About the turn of the century the whites were firmly entrenched in a position of complete supremacy. Together with the socially somewhat inferior Indo-Europeans (Eurasians) they formed the Civil Service, the army, the police force and the judiciary. In private enterprise even Indo-Europeans were hardly to be found in higher staff functions. Intermediate and clerical functions in government offices and private firms were also largely occupied by Indo-Euro-pean staff, owing to their advantage in the educational field. Inter-mediate trade of a middle-class character was mainly concen-trated in the hands of 'Foreign Orientals', among whom the

[1] Geertz, *The Social Context, op. cit.*, pp. 43–45.
[2] For this 'colour caste' concept I may refer to the third paper included in this volume, dealing with trading minorities.

Chinese group was by far the largest. The great majority of the 'Native' population group was relegated to small farming or to menial work as cheap labour in Western plantations or in urban sectors, such a public works or industry.

Outside the 'principalities' of Solo and Jogjakarta the only significant groups distinguishing themselves from the mass of the population were the *priyayi* (aristocracy) and the *ulama* (Moslem scribes). The former dominated the Indonesian sector of the dualistic Civil Service under a colonial system of 'indirect rule', while the latter either served as mosque personnel and advisers at the government courts, or occupied an independent position as religious teachers (*kyai*).

Within the Javanese villages there had always been some social differentiation, based on landownership.

First comes the group of villagers who own both fields and garden land plus a house on the latter. They are known as *gogols*. The *gogol* is a 'full peasant' in the sense that he has all the rights that a member of the *desa* may have and also shares in all the burdens. In the next lower group are the *stengah gogols*, or 'half peasants', who own garden land and houses, but no fields. The *menumpangs* are villagers who own houses, which, however, stand on the garden land of others. Still lower in rank are the villagers who live in others' houses and own neither house nor land of any kind. These are called *kumpulans* or *nusups*. The numerical proportion of these various groups is a good indication of the crowded condition of a village. If a *desa* or a whole district is divided into small holdings and has a large number of *stengah gogols*, *menumpangs*, and *nusups*, we may assume that the population exceeds the carrying capacity of the land. The excess population must rely in part or wholly upon wages for their livelihood.[1]

But since landlordism of the type prevalent in several Asian countries was largely absent in most parts of Java (only the Priangan area in Western Java showing a significant exception), the villagers, whether landowners or tenants, were equally to be reckoned among the 'mass of the population' separated by a wide gulf from the upper caste of Europeans who, in their large man-

[1] Pelzer, *op. cit.*, pp. 165–166.

sions and select clubs, kept themselves aloof from the main body of Javanese society.

During the period 1900–1930 some factors were operating to affect the rigidity of the colonial caste structure. Both economic development and education opened the way to social mobility for significant numbers of Javanese, particularly in the urban sphere. On the other hand, the traditional 'colour caste' structure blocked a full realization of the potentialities opened by the dynamic impact of modern colonial rule. According to an analysis by Philip Levert,[1] in the sugar plantations and factories the Indonesians were all but relegated to menial or minor administrative tasks. Clifford Geertz argues that

> by keeping their labor force maximally seasonal, their wages low and preventing mobility for Javanese upward through the ranks of their organization, the plantations encouraged the formation of a very large partial proletariat composed of worker-peasants who were neither wholly on the 'pre-capitalist' nor wholly on the 'capitalist' side of the dual economy, but who moved uneasily back and forth between the two in response to the movement of sugar prices.[2]

This policy was one of the main factors responsible for what Geertz calls 'the plantations' re-enforcement of the traditional village way of life'.

Again, the general atmosphere created by a colonial stratification according to skin colour was one of the factors preventing a rapid transformation of Javanese society throughout the ethical policy period.

3. Stagnation or dynamic development?

If we take into account the above factors making for increasing rigidity in the social system, should not the period be termed one

---

[1] Ph. Levert, *Inheemsche arbeid in de Java-suiker-industrie* (Native labour in the sugar industry of Java, doctoral thesis Wageningen School of Agriculture, Wageningen, 1934), pp. 107 ff., 295.

[2] Geertz, *op. cit.*, pp. 41–42.

of stagnation instead of accelerated development? Some dynamic developments did occur, however, during the ethical policy period, but such processes were much less directly influenced by the new Dutch policy than had been expected by its initiators. And in as far as Javanese society was transformed, the development took quite a different course from what had been foreseen by the leading Dutch politicians at the turn of the century.

The inadequacy of the conceptual framework in which the ethical policy period is visualized as a consistent sequence of events was clearly demonstrated by Professor Resink's attempt to conceive a different frame in which the period of accelerated growth is reduced to the years 1908–1928.[1] Resink, in so doing, tried to demonstrate that insofar as dynamic processes occurred they were produced by intrinsic social forces often in conflict with the colonial government's proclaimed aims, rather than by forces set in motion by policy-makers in the Netherlands.

In my opinion, the two viewpoints can be combined into a consistent whole. It is useful to view the ethical policy (ending with the world depression of 1930) as an entity if one wants to assess the prospects of a program of 'rapid development' initiated by a colonial power. It is instructive to see how far such a well-intended policy may be frustrated by the rulers' aloofness from the mass of the population. The ethical policy took for granted the existence of certain economic needs which in reality had first to be aroused among those for whom the measures were intended. On the other hand, it is interesting that in spite of those limitations, such a program may set in motion a number of social developments, some of them intentionally (for example by extending popular education), others unintentionally (for example the rise of nationalism stimulated by the very formation of a class of educated people). To use Raymond Kennedy's formula once again, in Indonesia as everywhere else education functioned as 'dynamite for the rigid caste system of colonies'.

We should also note that, independently from the official policy,

[1] G. J. Resink, *Java 1900–1930*, unpublished paper prepared for the Java Seminar organized by the Institute of Social Studies, The Hague, 1959.

during the period under discussion factors were operating to provide a dynamic impulse to some sectors of Javanese society because they appealed to already existing needs and had some relation to value-systems accepted among the social group concerned. Such processes could be conditioned by outside economic forces working more or less independently from the official ethical policy (such as the ever deeper penetration of a money economy into the Javanese villages), or they could be called forth by intrinsic forces operating within Javanese society (such as an increasing population pressure resulting in mass migration to the towns). Such processes could also be stimulated by political or cultural developments outside Indonesia, such as the Japanese victory over Russia in 1905, the Chinese Revolution of 1911, the Islamic reformist movement in Egypt, the Russian Revolution of 1917, Gandhi's non-cooperation movement in India.

Professor Resink is right in arguing that such independent processes were in the long run much more significant for the period under review than the initial colonial program. We shall have to analyse these dynamic developments in due order.

4. Dynamic processes

a. Urban social change

Generally speaking, this period should be seen as one during which new forces were set in motion, though partially outside the scope envisaged by those who first formulated an ethical policy. The development of urban life was one of the most significant processes during these years. Java, as visualized by the Dutch politicians around the turn of the century, was a predominantly rural country, where even the towns, all of them of a moderate size, presented a rustic outlook. This view influenced the way those politicians conceived the future of Java. A rapid urbanization process was outside the scope of their imagination. Still, it was precisely this process of urban development which, more than any other single factor, changed the character of the Javanese social structure, and in particular its system of social stratification. Though within the urban environment elements of stagnation and quasi-rural primitivity were apparent and though urban life was strongly influenced by the overall colonial structure with its 'colour caste' aspect, this urbanization process could still be viewed as the main factor stimulating the dynamic processes. But it was not the only one operative during that period.[1]

b. Islamic reform

Around 1900, Islam was looked upon by many Western observers, and even by a good many Indonesians from the *priyayi* elite, as a stagnant religion. Islam as practised at that time in Java was fettered by age-old traditions and burdened with a cumbersome heritage of mediaeval scholasticism. The ethical politicians expected that liberal education would succeed in transforming Indonesian society. But since a 'modern Indonesia, by definition, could not be an Islamic Indonesia nor an Indonesia ruled by the *adat* (customary law), it would have to be a Westernized Indonesia'.[2] But as a reaction to Western influences, and particularly to widespread missionary activities by the Dutch Protestant Church, Indonesian Moslems responded with a vigorous countercurrent in the shape of a preponderantly urban Islamic renaissance movement. By adapting their own value-system, as expressed in Islamic religion, to the requirements of a modern world, the Moslem reformists succeeded in unleashing a movement of rapid development without abandoning their spiritual basis and their identity

[1] The urbanization aspect has been specifically dealt with by The Siauw Giap: see W. F. Wertheim and The Siauw Giap, 'Social Change in Java, 1900–1930', *Pacific Affairs*, Vol. 35 (1962), pp. 223–248; The Siauw Giap, 'Urbanisatieproblemen in Indonesië' (Urbanization problems in Indonesia), *Bijdragen tot de Taal-, Land- en Volkenkunde*, Vol. 115 (1959), pp. 249–276; see also for this subject, *The Indonesian Town: Studies in Urban Sociology* (The Hague/Bandung, 1958); finally, I refer to the eighth paper of this volume.

[2] Harry J. Benda, *The Crescent and the Rising Sun: Indonesian Islam under the Japanese Occupation 1942–1945* (The Hague/Bandung, 1958), p. 26 (discussing Professor Snouck Hurgronje's views).

as true Moslems. Both in its political form as a pre-nationalist movement (*Sarekat Islam*) and in its cultural aspects as a movement for spiritual and social reform (*Muhammadyah*), Islamic modernism embodied at the same time a dynamic response to and a vigorous protest against the ethical policy.

c. Western education

The importance of Western education for the period under review is also undeniable. One of the striking facts about the growth of education was that, while the creation of village schools did not evoke a wide response (as they did not meet a live demand within the Javanese village community) the supply of other types of school education lagged far behind popular demand. School education became, especially among broad sections of the *priyayi* class, a key to upward mobility on the social ladder. All types of schooling which provided the diplomas required for government positions were in high demand. Frequently private initiative was in advance of the government in providing such educational opportunities, or remained active by supplying facilities for many children excluded from entrance to government schools or attracted by the better educational level achieved at certain private schools. In the field of education especially religious organizations of a denominational character were very active, among them the Protestant and Catholic missions, masonic organizations and the Islamic reform movement, *Muhammadyah*.

This mushrooming of Western-type schools produced a surplus of clerical skills. To quote Furnivall, 'the schools meet the demand for officials and subordinates in administration and Western enterprise and produce a supply in excess of the demand'.[1] Even those attending agricultural or technical schools tended to look for employment in the clerical sphere, which was more lucrative than native agriculture or crafts where there was little scope for the skills acquired at school. Moreover, a 'feudal' tradition made

---

[1] J. S. Furnivall, *Colonial Policy and Practice: A Comparative Study of Burma and Netherlands India* (New York, 1956), p. 404.

many young people favour types of employment in accordance
with the social value-scale which placed clerical work definitely
above manual labour.

The graduates of these schools began to compete primarily with
those groups (such as Eurasians and Menadonese or Ambonese
Christians) who had achieved during the nineteenth century a
near-monopolistic position in the field of government administration. The large numbers of educated Indonesians working in the
ever-extending government offices and large concerns under
Western management became a major factor in upsetting the
clear-cut colonial caste system in existence about 1900. Higher
education provided in the Netherlands or in Java also began to
threaten the traditional stratification system within Javanese
society by creating a class of 'new *priyayis*' in possession of certifi-
cates affording them a social and economic status at least equal to
that of 'old-style *priyayis*', who were still mostly employed in the
Civil Service. An academic degree could assure its holder the *ius
connubii* within the highest levels of Javanese aristocracy. Likewise, the spread of Western types of education among girls contributed to a collapse of the traditional social structure, emancipa-
ting many young women from their position of relative inferiority.
In general the traditional stratification according to birth was
gradually being replaced by one based on individual achievement.

Besides this widespread demand for the type of education promising entrance into government service, there were other groups
aspiring to social advance for their children along a different
road. Among the Chinese group, mostly occupied in commerce
and other middle-class functions of an independent character, a
desire to see their children admitted to government service was,
before the world depression of 1930, all but non-existent. On the
other hand, that group decidedly needed better and more advanced education than was provided by the colonial government at
the end of the nineteenth century. Therefore, an organization
(*Chung Hua Hui Kuan*) was formed providing educational facilities
on a *Chinese* cultural basis. Even after the government had reacted
by creating primary schools (with Dutch as a medium of instruc-

tion) intended especially for Chinese children, the private Chinese schools continued to absorb large numbers of children from the lower trading class, whose parents were not able to pay the high entrance fees for the Dutch-language government schools.

In the same way, around 1920, the *Taman Siswa* organization was founded to provide education on a national basis for Indonesian children. The *Taman Siswa* schools were not intended to prepare new applicants for the government service, nor did they accept governmental subsidies. Again, to a certain degree, both the *Muhammadyah* and the *Taman Siswa* schools embodied at the same time a response to and a protest against the official educational policy by providing educational facilities along lines different from those supplied by the colonial authorities.

d. Cultural revival

In the cultural field, too, dynamic developments occurred but they followed a course much at variance with the assimilation policy advocated by the founders of the Ethical Program. The Indonesian language became a vehicle for expressing cultural, political and social aspirations in accordance with current trends all over the world but generally in conflict with the colonial legacy, even if clothed in an ethical cloak. The modernization of the Malay language in order to adapt it to modern society was a process in which the Indonesians themselves led the way, though *Balai Pustaka* (the government Agency for Popular Literature) stimulated the development. In the *Taman Siswa* schools and other similar institutions attempts were made to adapt the Indonesian cultural heritage to modern life and at the same time to imbue the expression of Indonesian culture with a nationalistic, anticolonial spirit. Both the Westernists and the revivalists among the Indonesian intellectual youth were, above all, anti-assimilationists.

e. Social differentiation within the villages

The developments described above were largely urban-centered and affected the countryside only superficially. Nevertheless, the rate of change in village society during the period under review should not be underrated. But in the Javanese villages it was most of all the continuing penetration of a money economy which affected the traditional social structure. This thesis may appear to contradict the previous argument that the ethical policy period was one of stagnation and inertia in the villages, the only responses being static expansion and a system of shared poverty which amounted to an increasing rigidity of the traditional structure. To this objection one could reply, however, that the general picture as outlined above retains a certain validity against the background of the Ethical Program but should be revised by adding a few fine shades to bring out its relative insufficiency. The trend toward stagnation is only one part of the story.

First, the picture holds mostly for typical *sawah* areas where Western sugar plantations added to the rigidity of the economic system. But Java presents great regional differences which account for significant deviations from the general pattern outlined above. For example, areas not too far from large towns were much more influenced by factors radiating from the urban centres than distant regions. Likewise, the Priangan area (where landlordism was increasingly in evidence) felt the influences of a penetrating money economy more directly than regions where parcellation of land was steadily proceeding despite the official restriction upon sub-division of allotments under a system of 'communal' ownership.

Second, the process of levelling termed 'shared poverty' does not exclude the possibility that individuals respond positively to the stimuli of an expanding money economy. Many Javanese in the villages undoubtedly attained a more dynamic attitude toward economic life, among them those who migrated to a city and profited from the better opportunities for economic advance. Others were attracted by non-urban centres of Western enterprise, such as sugar factories and found employment there as full-time semi-skilled labourers. But the village society also afforded some opportunities, for example as small traders, cart-drivers, or tailors, for individuals of more than average energy. Agriculture offered opportunities for some who were keen to profit from the advice given by officials of the Agricultural Extension Service; after about 1920 this service had applied the 'personal approach' method advocated in 1927 by Professor Boeke as a general means for promoting welfare.[1]

Accordingly, social differentiation was probably greater in 1930 than it had been in 1900, as is suggested in the regional surveys undertaken by Van der Kolff and Burger. The former sees some indications that from 1900 to 1922 economic life had been developing in a more individualistic direction.

> It might prove that the higher class had advanced. In that case there is always this gain to be booked from a dynamical point of view, namely that in an amorphous mass a definite differentiation has set in, which is the beginning of all progress, including increased prosperity.[2]

Burger's data, comparing a few Central Javanese villages as they had been in 1868–69 with the situation in 1928–29, also point in the same direction.[3]

The village schools and 'continuation' schools, despite the primitive level of instruction which was restricted to the three R's, also helped to open up new opportunities for those young people who wanted to improve their social and economic status. Moreover, the existence of the village schools, where young teachers (largely of lower *priyayi* origin) wielded an authority which often surpass-

[1] *Indonesian Economics, op. cit.*, p. 36.
[2] G. H. van der Kolff, *The Historical Development of the Labour Relationships in a Remote Corner of Java as They Apply to the Cultivation of Rice* (New York, 1936), pp. 36, 41.
[3] D. H. Burger, *Rapport over de desa Pekalongan in 1868 en 1928* (Report on the desa Pekalongan in 1868 and 1928, Weltevreden, n.y.); Burger, *Vergelijking van den economischen toestand der districten Tajoe en Djakenan, Regentschap Pati, Afdeeling Rembang* (Comparison of the economic situation in the districts Tajoe and Djakenan, Pati Regency, Rembang Division, Weltevreden, n.y.), pp. 55 ff.; Burger, 'De desa Ngablak (Regentschap Pati) in 1869 en 1929' (Desa Ngablak, Pati Regency, in 1869 and 1929), *Koloniale Studiën*, Vol. 17 (1933), p. 232. See the table on the next page.

Profession	Number of individuals occupied			
	Desa Pekalongan		Desa Ngablak	
	1868	1928	1869	1929
Tailors	—	7	—	7
Goldsmiths	—	5	—	2
Carpenters	—	—	—	3
Traders	—	36	—	29
Cart-drivers	—	7	—	11

ed that of the elders in the village and were entrusted with inculcating in both boys and girls skills of which their parents were ignorant, was in itself a factor undermining the traditional social structure and its underlying value-systems.

Still, the characterization of the situation in the Javanese villages as one of stagnation remains valid insofar as the above individualizing and dynamic effects were, for the time being, restricted to a minority. As Boeke has pointed out, with a certain amount of exaggeration, the dynamic forces in the villages did not affect the mass of the population. Those profiting from a 'personal approach' were only the happy few. And while an increasing social differentiation helped a few individuals to rise on the social scale, to the rapidly growing mass of the population the impact of a money economy meant a harder plight, increased indebtedness and dependence on the *beati possidentes*, and a growing tendency 'to share food equally when one had it and to share its absence equally when one did not have it'.[1]

The following table, based on an official report from 1926, provides a rough picture of the social stratification system in the Javanese countryside at the end of our period.[2]

[1] Clifford Geertz, 'Religious belief and Economic Behavior in a Central Javanese Town', *Economic Development and Cultural Change*, Vol. 4 (1956), p. 141.

[2] J. W. Meijer Ranneft and W. Huender, *Onderzoek naar den belastingdruk op de Inlandsche bevolking* (Inquiry into the tax burden on the Native population, Weltevreden, 1926), p. 10; W. F. Wertheim, *Indonesian Society in Transition: A Study of Social Change* (Second Ed., The Hague/Bandung, 1959), p. 112.

	Percent of total population*	Household income per year (in guilders)
Officials, native chiefs, teachers of religion	4.0	
Permanent workers in European and Chinese enterprises	2.4	370
Wealthy farmers	2.5	1090
Middle class farmers	19.8	300
Poor farmers	27.1	147
Share-croppers, having no property of their own	3.4	118
Labourers on native holdings	12.4	101
Native wholesale merchants and industrialists	0.3	1130
Retail dealers, artisans	5.9	248
Coolies	19.6	124
Miscellaneous	2.6	—
	100.0	

* From this table we can calculate that the landless peasants and coolies amounted to 37.8 percent of the village population; by adding the poor farmers or semi-proletarians we arrive at a total of poor people amounting to 65 percent.

f. From communalism to organization

Despite the existence of a few factors making for increasing rigidity in the traditional village social structure, the general tendency was one of decay of the existing communal ties. The introduction of a money economy transformed many relationships based on mutual aid into contracts of a financial character. Greater mobility loosened the existing bonds between the individual and his village community. Several customs in connection with land-ownership or cattle decayed, and the social status of the elders, the traditional upholders of the ancient *adat*, crumbled. Yet, at the same time, the first beginnings of a new collective consciousness became visible. The rise of all kinds of trade-unions and voluntary organizations was mainly an urban phenomenon but the influence of this organizational growth radiated from the towns into the countryside. One of the most striking phenomena was the rapid expansion of the *Sarekat Islam* movement among the Javanese peasantry. The huge following that this organization was able to collect within a few years (allegedly over two million) was a sign that new collective ties of an organizational kind were in accordance with a deeply felt need among many villagers. The religious tinge of this new bond appealed to the existing value-systems at the rice-roots level. As a pre-nationalist movement, *Sarekat Islam* at the same time gave vent to a general desire among the peasantry to identify themselves with those defending their own value-systems against the colonial government and its representatives.

One of the striking facts about this rapid expansion of the *Sarekat Islam* movement was the readiness of the peasantry to accept the leadership of an urban class of Western-educated people. This proved that the old-style aristocracy, through its association with colonial rule, was gradually losing its grip upon Javanese society. On the other hand, the traditional opponents of the aristocracy, the rural *kyais* (religious leaders), could retain their influence only by joining the urban-led Islamic organization.

Another sign that new collective ties were beginning to replace the old communal bonds was provided by the rapid rise of a trade-union movement, in particular among the workers in the sugar plantations. This incipient proletariat of peasant origin, uprooted by the impact of wage labour, was the first to organize on a large scale. Despite the usual weaknesses and shortcomings of these young organizations, their rapid growth was again a sign of a new social consciousness, directing itself against the very economic forces which had called this new labour class into existence.

g. Development from regionalism to nation-wide group solidarity

Finally there is one dynamic development within Javanese society which we should not overlook. At the turn of the century, group cohesion among the inhabitants of Java, as a rule, did not extend beyond local or familial boundaries. Where there was a broader group-consciousness, it seldom extended beyond speech-groups, such as Javanese, Sundanese or Madurese. The only spiritual bond linking together Indonesians from different parts of the archipelago, and all of them to the outer world, was the Islamic faith. Despite the many divisions within Islam, with its manifold schools and mystic sects, there was an underlying unity of the *Ummat Islam*, the community of all Moslems. But this latent unity was not yet expressed in adequate organizational forms.

The same phenomenon was prevalent among minority groups such as the *singkeh* Chinese (*i.e.* the first generation of migrants from China) who were also mostly organized on a local base and divided according to speech-groups. Even among the Indo-Europeans (Eurasians), who were a rather mobile group within the archipelago owing to the fact that many of them worked in government offices and were subjected to frequent transfers, local differences and group allegiances were in evidence.

When the government started to create representative, consultative or legislative bodies, they were first of all established in the local sphere in order (as it was stated) to educate the Indonesians in political affairs in a sphere which did not extend beyond their supposedly rather limited outlook.

The spontaneous growth of a group-solidarity, rapidly extending to a nation-wide scale – which could be also termed a development from a restricted 'particularism' toward a broader one, bordering on a quasi-'universalism' – was one of the most striking developments during the period. The first group to organize itself on a broader, more-encompassing basis, were the Chinese. The formation of the *Chung Hua Hui Kuan* in 1901 is a case in point. Lea Williams has discussed many aspects of this broadening base of Chinese group life during the period from 1900–1916.[1] The traditional organizations, mostly based on separate speech-groups, and some of them assuming the underground form of 'secret

[1] Lea E. Williams, *Overseas Chinese Nationalism: The Genesis of the Pan Chinese Movement in Indonesia, 1900–1916* (Glencoe, 1960).

societies', were gradually replaced by all kinds of modern unions, which encompassed the Chinese living throughout Java and brought them together into nation-wide organizations. This trend could be distinguished both among the China-born *singkehs* and among the Indonesia-born *peranakans*. Among the Indo-Europeans the trend toward large nation-wide organizations became equally apparent. The best-known organization of this type was the *Indo-Europees Verbond* (1919), though it already had predecessors in such movements as the *Indische Bond, Indische Partij* and *Insulinde*.

Among the Indonesians, the creation of *Budi Utomo* (1908) was highly significant. Though inaugurated by Javanese, it did not choose *Javanese* as its medium, but *Malay*. This choice was a symbol of a desire to encompass all the people in Java regardless of their speech-group. A few years later *Sarekat Islam* was established as a nation-wide organization. In it Islam still was functioning as a pre-nationalist ideology, but by 1930, after both the organizations on a religious basis and those on a communist basis had met with serious set-backs and the communists had even suffered a major defeat in the suppressed rebellions of 1926–1927, nationalism was finally adopted as the leading ideology for the time being. In the same vein, all kinds of organizations (cultural, religious, youth groups, women's organizations) were increasingly conforming to the pattern of nation-wide group life.

Meanwhile, the colonial government had been forced to create avenues for the expression of nation-wide political aspirations and to abandon its policy of 'local education towards self-government' by calling into life the *Volksraad*, first as a consultative and later as a co-legislative body. The rapid development of nationalist feelings had made the establishment of this body overdue as early as 1918. All attempts to introduce an 'assimilationist' policy were crushed by the rising tide of nationalism.

5. *Conclusions*

These were a few among the most striking signs of a growing dynamic impulse which made itself felt within Javanese society. The period between 1900–1930 can thus rightly be called a period of 'rapid development'. But the development was largely independent from, and in certain respects opposed to, the forces which had originally formulated a reform program. All the dynamic processes mentioned in the previous pages tended to combine into a strong nationalist movement, Western-inspired as far as ideology was concerned but at the same time directed against the very colonial power which had produced the new forces unwittingly and unwillingly.

> Western education and welfare legislation, however well intended they had been, had combined in unloosing a whirlwind of unexpected and highly perturbing repercussions which seemed to threaten the very foundations of colonial society. The tides of change, in other words, were running faster than ever before, but they were to all intents and purposes spilling over the banks chartered by the proponents of the Ethical Policy.[1]

The ultimate cause of this devious and even abortive development, however, should not be sought exclusively in the fact that the Ethical Program was formulated by a colonial government aloof from the population for whom the policy was intended and defending economic interests partly opposed to those of the masses. A further cause may have been the fact that the Ethical Program, despite its more or less revolutionary appeal, did not aim at a wholesale transformation of Indonesian society. The changes it attempted to bring about were of a partial nature and did not affect the totality of the economic and social structure. Industrialization, as far as its realization was included in the economic program of some of the ethical politicians, remained throughout the period under review a half-hearted attempt. Strong interest groups opposed any idea of industrial development on a larger scale.[2] The economist Van Oorschot pointedly called the period, as regards industrial development, 'a paper period'.[3]

[1] Benda, op. cit., p. 36.
[2] The Dutch policy with respect to industrial development in Indonesia has been discussed at greater length by The Siauw Giap in the version published in *Pacific Affairs:* see Wertheim and The, *loc. cit.*, pp. 236 ff.
[3] H. J. van Oorschot, *De ontwikkeling van de nijverheid in Indonesië* (The devel-

As a consequence, dynamic processes outside the scope of the Ethical Program could develop in sectors of the Javanese society which had been completely left out of consideration by the Dutch policy-makers, and were liable to unleash forces aiming at a total transformation of the society.

The experience of the 1900–1930 period in Java thus appears to lend additional support to the thesis elaborated by Margaret Mead that overall change may, under certain circumstances, occur with less friction than partial change.[1]

opment of industry in Indonesia, doctoral thesis Rotterdam School of Economics, The Hague/Bandung, 1956), pp. 18 ff.
[1] Margaret Mead, *New Lives for Old: Cultural Transformation – Manus, 1928–1953* (London, 1956).

The paper on 'The sociological approach to Indonesian history' has originally been written in 1959, as a contribution to a Symposium on Indonesian historiography, which was at that time intended to be published simultaneously in an English and an Indonesian version.

The English volume, edited by Soedjatmoko, Mohammad Ali, G. J. Resink, and G. McT. Kahin, is being published in 1964 by Cornell University Press, with the title: *An Introduction to Indonesian Historiography*; the present essay is being incorporated as Chapter 18 ('The Sociological Approach'). It has been somewhat revised to bring it more up-to-date.

The publishers kindly agreed with inclusion within the present volume.

ELEVEN

THE SOCIOLOGICAL APPROACH
TO INDONESIAN HISTORY

Until 1930 there was a good deal of confusion about the character of what was called 'Hindu colonization' in Java. Besides the 'Greater India' concept of some Indian historians, who simply attributed the Hindu influence in large parts of Southeast Asia to political domination from India (a concept which, however, found no corroborating evidence in historical sources), there was a view more generally accepted among Dutch historians that Hindu influences in Indonesia could be fully accounted for by the presence of large colonies of Indian traders, some of whom had assumed power as Hindu kings.

In 1934, however, a young Dutch sociologist, Jacob C. van Leur, demonstrated that the latter view was equally inadequate.[1] If one kept in mind the type of society the so-called Hindu-Javanese in the early centuries of the Christian era were living in, one arrived at the conclusion that Hindu-Javanese civilization could never have been brought there by plain Indian traders. In view of the kind of people the travelling traders from India were – pedlars, crowded in large numbers on the ships and in the harbours – it seemed to Van Leur highly improbable that they had been the transmitters of Brahmin hierocratic civilization which was the essence of Hindu influence on Java. The social distance between the trader class and the rulers was, in Van Leur's view, much too wide to make such a hypothesis probable. The places where the Hindu culture was centered also contradict the traditional view: the Hindu influence did not make itself felt primarily along the coasts of Java, where the traders were to be found in

[1] J. C. van Leur, *Indonesian Trade and Society: Essays in Asian Social and Economic History* (The Hague/Bandung, 1955).

large numbers, but in the courtly centres in the interior. It is there that one has to look for the remains of the grandiose Hindu temples.

According to Van Leur the transmitters of Hindu civilization were a small group of influential Brahmins, who were summoned by Indonesian princes to their courts for their powers of consecration and perhaps also their chancellory skills. Their work was, as in India, above all the legitimation of the ruling dynasty, the provision of mythological sanction to genealogy and tradition. Thus, sociological analysis according to the 'idealtypic' method propagated by Max Weber helped Van Leur to arrive at a reinterpretation of the published sources on Hindu-Javanese history. It was a great victory for the sociological approach as such that his findings were essentially corroborated by research independently undertaken by Professor Bosch with a different method, that of archeology and the history of art.[1] Van Leur's success in challenging the view generally held among Dutch historians is an outstanding example of the significance of the sociological approach to Indonesian historiography.

However, Van Leur was not the first to apply a sociological analysis to Indonesian history in line with Max Weber's methodology. Already in 1919, the Dutch radical D. M. G. Koch had attempted to analyse the Indonesian nationalist movement in terms of the sociology of religion, as elaborated by Max Weber in *The Protestant Ethic and the Spirit of Capitalism*.[2] Koch concluded that a parallel could be drawn between the *Sarekat Islam* movement and Protestantism as it had developed in Western Europe in the fifteenth and sixteenth centuries. In both instances, according to Koch, an incipient bourgeoisie attempted to build up a new ideology, more in harmony with the requirements of their way of life. Just like in the years of the rise of Protestantism in Holland

[1] F. D. K. Bosch, *Het vraagstuk van de Hindoe-kolonisatie van de Archipel* (The problem of Hindu colonization in the archipelago, inaugural address Leiden University, Leiden, 1946.)

[2] Max Weber, *The Protestant Ethic and the Spirit of Capitalism* (Fifth Ed., New York/London, 1956).

the cloth manufacturers had led the way in developing a new attitude toward religious values, in Java the *Sarekat Islam* movement had been inaugurated by *batik* (printed cotton) industrialists and traders. In both instances, a new attitude toward labour,[1] interpreted in religious terms, was one of the most important signs of a new *Wirtschaftsgeist*, which became transparent in the religious outlook of the social groups concerned.

This sociological interpretation of the Indonesian nationalist movement was included in an official report which was published anonymously.[2] This first attempt to apply a sociological methodology to Indonesian society met with much criticism on the part of the Dutch-language press, the colonial government being accused of having published a 'Marxist' paper.[3] It was not to remain the only occasion when critics would appear to overlook the difference between quasi-Marxist stereotyped evolutionism and a Weberian 'idealtypic' analysis giving full scope to social environment and the constellation of time factors.[4]

The two above examples of sociological analysis illustrate the different function of this methodology according to the period of Indonesian history to which it is applied. For more recent times the sociological approach merely adds a new frame of reference and contributes to a deeper insight, without necessarily disclosing new unknown facts. But for the earlier periods, where source materials are scarce and not seldom obscure, ambiguous, or unreliable, the sociological approach may open up completely new

---

[1] For the different attitudes towards labour in general, see Jan Romein, 'Het arbeidsbegrip in Oost en West' (The concept of labour in East and West), one of the chapters of his *In de ban van Prambanan: Indonesische voordrachten en indrukken* (Under the spell of Prambanan: Speeches and impressions from Indonesia, Amsterdam, 1954).

[2] *Mededeelingen omtrent onderwerpen van algemeen belang* (Informations about subjects of general interest, Weltevreden, 1920); see also D. M. G. Koch, *Verantwoording: Een halve eeuw in Indonesië* (Justification: Half a century in Indonesia, The Hague/Bandung, 1956), pp. 108 ff.

[3] Koch, *op. cit.*, pp. 112 ff.

[4] Clifford Geertz, in his review of W. F. Wertheim, *Indonesian Society in Transition*, in *Indonesië*, Vol. 10 (1957), pp. 85, 87.

vistas, as was the case with Van Leur's 'new look' at Hindu-Javanese history.

The only sociologist who has occupied himself with early Indonesian history as intensively as with more recent periods is the late Professor B. Schrieke.[1] In his studies dealing with contemporary history,[2] he provides the reader with many illuminating insights into the dynamic forces operating in Indonesian society, without pretending, however, to shed a new light upon the historical chain of events. Insofar as he brings to light facts hitherto unknown, he is applying the usual historical method. The sociological approach is, nonetheless, useful in providing a new enlightening interpretation of facts of common knowledge or in focussing attention on historical occurrences previously neglected or overlooked. For example, Schrieke's analysis of those social groups in Menangkabau either sympathetic or inimical to the Communist movement, in a period of transition from traditionalism to individualism, may help the reader to get better understanding of the motive forces behind the revolutionary actions of January, 1927.

The fruitfulness of Schrieke's approach to earlier periods of Indonesian history, however, still exceeds the significance of the contribution he made in his treatment of recent developments. A good instance is provided by his discussion of the political structure of the seventeenth-century kingdom of Mataram.[3] From Schrieke's description of that kingdom, the picture arises of a true 'patrimonial bureaucratic state', in the Weberian sense.[4] As is the case in nearly every pre-Napoleonic state, 'the component parts

[1] See volumes 2 and 3 of the Selected Studies on Indonesia by Dutch Authors: B. Schrieke, *Indonesian Sociological Studies. Selected Writings*, Part One (The Hague/Bandung, 1955), and *Indonesian Sociological Studies. Selected Writings: Ruler and Realm in Early Java*, Part Two (The Hague/ Bandung, 1957).

[2] The most important one is 'The Causes and Effects of Communism on the West Coast of Sumatra', in *op. cit.*, Part One, pp. 85 ff.

[3] Schrieke, *op. cit.*, Part Two, in particular pp. 217 ff. See also *op. cit.*, Part One, 'The Native Rulers', pp. 184 ff.

[4] See Max Weber, *Wirtschaft und Gesellschaft* (Second Ed., Tübingen, 1925).

of the kingdom display a loose coherence'.[1] Mangkurat I (1646–1677) made an energetic attempt to put the idea of the 'state' into practice. Whereas his predecessor, Sultan Agung (1613–1646), had forced the subjected local princes to remain at the court and attempted to tie them through marriage alliances in order to keep them under control, thus transforming the independent landed aristocracy into a court nobility, Mangkurat I applied other means, listed by Weber, to check centrifugal tendencies. After having summoned the subjected aristocracy to court, he deliberately destroyed the whole group, 'and placed the administration of the provinces in the hands of *ministeriales*, whom he constantly replaced in order to nip in the bud any aspirations to independence'.[2]

Mangkurat attempted to bring about certain innovations of the state structure. He made foreign trade a state monopoly and tried to introduce taxation in money in order to transfer its revenue from the provinces to the central government. But the attempt to form a state out of a society based on a goods economy and with an underdeveloped system of communications inevitably failed, and ended in a debacle.[3] But it is curious to note that Mangkurat I, who was painted in traditional history writing in the blackest of colours, appears from Schrieke's analyses as an innovator who was, in some respects, even ahead of the contemporary Company's rule which restored the *ministeriales* to a position of an old-style landed aristocracy.

It is more important still that in Schrieke's view conditions in the Moslem kingdom of Mataram were not essentially different from those prevalent in earlier centuries. From the political structure as he found it in the seventeenth century Schrieke tried to read back into the pages of history dealing with earlier 'patrimonial bureaucratic states' in Java, on which we are not so well informed, and his analysis helps to illuminate what must have taken place in those earlier times. It is a great advantage of the sociolog-

[1] Schrieke, *op. cit.*, Part One, p. 184.
[2] *Ibidem*, p. 184.
[3] *Ibidem*, p. 184–185.

ical, 'idealtypic' approach that it helps to reconstruct conditions prevailing in periods on which source materials are scarce and obscure.

Schrieke concludes (and his conclusion would appear to be essentially valid for any 'patrimonial bureaucratic state') that

> whatever system was applied – whether the landed nobility were retained as vassals, members of the royal family were established as local administrators, or the territory was put in charge of officials, – the ties which held the various parts of the realm together were always comparatively loose. What we have found taking place during the reign of Sultan Agung can be expected just as well during the reign of an Ayam-Wuruk, a Krtanagara, a Jayabhaya, an Erlangga, or a Sinḍok.[1]

It seems to me that the typology of the early Indonesian bureaucratic structures as elaborated by Schrieke may provide a clue to solving the dissensions among historians about the extent of Majapahit's rule.

While according to traditional history writing the empire of Majapahit extended its rule, at the pinnacle of its glory, over a large part of the archipelago, in recent years this view has been challenged by Professor Berg, who doubts whether Majapahit ever achieved supremacy over other islands than Java, Madura and Bali.[2]

A sociological approach to this problem may reduce the dispute to a matter largely of terminology. If one keeps in mind the type of political power held by the rulers of those early kingdoms, it becomes evident that any idea of an empire comparable with our modern national states would appear an anachronism. The only territory where the ruling prince held real power, comprised the crown lands (*nagaragung*) surrounding his *kraton*. In more distant regions, the actual ruler was a provincial governor, whether he was a relative of the prince, a member of the native landed aristocracy, or a *ministerialis* appointed by the prince. It was the gover-

---

[1] Schrieke, *op. cit.*, Part Two, p. 221.

[2] C. C. Berg, 'De Sadeng oorlog en de mythe van Groot Majapahit' (The Sadeng war and the myth of Great Majapahit), *Indonesië*, Vol. 5 (1951–52), pp. 385 ff.

nor with his underlings who was entitled to levy taxes and services from the subjected rural population.

In general, his main obligation toward the sovereign was to pay homage and tribute at the yearly ceremony in the court capital, described with such a wealth of colour in the *Nagarakrtagama*. In addition, he had to provide labour and military assistance when summoned by the ruling prince. The periodical inspection tours through the country by the sovereign and his retinue, also related in the *Nagarakrtagama*, were mainly intended to impress his power upon the governors and the local population and to ensure that the former would not skip their obligations toward the ruler. The spies sent out from the *kraton* in all directions served to report to the king any indications that the governors might be behaving too independently. If necessary, a military expedition was sent out to remind the vassal of his obligations.

Under such conditions the distinction between 'internal' and 'international' relations was a fluid one. There was a sliding scale of relationships between rulers, ranging from complete subordination to full equality. The rulers, who considered themselves the pivots of the world (*Paku Buwana*), were prone to consider a trade mission sent by a prince 'abroad' a tribute duly paid to their supreme power. Nevertheless in order not to lose face they would entertain the mission in a liberal manner and offer precious gifts in return. But for the historian it is difficult to decide where political rule ends and where plain trade begins. Schrieke describes in a colourful manner how the kings of seventeenth-century Mataram attempted to impose their power upon the coastal rulers outside Java, as 'lords of thirty-three islands', and how those rulers attempted to shirk the obligation of making a personal appearance and to send ambassadors instead, to the *susuhunan*'s displeasure.[1]

In this light it seems as inappropriate to imagine an empire of Majapahit extending its power over the whole archipelago as to deny a certain subordination of the Sumatran coastal rulers to

[1] Schrieke, *op. cit.*, Part Two, pp. 221 ff.

the king of Majapahit, evidenced by the punitive expedition after
the ruler of Srivijaya had attempted to establish direct relations
with the Chinese emperor, an event duly recorded in the Ming
chronicles.[1] It is impossible to conceive the ancient world in terms
of clear-cut national boundaries as exemplified by our maps dividing up the whole world into political units coloured yellow,
green, or pink. The modern state of Indonesia has as little relationship to early Majapahit as present-day 'Smaller Europe' to the
mediaeval Roman kingdom of Charlemagne, the only real link
being in either case a powerful political myth.[2]

Thus, the sociological approach may help the historian to gain
a relativistic view of early political structures in Indonesia, in the
same way as an approach from the angle of international law
may help him to achieve a more balanced conception of the
Netherlands East Indian colonial structure.[3]

A different approach which could equally be called, with some
reservations, a 'sociological' one, has been followed by a few
writers who treat Indonesian history from a Marxist point of
view. An outstanding example of this kind of treatment is to be
found in a study written by Rutgers, a Dutch Marxist, in co-operation with Huber (sometimes spelled Guber), a Russian histo-

[1] W. P. Groeneveldt, 'Notes on the Malay Archipelago and Malacca: Com-
piled from Chinese Sources', *Verhandelingen Bataviaasch Genootschap*, Vol. 39
(1880), p. 69.
[2] G. J. Resink, 'Tussen de mythen' (Between the myths), *De Nieuwe Stem*,
Vol. 7 (1952), pp. 346 ff.
[3] See Resink's following publications: 'Veronachtzaamde uitspraken' (Neglected pronouncements), *Indonesië*, Vol. 8 (1955), pp. 1 ff.; 'Onafhankelijke
vorsten, rijken en landen in Indonesië tussen 1850 en 1910' (Independent princes, realms, and lands in Indonesia between 1850 and 1910), *Indonesië*, Vol. 9
(1956), pp. 265 ff.; 'Uit het stof van een beeldenstorm' (Out of the dust of an
iconoclasm), *Indonesië*, Vol. 9 (1956), pp. 433 ff.; 'Een cadens van Colijn' (A
cadenza from Colijn), *Indonesië*, Vol. 10 (1957), pp. 246 ff. The above essays
will shortly be published in English translation in G. J. Resink, *Indonesia's
History Between the Myths*, to appear as Volume Seven in the series Selected
Studies on Indonesia.

rian.[1] In this work an attempt was made to interpret Indonesian history in terms of class struggle and dialectics, on the lines of historical-materialist thought. In a few interesting pages the authors, for example, take issue with Van Leur's view of pre-colonial Indonesia. According to the writers, some Indonesian coastal kingdoms were on the verge of a truly capitalistic evolution in the direction of a bourgeois society when Dutch colonial monopolistic policy, supported by naval military power, nipped in the bud such autochthonous tendencies.[2] The general contribution of this approach to Indonesian history consisted in deflecting the attention from purely incidental facts largely dealing with personalities to the underlying dynamic social forces rooted in the basic economic structure.

Finally, some special attention has to be devoted to De Kat Angelino's *magnum opus* which was more or less intended as an official view of the aims and policies of the Netherlands East Indian government.[3] Although not dealing with Indonesian historiography in particular, it was still a significant attempt to analyse many aspects of social development in Indonesia on the basis of a broad knowledge of recent literature on sociology and cultural anthropology. For example, Durkheim was quoted to support the author's view that Indonesian rural life was moving from a state of uniform 'mechanic solidarity' toward 'organic solidarity' in a more diversified society.[4] Very enlightening is his treatment of the character of towns in pre-modern Asia. He quotes Oswald Spengler's words: 'They are centres of the landscape, they do not

---

[1] S. J. Rutgers and A. Huber, *Indonesië*, Part One (Amsterdam, 1937). See also the post-war publication by Rutgers, *Indonesië: Het koloniale systeem in de periode tussen de eerste en de tweede wereldoorlog* (Indonesia: The colonial system in the period between the two World Wars, Amsterdam, 1947), which was intended as a continuation of the former work.

[2] Rutgers and Huber, *op. cit.*, pp. 37 ff., in particular pp. 51 ff.

[3] A. D. A. de Kat Angelino, *Staatkundig beleid en bestuurszorg in Nederlandsch Indie*, Two Parts, in Three Volumes (The Hague, 1929/30). In an abridged form published in English, as *Colonial Policy*, Two Volumes (Amsterdam/Chicago, 1931).

[4] *Op. cit.* (Dutch Ed.), Part One, p. 109.

inwardly form worlds. They have no soul'. In general, they are mere agglomerations of villages and separate quarters.[1]

Yet whereas the works of Van Leur and Schrieke, despite some outmoded aspects, are still of absorbing interest to the present-day reader, De Kat Angelino's contemporary work, notwithstanding its positive qualities and the high level of learning to which it bears testimony, reeks of dust and camphor. Evidently sociology cannot stand a blend with official ideology. Sociology, if it is to serve any purpose, has to be independent and critical.

At the time when Koch, Schrieke, and Van Leur published their pioneering studies, sociology was only beginning to get a foothold in the Dutch academic world. Since the Second World War, sociology has become the vogue of the day. Thus, it is understandable that a much greater number of scholars, both Indonesian and others, have devoted themselves to sociological studies with respect to Indonesia. However, whereas in the pre-war studies sociology had won its greatest successes in its application to early history, the post-war studies of this kind have dealt mostly with more recent periods of Indonesian history. This can be partly accounted for by the fact that sociological analysis of recent periods has sometimes been linked up with actual field research. For example, Clifford Geertz's analysis of the non-aristocratic elements of Javanese society in terms of a *santri* civilization centered in the bazaars as opposed to an *abangan* sphere characterized by the people's clinging to Javanese tradition, their stress upon communal values, and their 'shared poverty' pattern was derived from the field research undertaken by a team of the Massachusetts Institute of Technology engaged in the 'Modjokuto' project.[2] Ten Dam's analysis of the processes underlying social

---

[1] *Ibidem*, p. 117.

[2] I may mention the following studies by Clifford Geertz: 'Religious Belief and Economic Behavior in a Central Javanese Town: Some Preliminary Considerations', *Economic Development and Cultural Change*, Vol. 4 (1956), pp. 134 ff.; *The Social Context of Economic Change: An Indonesian Case Study* (mimeographed paper M.I.T., Cambridge, Mass., 1956); *The Development of the Javanese Econ-*

stratification within a village in Western Java and bringing about
a differentiation of cultural values according to social status
connected with the stratification pattern, was derived from the
field work undertaken under his guidance by a team of students
at the Faculty of Agriculture in Bogor.[1] In the last few years the
number of studies based on field research in Indonesia, some of
them by Indonesian scholars, has appreciably increased.[2]

But quite apart from actual sociological research, the post-war
generation of sociologists has felt much attracted by historical
developments over the past hundred years, on which source
materials are abundant. The literature on social developments
which appeared since World War II deals extensively with such
aspects as the colonial stratification system,[3] the Islamic reform
movement,[4] the process of urbanization,[5] the evolution of labour

---

omy: A Socio-Cultural Approach (mimeographed paper, M.I.T., Cambridge,
Mass., 1956); *The Religion of Java* (Glencoe, 1960); *Peddlers and Princes: Social
Development and Economic Change in Two Indonesian Towns* (Chicago/London
1963). Studies by other members of the team have been published since,
and several of them are still to appear.

[1] H. ten Dam, *Desa Tjibodas* (Bogor, 1951); Ten Dam, 'Cooperation and
Social Structure in the Village of Chibodas', in: *Indonesian Economics: The
Concept of Dualism in Theory and Policy* (The Hague, 1961), pp. 347 ff.

[2] See for example, Selosoemardjan, *Social Changes in Jogjakarta* (Ithaca, 1962);
Leslie H. Palmier, *Social Status and Power in Java* (London, 1960); Donald E.
Willmott, *The Ch nese of Semarang: A Changing Minority Community in Indonesia*
(Ithaca, 1960); Kampto Utomo, *Masjaraka: Transmigran Spontan Didaerah W.
Sekampung (Lampung)* (Spontaneous transmigrants' settlements in the Way
Sekampong department of the Lampong area, doctoral thesis Faculty of Agri-
culture, University of Indonesia, Jakarta, 1957).

[3] Raymond Kennedy, 'The Colonial Crisis and the Future', in: R. Linton
(ed.), *The Science of Man in the World Crisis* (New York, 1945), pp. 306 ff.; D. H.
Burger, 'Structuurveranderingen in de Javaanse samenleving' (Structural
changes in Javanese society), a series of articles in *Indonesië*, Vol. 2 and 3
(1948–49 and 1949–50); Wertheim, *Indonesian Society in Transition: A Study of
Social Change* (Second Ed., The Hague/Bandung, 1959); Leslie Palmier, 'Aspects of Indonesia's Social Structure', *Pacific Affairs*, Vol. 28 (1955), pp. 117 ff.

[4] C. A. O. van Nieuwenhuijze, *Aspects of Islam in Post-Colonial Indonesia: Five
Essays* (The Hague/Bandung, 1958); Harry J. Benda, *The Crescent and the
Rising Sun: Indonesian Islam under the Japanese Occupation 1942–1945* (The Hague/

relationships,[1] differentiation of social roles according to age group and sex,[2] and many other aspects of Indonesian society. Whereas the approach of pre-war sociologists was largely inspired by Weber's methodology, modern writing on Indonesian society is profusely making use of the conceptual framework and terminology developed by Anglo-Saxon schools of sociological thought. I mention the 'colour caste' terminology, adopted by the present author from American writers on the Negro problem; Geertz's attempt to analyse social change in Java in terms of Talcott Parsons' theory of social interaction;[3] or Willmott's effort to fit in his materials with theories of socio-cultural change developed by American scholars.[4]

In some cases new or somewhat modified conceptual tools have been developed by sociologists dealing with the Indonesian scene. The 'shared poverty' concept elaborated by Geertz and the 'mestizo culture' coined by the present writer are both a case in point. Highly significant are Clifford Geertz's attempts to develop Goldenweiser's concept of 'involution' as a useful tool for

Bandung, 1958); Clifford Geertz in his various studies on 'Modjokuto' mentioned on p. 248 in note 2; Wertheim, *op. cit.*

[5] Wertheim, *op. cit.*; Geertz, in his various 'Modjokuto' studies; The Siauw Giap, 'Urbanisatieproblemen in Indonesië' (Urbanization problems in Indonesia), *Bijdragen tot de Taal-, Land- and Volkenkunde*, Vol. 115 (1959), pp. 249 ff. See also *The Indonesian Town: Studies in Urban Sociology* (The Hague/Bandung, 1958) for significant pre-war studies on this subject.

[1] Bruno Lasker, *Human Bondage in Southeast Asia* (Chapel Hill, 1950); Wertheim, *op. cit.*

[2] G. Bateson and M. Mead, *Balinese Character: A Photographic Analysis* (New York, 1942); Cora Du Bois, *The People of Alor: A Social-Psychological Study of an East-India Island* (Minneapolis, 1944); H. Th. Chabot, *Verwantschap, stand en sexe in Zuid-Celebes* (Kinship, status and sex in South Celebes, Groningen/Jakarta, 1950); Wertheim, 'De generatiestrijd buiten de Westerse cultuurkring' (The clash between generations outside the Western cultural area), in: *De wereld der mensen: Sociaal-wetenschappelijke opstellen aangeboden aan Prof. Dr. J. J. Fahrenfort* (The world of man: Essays in the social sciences, dedicated to Professor J. J. Fahrenfort, Groningen/Jakarta, 1955), pp. 168 ff.

[3] See Geertz, 'Ritual and Social Change: A Javanese Example', *American Anthropologist*, Vol. 59 (1957), pp. 32 ff.

[4] Willmott, *op. cit.*, pp. 303 ff.

understanding the process of increasing rigidity in Javanese society[1] or his effort to apply a 'more dynamic functionalist approach' to Javanese society than usual among social anthropologists in order to deal more adequately with processes of social change.[2]

The suggestion by the present author of a historical chain from communities via individuals toward modern collective organizations to replace the traditional *Gemeinschaft-Gesellschaft* dichotomy proposed by Tönnies may be seen as an attempt to refine the framework of recent social history. In the same vein a historical sequence has been elaborated by the present author, starting from a recognition of status according to birth via status based on achievement toward status derived from membership in collective organizations.[3] The traditional view of society as a complex and fully integrated structure is being replaced by one which starts from the assumption, that there exist opposing value systems and veiled protest elements against the dominant system of hierarchy in any social structure.[4] This concept of the existence of 'counterpoints' in any society, more often than not manifesting themselves in a veiled form, may prove a significant contribution to the study of historical processes. For example, the interpretation of messianic cults as disguised movements of social protest may add to our insight into such phenomena.[5]

At the same time, this type of sociological analysis may draw attention to source materials hitherto largely neglected. Myths,

[1] Geertz, *The Development of the Javanese Economy* (*op. cit.*), pp. 29 ff.
[2] Geertz, 'Ritual and Social Change', *loc. cit.*, pp. 34–35.
[3] This view is somewhat related to Talcott Parsons' distinction between allocation of status by ascription and by achievement; but the historical sequence suggested is a departure from Parsons.
[4] Wertheim, 'Het contrapunt in de samenleving' (The counterpoint in society), in: *Weerklank op het werk van Jan Romein: Liber amicorum* (Resonance upon Jan Romein's works: Liber amicorum, Amsterdam, 1953), pp. 210 ff. See also Wertheim, 'De generatiestrijd buiten de Westerse cultuurkring', *loc. cit.*; I may also refer to the second paper in the present volume, dealing with society as a composite of conflicting value systems.
[5] Peter Worsley, *The Trumpet Shall Sound: A Study of 'Cargo Cults' in Melanesia* (London, 1957).

tales, or fiction may provide strong indications for the existence
of such counterpoints against the dominant hierarchical values.
Sundanese tales of the *kabayan* type reveal the existence of a hidden protest against the prevailing class hierarchy and the domination of the elders. Jokes common in Balinese theatre performances may disclose an institutionalized form of reaction against
the rigid social order.[1] The *Lay of Jaya Prana* gives a vivid expression to hidden discontent with the imposed caste order of Balinese
society.[2] With many reservations, modern fiction may equally
provide material which is useful for sociological and historical
analysis of Indonesian society.[3]

Thus it would seem as if the sociological approach had made an
unqualifiedly positive contribution to Indonesian historiography.
Still, it becomes increasingly evident that the advantages to be
derived from this approach have also certain limitations. It is
significant that two of the pre-war classics presented in this article
as outstanding examples of sociological analysis have been recently submitted to a thorough criticism by well-qualified *pur sang*
historians.

One of the main themes of Van Leur's analysis of Indonesian
society is a wide gulf allegedly existing between on the one hand
the ruling aristocracy of the coastal towns supplemented by a
restricted patrician class conforming as far as possible to the
aristocratic way of life, many of them incidentally engaged in
trading as owners or participants of cargoes and ships, and on the
other hand the numerous class of pedlars actively engaged in
professional trade, who crowded the ships and travelled along
with their bundles and loads representing, as a rule, a high value
in a small volume. The *popolo grasso* as opposed to the *popolo minuto*

---

[1] Wertheim, 'Het contrapunt in de samenleving', *loc. cit.*
[2] C. Hooykaas, *The Lay of Jaya Prana: The Balinese Uriah* (London, 1958).
[3] Lily Clerkx, *Mensen in Deli: Een maatschappijbeeld uit de belletrie* (People in
Deli: A picture of society from belletristic sources, mimeographed paper no. 2
of the Sociological-Historical Seminar for Southeast Asia, University of Amsterdam, n.y.).

has been a significant element in both Van Leur's interpretation of Hindu-Javanese history and his view on later periods of Indonesian history.

A Dutch historian, Mme M. A. P. Meilink-Roelofsz, has recently attempted to test Van Leur's picture of early Indonesian trade and society on the basis of historical sources, among them Tome Pires' *Suma Oriental*, in a doctoral thesis defended at the University of Amsterdam.[1]

Without attacking Van Leur's general view of the social structure of early Indonesian society Dr. Meilink still succeeds in establishing that the gulf assumed by Van Leur is much less absolute and unbridgeable than alleged in this work. According to Pires' description of early-fifteenth-century Malacca – which had not yet been unearthed at the time of Van Leur's and Schrieke's writing – there was a gradual scale leading from the small pedlar to the merchant-gentleman, who was included by Van Leur with the *popolo grasso* as a patrician whose way of life was nearly aristocratic. Dr. Meilink also points out that not all the traders travelling with their cargoes belonged to the pedlar type. There were many who leased a *petak*, a part of the ship's hold, from the *nachoda* (captain). Further, Dr. Meilink does not agree with Van Leur that the trade carried on in Southeast Asia was exclusively one of high-quality goods. Bulk trade had equally its place in the general trade movement.

All in all, the main objection of Dr. Meilink to Van Leur's view is that in his effort to draw an idealtypic picture of early Indonesian society he has too much forced the historical facts to fit his theory, tending to neglect the fine shades.

Although the idealtypic approach is not intended to provide a true picture of 'reality', in its tendency to simplify reality in order to make it accessible to our comprehensive faculties it still may seduce its followers into distorting the object matter of historians. Historical science, in its stress upon the incidental flow

[1] M. A. P. Meilink-Roelofsz, *Ancient Trade and the European Influence in Indonesia between 1500 and 1630* (The Hague, 1962); see also *The Suma Oriental of Tomé Pires and the book of Francisco Rodrigues* (London, 1944).

of events, is less prone than sociology to indulge in sweeping generalizations which have an attractive look but are not immune from the danger of too far a departure from the firm ground of historical evidence.[1]

However, if we think of the sweeping generalizations by the historians Van Leur was coming up against in his writings – as for instance the 'Hindu colonization' of Java! – we begin to doubt whether sociologists are the only ones who are in danger of indulging in unwarranted simplifications.

In general, it can be stated that the sociological approach is especially dangerous in fostering over-simplification, when sociologists attempt to analyse social reality in terms of a dichotomy. *Gemeinschaft – Gesellschaft, popolo grasso – popolo minuto, santri – abangan*, landowners – landless people, Western – Eastern, universalism – particularism: these are a few of the distinctions used in current sociological literature dealing with Indonesia. By and large, such distinctions have only a heuristic value to promote a certain initial understanding and to formulate a working hypothesis for further research. As a rule, such a dichotomy will prove, in the long run, too rough for a deeper understanding, and a more graded scale of possibilities will have to be elaborated to leave room for the fine shades. Especially for a more dynamic approach, as required for modern historiography, the tools of sociology may still be too primitive.

A second example of historical criticism of pre-war sociological studies is to be found in Van Niel's analysis of the *Sarekat Islam* movement.[2] Van Niel takes issue with Koch's attempt to view *Sarekat Islam* primarily as a bourgeois movement comparable with sixteenth-century Protestantism. In his opinion, which is based on an impressive body of biographical information on the

[1] See for the relationship between general concepts and detailed historical research in general: Romein, 'The Common Human Pattern: Origin and Scope of Historical Theories', *Journal of World History*, Vol. 4, no. 2 (1958), pp. 449 ff.

[2] Robert van Niel, *The Emergence of the Modern Indonesian Elite* (The Hague/ Bandung, 1960), pp. 103, 113 ff.

leading nationalists of that period, the term bourgeois would appear less appropriate to designate a social group mostly belonging to the *priyayi* elite and in general not engaged in trade but in white-collar functions. In this case, the criticism by the historian is primarily levelled against a tendency of sociologists to look for historical parallels and to reduce phenomena from societies far apart in space and time to an aggregate denomination.

But again the sociologists were not the only ones or the first, to draw parallels. It was the historian Geerke who thought fit to compare Coen with Mussolini;[1] and it is the historian De Graaf who draws a comparison between the disintegration of the Mataram empire and similar developments in Western Europe during the early Middle Ages.[2] Comparison of processes in Indonesian history with similar processes elsewhere may yield fruitful insights, provided that the categories used are truly universal, and that the simplifying, idealtypic characterization is being refined by taking full account of the time factor, discussed by Professor Romein in an enlightening study.[3] The historian could, in this way, help and correct the sociologist who may tend to look too much for generalities and to overlook specific factors.

Thus, the ultimate value of the sociological approach to historiography has still to be established. Nevertheless, its influence upon Indonesian history writing is already undeniable. The fact that a doctoral dissertation has been written by a historian with the outspoken aim of testing the sociological hypothesis of Van Leur is significant of the importance attached to his views in historical circles. Sociologists are likely to continue their efforts to treat

---

[1] H. P. Geerke, *Jan Pieterszoon Coen: De baanbreker in ons Indië* (Jan Pieterszoon Coen: The pioneer in our Indies, Utrecht, 1929), p. 230.

[2] H. J. de Graaf, *Geschiedenis van Indonesië* (History of Indonesia, The Hague/ Bandung, 1949), p. 207.

[3] To be included in Soedjatmoko *c.s.* (ed.), *An Introduction to Indonesian Historiography* (Ithaca, 1964), as Chapter 20, with the title 'The National and Social Revolution in Asia and the Time Factor'.

Indonesian history from a sociological point of view. But modern historians are equally likely to insert sociological viewpoints in their treatment of Indonesian history.[1] If they do not, their work is bound to be thought, as it were, incomplete.[2]

Modern thinking is so much imbued with sociological elements and jargon that present-day historians will inevitably be influenced by sociological thought, even though they remain, rightly, critical toward specific theories and views expressed by sociologists. They will, not unlike Monsieur Jourdain, write sociology even without knowing it.

Whether the historians accept or reject concrete theories or views emanating from sociologists, the sociological approach has forever added a new dimension to historiography.

---

[1] See for example Benda, *op. cit.*; Van Niel, *op. cit.*
[2] As is for example the case with De Graaf, *op. cit.*

Betting on the Strong? has been conceived as a concluding chapter, especially written with the present volume in view.

TWELVE

BETTING ON THE STRONG?

The preceding chapters were largely devoted to a study of social processes demonstrable in the past. Historical experience was submitted to an analysis in terms of sociological theory. In most of the previous essays hardly any attempt was made to predict future trends on the basis of past experience or to discuss practical policies prescribed by the acquired insight. In this concluding chapter, therefore, a tentative projection of past trends into the future appears appropriate.

It is not customary for human beings to learn from the lessons taught by history. The human mind is mostly moulded in such a way as to protect it from disturbing, uneasy thoughts. In interpreting historical evidence we tend to make it serve as a confirmation of firmly rooted beliefs and pre-conceptions.

On the other hand, writing of history more often than not performs the function of an allegory. Historians are quite often Cassandras without knowing it. They present their historical images and interpretations as lessons for future conduct, hoping that at least a few will stop and listen. Let it be so: I venture to make the 'lesson' inherent in my interpretation of the past explicit. It is up to the reader to take the lesson – or to leave it.

As a starting-point for my tentative projections into the future I should like, then, to hark back to the concept of 'dialectics of progress', launched by Jan Romein. In the first chapter of the present volume I ventured to substitute Romein's view of the process of human evolution for an outmoded concept of a gradual unilinear development. I made use of the concept of 'involution' elaborated by Clifford Geertz to show that, in actual history, many social processes cannot possibly be viewed as fitting in an evolutionary pattern, since they rather manifest a reverse trend, an over-specialization in a direction which is essentially anti-developmental. The complementary element of the dialectics of progress consists, however, of processes which show an acceleration in social change and economic development. Relative backwardness – this is the core of Romein's thesis – may function as a spur to accelerated development, and a high stage of development as a retarding factor. Short-cuts from lower to higher stages are possible as alternatives to gradual development; an involution-revolution pattern may alternate with a process of gradual evolution.

Though the selection of papers included in the present volume has not been specifically guided by a purposive design to illustrate this central thesis, most of them may serve as contributions to a further development of the basic idea. The second chapter provides an analysis of the contrapuntal elements present in any society, which in turn may contain the germ of dynamic, revolutionary change. The third chapter, dealing with trading minorities, indicates a parallel between present developments in Southeast Asia in connection with the situation of the local Chinese, and the Jewish problem in many parts of Europe. But the analysis also shows that the attainment of national independence does not necessarily imply a stride toward the achievement of universalistic human values; the strongly particularistic and racialistic attitudes shown by the ruling classes of most of the new nations disprove any pre-conceived model of gradual evolution in the field of human relations. The fourth chapter, dealing with nationalism and leadership, attempts to outline some of the social and political processes engendering new revolutionary trends after the achievement of independence. Its purpose is to contribute to a deeper insight into the reasons why the course taken by the 'new emerging forces' is so different from the model set by the 'old established' ones.

The following chapters likewise attempt to demonstrate why, in twentieth-century South and Southeast Asia, the parallel with earlier developments in the Western world is only partially valid. In the fifth chapter the present author tries to establish this in

relation to the corruption issue; the sixth and seventh draw a
parallel with the rise of Western Protestantism. The eighth draws
a similar parallel with respect to urban development; it shows the
involutionary character of the urbanization processes in Indonesia and in India and tries to assess the type of modern planning
needed for a radical reversal of these involutionary trends. In a
similar way the previous chapters had shown why a simple copying
of Western nineteenth-century bureaucratic practices would not
do; or why religious reform of a bourgeois type fails to achieve a
wholesale renovation of society comparable to the achievement
of the Christian Reformation in the West.

The ninth chapter demonstrates the involutionary trends inherent in the type of internal migration practised in post-war
Indonesia. Its argument boils down to the thesis that, as far as
the overpopulation problem of Java is concerned, a solution
could only be found by applying the adage: *aux grands maux les
grands remèdes*. The tenth chapter reinforces this argument by
analysing social processes in Java during the 'ethical policy'
period; it culminates in the thesis forwarded by Margaret Mead,
that overall change may occur with less friction than partial
change, contrary to the ideal of gradual evolution generally
adhered to by cultural anthropologists. Once again, a half-way
solution proves to be no solution at all.

Finally, the eleventh chapter attempts to establish to what
extent the use of parallels based on sociological typology is generally admissible for a historian. It appears that one of the main
obstacles to a simplistic application of parallels is to be found in
the varying constellation of social elements, owing to the operation of the time factor. This factor causes any repetition of the
original model to develop in a different tempo – sometimes a
process may be strongly retarded, in other cases it may be much
accelerated. Here, again, a simplistic evolutionary view, which
takes for granted 'that it takes three generations to make a
gentleman' – or three centuries to form a modern nation – would
appear to fall short of the sociological insight needed to understand the intricacies of human history. The identical and the

individual elements in human history can never be separated; and any attempt at drawing parallels with processes in the past has to be guided by a full comprehension of the uniqueness which is no less inherent in the flow of history than its correspondence to repetitional patterns and models which are the subject matter of sociological research and typology.

I must now demonstrate that this way of viewing history could be helpful in formulating policies for the future.

The difficulty of bringing about a 'take-off' in the non-Western world is being realized more and more clearly by modern economists. The impossibility of simply copying the Western model of economic development is hardly challenged any more. It is the omnipresent rural poverty combined with a rapid natural increase which reduce to nought any attempt at bringing about a take-off by conventional means. Even the numerous economists who do not share the pessimistic outlook of the late Professor J. H. Boeke as to the capacity of Asian societies to overcome the present impasse, have to acknowledge the 'vicious circle' character of the actual state of the rural economy. Radical innovations are needed to increase agricultural *per capita* production. But poverty and ignorance are severe impediments to introducing innovations. Lack of response from the poor masses to all well-intentioned governmental measures is among the most serious obstacles to economic development.

This is why many of those who are seriously concerned with the 'take-off' problem tend to look for specific agents for introducing the innovations wanted. It is the more advanced farmers who are almost automatically being selected as such. It is they who show a greater responsiveness to all kinds of innovations and technical improvements and who are much easier to approach for government agencies or special services. Such an approach starts implicitly from the assumption that the advanced farmers will set an example to the poorer sections, who are expected to follow the model which they are able to observe from close by. The innovation is intended to spread, like an oil-stain, to other layers of rural society.

It is this approach which could be called: *betting on the strong*.

It is obvious, that the underlying philosophy of this approach is an inherent belief in gradual evolution. It is assumed that the process of spreading knowledge and technical progress cannot be but a gradual one, and that the best agents for this evolutionary process have to be looked for among the most advanced individuals in rural society. In the village sphere this group generally consists of those well-to-do farmers who have enjoyed sufficient education or had enough contacts with urban elements to respond positively to all kinds of suggestions for the improvement of their production techniques.

In the former Saurashtra State in Western India even a special registration of so-called 'progressive farmers' had been introduced, as the prospective agents of a Community Development scheme. I quote from an official government report:[1]

A Progressive Farmer should:
(1) possess at least 2 acres of land for irrigation and eight acres of land for dry farming and if irrigation is not possible in any area, he should have 16 acres of land for dry farming;
(2) have at least one pair of good bullocks;
(3) have at least one cow preferably of good Gir breed or of local breed or he should arrange to have one as early as possible in case he has none;
(4) have planted at least five trees on his farm or should have given an assurance of doing so at the earliest;
(5) have dug at least two systematic compost pits either on his *wadi* of field, or he should give an assurance of doing so at the earliest;
(6) have taken all possible measures to prevent erosion of his land;
(7) have adopted improved agricultural practices by taking advantage of agricultural research;
(8) be a member of any one cooperative society or should enrol himself as such within a year of his having been registered as a progressive farmer; and
(9) use improved and selected variety of seeds for sowing.

These progressive farmers were afforded preferential treatment by the governmental services.

[1] Report of the Team for the Study of Community Projects and National Extension Service, Vol. 3, Part 1 (New Delhi, 1957), pp. 254-255.

Progressive farmers should ... be given preference in the matter of supply of improved seeds, fertilizers, technical advice and guidance and other facilities available from the State. Every progressive farmer will thus serve as an experimental and research centre spread all over the rural areas, and will be an effective instrument of propagating improved agricultural practices. Such a scheme has certain definite advantages over any scheme worked by the department in that the agriculturist will have greater faith and confidence in the results obtained on the fields of his fellow-cultivators which he will readily adopt.

This special reliance on the 'progressive' farmer is typical of the general Indian approach to rural society. Dube also found, in his survey of the Community Development scheme as applied in a certain village, that

the Project hoped to be able to work intimately with a smaller group of individuals who were expected to function as local agents of change. For this purpose persons occupying existing positions of leadership in the village as well as traditional leaders were to be used. The underlying assumption in this approach was that if leaders could first be converted to the ideology of change, the task of converting the rest of the community would be greatly facilitated. Implied in this assumption was the belief that people normally looked to this group for guidance and would automatically start emulating their example once they adopted the new practices. It was also hoped that by making them a link between the officials and the people some of the difficulties in communication would be appreciably reduced.[1]

Dube also points out, that among those

included in the category of 'traditional leaders' were the important and influential people in the village. Naturally most of them were from the dominant land-owning group.[2]

I remember once having read that an Indian writer divided the rural people into two types: the hens and the ducks. The hens are those, who run, who are 'progressive'. The ducks are the mass of the people. They move slowly and heavily. The Indian authorities rely on the hens: they are *betting on the strong*.

[1] S. C. Dube, *India's Changing Villages: Human Factors in Community Development* (London, 1960), p. 124.
[2] *Op. cit.*, p. 125.

The *betting on the strong* principle has been, for a long time, a controversial issue in the literature devoted to Indonesian economics. In his doctoral dissertation of 1910 based on printed sources and not on personal experience in the colony, J. H. Boeke had expressed a distrust of the 'well-to-do Natives', among whom many *hadjis*, as agents for economic development. Their progress would only amount to a situation in which 'the rich grow richer and the poor grow poorer'.[1]

Paradoxically enough, Boeke himself, after a prolonged stay in Indonesia, reversed his stand in 1927. At that time he did not see any possibility of promoting native welfare except through the intermediary of a small elite, consisting of 'the vigorous, energetic, advanced elements' in Indonesian rural society. These wealthier landowners working their way upwards should not be blackened and branded as usurers and bloodsuckers.[2]

These elements of rural society should be approached by the specialized welfare agencies in a way which Boeke called 'person-centered'. Not compulsion, but patient persuasion should be the method used by the welfare agencies; and the effort should not be directed towards the poor masses, in order to get certain 'objects' done, but towards individuals differentiating themselves from the mass by certain personal qualities. The basic assumption is, evidently, that the improvement of native welfare cannot be but a slow, gradual process. The person-centered welfare policy should be led, above all, by 'faith and patience'.[3]

At the time when Boeke expressed these thoughts, the Agricultural Extension Service in the Netherlands East Indies had already embarked upon a policy which was also primarily directed towards the more advanced farmers, whose example was expected to spread automatically, according to what was called an 'oil-stain system'.[4]

[1] *Indonesian Economics: The Concept of Dualism in Theory and Policy* (The Hague, 1961), p. 33.
[2] *Op. cit.*, pp. 36–37.
[3] *Op. cit.*, p. 298.
[4] *Op. cit.*, p. 36.

It is of minor importance that Boeke, adding a new paradox to the existing one, appears in his later publications to have reversed his stand once more.[1] Promoting the economic welfare of the masses did not seem to him to be any longer within the range of human possibilities, when he, in 1948, declared the poverty of the masses of Asia unchangeable, at least as far as the densely populated areas are concerned.[2] Probably this explains why also the gradualistic approach to rural society, via well-to-do advanced farmers, no longer occupies an essential part in his later publications.

What matters more is how the oil-stain approach, actually applied by the Agricultural Extension Service in Indonesia, worked out in practice. The fruits of such a policy, as recorded by H. ten Dam in a study of Western Java village Tjibodas, are far from promising.[3] In this village it is with the large landowners – comprising roughly one and a half *per cent* of the total village population – that the representatives of the government agencies came into personal contact. It is they who profited most from all kinds of facilities provided by the Agricultural Extension Service. It is they who, through a co-operative society in which they had the largest stakes, got artificial fertilizers and chemical preparations, needed for the cultivation of profitable commercial crops, such as potatoes and cabbage, at prices set by the Extension Service.

[1] *Op. cit.*, pp. 40 ff.

[2] J. H. Boeke, *The Interests of the Voiceless Far East: Introduction to Oriental Economics* (Leiden, 1948), p. 88: 'It will be necessary to acquiesce in the immutability of the dualistic character of the densely populated oriental countries, in the perpetuation of the subsistence economy of the rural masses.' Still, he clung to his view 'that a welfare policy, conducted with true economic insight, has to be aimed at the individuals conversant with the Western conception of life. These individuals should be stimulated to independent effort and to the achievement of the possibilities of economic development offered by their country' (*op. cit.*, p. 90). The difference with the author's stand in 1927 seems to be that he no longer believed in an oil-stain effect, not even in the long run.

[3] H. ten Dam, 'Cooperation and Social Structure in the Village of Chibodas', in *Indonesian Economics* (*op. cit.*), p. 345–382.

There was a group of smaller independent farmers with economic holding, of whom a number attempted to follow the example of large landowners. If they grew cabbage and potatoes, their profits were frequently lower than those of the large landowners since they had to pay higher commercial prices for fertilizers and chemicals. The prices they had to pay for these items were excessive because they obtained them from large landowners, who in turn bought them at reduced prices from the Extension Service.

But even when taken together, the large landowners and the independent farmers do not exceed ten per cent of the total village population. The great majority, the farm hands and the part-time farmers with uneconomic holdings who have to work for the larger landowners as wage labourers or share-croppers, do not profit at all from the manifold innovations introduced in local agriculture. They simply lack the amount of land and the capital needed for imitating the farming methods introduced by the Extension Service. The oil-stain stops at the ten per cent level. Ten Dam even mentions the possibility that the farm hands are worse off since the creation of the co-operative, 'since relations with the co-operative are much more businesslike and impersonal than the master-servant relations between a farmer and his hired hands'.[1]

Tjibodas is certainly an extreme case in certain respects. In most other villages of Java the percentage of landless people and of peasants with uneconomic holdings is decidedly lower, and the antithesis between the landed and the landless may be less sharp.[2] But the general tendency pointed out by Ten Dam, is manifest in many parts of Java.[3]

Boeke's prophecy, pronounced as early as 1910, appears to have come true: as a consequence of a policy of *betting on the strong* the

---

[1] *Op. cit.*, p. 380.

[2] *Op. cit.*, pp. 61–62.

[3] See for example Ina E. Slamet, *Pokok² pembangunan masjarakat desa: Sebuah pandangan anthropologi budaja* (Basic elements of the structure of village society: A cultural anthropologist's view, Jakarta, 1963), pp. 19 ff.

rich grew richer and the poor grew, if not poorer, then at least more numerous – and more restive.

This is exactly what happened in India whenever the *betting on the strong* approach was attempted. Dube assesses the results of the Community Development Project in the villages investigated by him, as far as the agricultural extension work is concerned, as follows:

> A closer analysis of the agricultural extension work itself reveals that nearly 70 per cent of its benefits went to the *élite* group and to the more affluent and influential agriculturists. The gains to poorer agriculturists were considerably smaller. Being suspicious of government officials they did not seek help from the Project as often. As this group had little influence in the village and outside, and was in no position to offer any material help in the furtherance of Project objectives, the officials largely ignored it. For the economic development of this group, as well as for that of the artisans and agricultural labourers, no programmes were initiated by the Project.[1]

Dube points out the mistake inherent in the assumption that 'progressive farmers' would be the 'accepted leaders' of village society.

> The village looked to them for guidance in its general relationship with the urban areas and the officials, and their help was sought in legal matters, in contacting and influencing officials, and generally in facing problems that arise out of contact between the village and the outside world. They were not necessarily looked upon as leaders in agriculture, nor were they in any sense decision makers in many vital matters concerning the individual and his family. Because of their association with the officials and the urban ways of life these leaders as a group had come to possess a special status within the community, but the average villager did not trust them without reservations.[2]

Since most of these 'traditional leaders' chosen as a link between the officials and the people were from the dominant land-owning group,

> the undue emphasis in working with 'traditional leaders' was construed by some villagers as an effort on the part of the government to maintain a *status quo* in the internal power relations within village communities and indi-

[1] Dube, *op. cit.*, pp. 82–83.
[2] *Op. cit.*, p. 125.

rectly as a step to support the domination of the landowning groups. Thus the policy of the government on the subject of leadership seemed contradictory and confusing.[1]

But the main obstacle to the oil-stain effect can be reduced to the obvious cause that following the example of the 'progressive farmers' presupposes the possession of sufficient land and capital, besides the required 'progressive' outlook and a mental preparedness to follow the example of the 'strong'. Those possessing uneconomic holdings are excluded anyway from that possibility. They are more likely to be forced, in the long run, to sell their holdings in order to pay off debts. The larger landowners, profiting from technical innovations, may be tempted to extend their holdings; a 'progressive' outlook as far as farming technique is concerned, is by no means a guarantee for a 'progressive' outlook as far as principles of social justice are concerned.

The prospect is still more complicated by the existence of a large category of landless farm hands. Can they be expected to profit from the improvements in farming techniques, introduced by their wealthier masters-landowners? First, it is not at all certain that the larger landowners working with paid labour will be among those readily accepting innovations. According to Dube, 'most substantial landowners, until recently, did not take enough personal interest in what was being done in their fields. The work was largely left to unskilled labourers, who preferred working along traditional lines'.[2] But even apart from that, in a situation in which there is no dearth of cheap labour, the type of improvement profitable for a landowner will at best aim at increasing the productivity per acre; there is no incentive at all to increase *per capita* production. And if the production per acre is being raised, it is not at all certain, that real wages for the landless labourers (or the shares for the sharecroppers, where such sharecropping contracts are legally allowed or illegally practised) will reflect the upward trend of production. There is a wealth of evidence to indicate that on the average real wages in rural India

[1] *Op. cit.*, p. 125.
[2] *Op. cit.*, p. 65.

have not appreciably increased since independence.[1] Over against certain local increases of rural employment opportunities, largely as a consequence of the introduction of irrigation works, we have to take account not only of the strong social, political, and economic position of the landowning castes in the countryside, but of the rapid natural increase of the population in the rural areas.

Only by absorbing most of the natural increase of the rural population in non-agricultural occupations could a mounting productivity per surface area, in the long run, be turned into higher real wages for agricultural labour, through a raising of *per capita* production. In order to make mechanization of agriculture profitable the absolute number of people dependent on agriculture would even have to be reduced, except inasfar as a reclamation of waste lands could increase the total cultivated area. But even the former condition – an approximately stationary population engaged in farming – is far from being realized in most parts of India, since urbanization and industrialization are developing much too slowly to be able considerably to reduce the percentage of the total population employed in agriculture, let alone to absorb the natural increase.

It has been suggested that, for some decades before the war, 'the farms appear to have retained an approximately constant or slightly increasing proportion of the population'.[2] And as far

[1] See for example V.K.R.V. Rao (ed.), *Agricultural Labour in India* (Bombay, 1962), with a detailed analysis of the discrepancies between the conditions of agricultural labour as revealed in the Report of the Second Agricultural Labour Enquiry (1956–57) as compared with those available from the First Enquiry (1950–51). There is a difference of opinion among Indian experts as to the question whether the deterioration is real or only apparent, as a consequence of changes in definition. But, however this may be, up till now there is little reason to assume that the overall condition of the agricultural labourers has undergone any appreciable improvement, if we read in the *Times of India* of 26 August, 1963, that 'at least one person out of ten in the rural areas earns only a little more than three annas a day'.

[2] Ansley J. Coale and Edgar M. Hoover, *Population Growth and Economic Development in Low-Income Countries: A Case Study of India's Prospects* (Princeton, 1958), p. 133.

as available sources indicate, after a period of accelerated migration to urban centres during the war and the partition disturbances, the percentage of urban population in relation to total population has again remained nearly constant in the period 1951–1961.[1] And it is not very likely that in the Indian villages the percentage of those primarily dependent on agriculture would have been appreciably reduced during that period.

The conclusion to be drawn from this constellation is obvious. Modern farm techniques are not likely to spread in a situation in which cheap agricultural labour is abundant. The gains to be derived from 'community development' largely aimed at the 'progressive farmers' will predominantly accrue to a restricted landowning group. A *betting on the strong* policy is likely to amount to a policy of *the devil take the hindmost*. In countries where these 'hindmost' are restricted in numbers, a large proportion of them may be driven away from the countryside to seek employment in an urban sphere; the remaining ones may, if they are not too numerous in comparison with the land surface available for cultivation, profit in the long run from the increased productivity per surface area and eventually learn improved farming techniques from the more prosperous farmers.

But in countries where the 'hindmost' form a large majority, either as peasants with uneconomic holdings or as landless labourers, the *betting on the strong* policy cannot work. The large

[1] *India: A Reference Annual–1963*, Delhi (1963), p. 20, Table 15.

Rural and Urban Population (1921–1961)

	Percentage of total population	
	Rural	Urban
1921	88.6	11.4
1931	87.9	12.1
1941	86.1	13.9
1951	82.7	17.3
1961*	82.0	18.0

* Excludes Goa, Daman and Diu.

masses of the rural population are, for the time being, tied to their traditional rural occupations as farm hands or sharecroppers, which means that a gradual oilstain-like spread of modern farming techniques to them is out of the question. These poor masses form a drag upon any attempt to solve the rural problem in a gradual way. Tarlok Singh recognizes that the Indian Five Year Plans 'were weak in dealing with the problem of landless labour, but it was thought that with the growth of the economy as a whole, increase in the productivity of land, development of cooperation and changes in the agrarian structure, this problem might become more manageable'.[1] In actual fact this proved to be a miscalculation. The problem has become less and less manageable, since this neglected sector had a stagnating effect upon the whole economy.

Where the actual trend could, rightly, be termed one of 'involution', a policy based on evolutionary principles is bound to fail.

The underlying philosophy of the Indian Community Development Program has been aptly circumscribed by Phillips Ruopp:

> The developmental differs radically from the cataclysmic, with the latter's delusive appeals to violent action. Development is gradual, but it is not a gradualness that lends itself as an excuse for inaction. It means growth, but it must be growth cultivated by unequivocal and constant witness to justice, liberty, and compassion.[2]

On the basis of the foregoing analysis we should reconsider this thesis in the light of actual experience in countries like Indonesia and India, which shows that a 'pre-take-off' situation is not necessarily one of 'accelerated development' but sometimes rather the reverse.

The inappropriateness of the *betting on the strong* principle finds a fitting parallel in international economics. Britain was the

[1] Tarlok Singh, *Agricultural Policy and Rural Economic Progress*, Presidential address to the All India Agricultural Economics Conference, December 25, 1962.

[2] Phillips Ruopp (ed.), *Approaches to Community Development: A symposium Introductory to Problems and Methods of Village Welfare in Underdeveloped Areas* (The Hague/Bandung, 1953), p. 18.

first country to develop modern industry. It aspired to becoming 'the workshop of the world'. Far from actively supporting the other countries' attempt at following its example, it tried to prevent the spread of industry. Any effort at industrial development outside Britain had to be achieved by a long term policy aimed at outdoing Britain's initial advantage and at protecting the newcomer's home industry against foreign competition. This is the way Germany, the United States, and Canada succeeded in building up an economic apparatus of similar strength as Britain. Instead of *betting on the strong*, in international economics *betting on the backward* appeared a more promising policy to make the backward strong. If the *betting on the strong* principle held true, it would amount, on a world scale, to further developing the already developed countries under the assumption that the thus acquired economic potential would automatically spread to the underdeveloped part of the world and that the backward countries would be able to follow the example of the developed ones.

Actual developments prove, time and again, that no automatical spread of the industrial potential to the underdeveloped part of the world is bound to occur. Despite a prevailing official international ideology stressing aid to be extended by developed countries to the underdeveloped ones, in actual practice the industrial world has not shown any great desire actively to promote the industrial advancement of the non-industrial world – though the experience in the Western world should have made clear long ago that the dwellers of a modern industrial country are, in the long run, far better customers for industrial goods than an impoverished peasantry. The gap between the price level of industrial goods and of raw materials has tended to increase since the end of the Second World War, and at the same time the cleavage between the welfare level of the industrial and the non-industrial world, if anything, has widened even further. The term 'countries in a process of accelerated development' amounts to a euphemism. If 'automatism' is allowed to work, the only effect is, as in the Asian countryside, that the rich become richer and the poor become, if not poorer, then much more numerous

– and much more restive. No advanced country is willing to part with its monopolistic advantages, in the same sense as no advanced farmer is prepared to part with his virtual monopoly in the realm of agriculture.

The analogy extends still further: in the cases in which non-industrial countries have succeeded in releasing a true take-off, they have done so largely on their own strength and with limited foreign assistance. In order to achieve this end, they had to curb the power of those foreign interests which were interested in essentially preserving the *status quo*. The amount of state interference needed to achieve a certain amount of autarchy and economic independence has considerably risen since the first competitors of Britain started on the road towards industrial development. The industrial revolution in Russia, the only major country which has thus far completed a take-off in the twentieth century, was even accompanied with a political and social revolution of an unprecedented magnitude. Only by a complete overhaul of the existing social structure and by an all-out mustering of the potential productive forces could the backwardness of the Russian economy be overcome. And the amount of directed planning, revolutionary zeal, lasting endurance, and inventive capacity needed to effectuate a true take-off in China appears again by far to exceed all previous instances.

The parallel with the agrarian situation in Asian countries seems obvious. If an evolutionary way out of the agrarian impasse is blocked because of involutionary tendencies, only a revolutionary response to the existing challenge seems appropriate. No more than in the realm of overall industrial development is an evolutionary course in the Asian countryside, via capitalistic enterprise, within the range of possibilities. Those who tend to view the formation of a class of capitalistic farmers as a pre-condition for further advances on the road to socialism and collectivism overlook the true character of the 'dialectics of progress'.

There are indications that it is this issue which is basic in the Sino-Soviet controversy. The Soviets consider the Indian achievement since independence with a favourable eye, since they expect a further gradual evolution toward socialism, in which extensive Soviet aid may even contribute to a development in which India could dispense with a truly revolutionary course. Ironically enough, they thus forsake their own past, which amounts to a forceful elimination of the strong landowner, the *kulak*.[1] The *betting on the strong* policy, applied in India, in certain respects resembles the agrarian reforms introduced by the Russian prime minister, Peter Stolypin, about 1910. The results of the Stolypin legislation can be compared with what happens after the agrarian reforms in India: 'the strong and sober among the peasants, upon whom Stolypin proposed to build, appeared to be benefiting, as the strong and sober – fortified by the science of arithmetic – usually do, in their dealings with those who are neither strong nor sober, or not arithmetically minded'.[2] The consequence of this experience was that in 1917 the Provisional Government repealed the Stolypin legislation; and even during the N(ew) E(conomic) P(olicy) period of 1921–1926 the *kulak* were not allowed to regain anything like the political power and social prestige which they would have acquired if the Stolypin reforms had been allowed to last.

On the other hand, the Chinese stand is that countries like India have not yet taken a real step on the road towards socialism. They are reminded of what happened in their own country dur-

---

[1] It does not follow that the densely populated countries of Asia could simply imitate the Russian model. The Soviet agricultural policy has remained largely extensive, the main emphasis being laid thus far upon mechanization, which means an approximately constant yield per surface area to be achieved with a decreasing labour force. The surplus labour could be drained off by an expanding industry. In Asian countries where involution prevails intensification of agriculture, that is to say increased yields per surface area, will remain indispensable for a long time to come, in addition to a great effort towards industrial development. This explains why the Chinese, in contrast with the Soviet model, stress 'walking on two legs'. Moreover, the Soviets appear to have discovered now that expanding extensive agriculture has a limit.

[2] John Maynard, *The Russian Peasant and Other Studies*, Third Ed. (London, 1943), p. 60.

ing the rule of the Kuo-min-tang. In their view, without a radical social revolution no progress in the economic field can be achieved. In this revolution an essential role has to be played by the poor peasantry.

Actual developments in Asian countries appear to bear out the basic soundness of the Chinese view. It would be perilous to speculate about the ultimate shape which the agrarian revolutions in Asian countries will assume. It is probable that the actual content of each revolutionary development will depend on the special rural and political conditions in the relative country and on the time factor, that is to say, on the moment when the revolutionary movement will occur. But this much could be stated, that the pre-condition to such an agrarian revolution will be the elimination of the well-to-do farmers as a power group. No truly effective agrarian reforms or co-operative movements will be possible if these *kulak* are allowed to counteract or dodge the reforms, or to compete with the co-operative society. Because of their strength they are dangerous to any movement pursuing a policy which aims at improvement of the living conditions for those who form the poor majority in the village. Only if they are willing to co-operate, that is to say, if they show themselves true 'progressive' farmers, can their forceful elimination, such as happened in the Soviet Union between 1927 and 1932, be prevented and could their capabilities as advanced farmers be used in the process of agrarian reform.

The violence of the revolution will depend on their readiness to be geared in with the revolutionary course of economic development

Betting on the strong is bound to fail in the prevailing conditions of most countries of Asia. The policy to be pursued instead is one of *betting on the many* – who will be made strong, mainly through organization and intensive education toward efficiency and self-reliance.

But only through a grasp of the basic idea of the dialectics of progress could be acquired a firm belief that the backward masses actually are a potential strength; and that they will soon be able to outdo the former *kulak* not only in devotion to society but in technical and administrative ability as well. Since the beginning of the twentieth century throughout the non-Western world those who are *betting on the many*, that is to say, who truly believe in human beings and promote their emancipation from all kinds of bondages, are patently on the winning side.

INDEX OF NAMES